Oxford Studies in Political Philosophy

Oxford Studies in Political Philosophy

Volume 6

Edited by

DAVID SOBEL, PETER VALLENTYNE,
AND STEVEN WALL

OXFORD
UNIVERSITY PRESS

OXFORD

UNIVERSITY PRESS

Great Clarendon Street, Oxford, OX2 6DP,
United Kingdom

Oxford University Press is a department of the University of Oxford.
It furthers the University's objective of excellence in research, scholarship,
and education by publishing worldwide. Oxford is a registered trade mark of
Oxford University Press in the UK and in certain other countries

First Edition published in 2020

Impression: 1

Published in the United States of America by Oxford University Press
198 Madison Avenue, New York, NY 10016, United States of America

British Library Cataloguing in Publication Data
Data available

Library of Congress Control Number: 2019947968

ISBN 978-0-19-885263-6 (hbk.)
ISBN 978-0-19-885264-3 (pbk.)

DOI: 10.1093/oso/9780198852636.003.0001

Printed and bound in Great Britain by
Clays Ltd, Elcograf S.p.A

Preface

The chapters collected here were first presented, in June 2018, at the sixth annual Workshop for Oxford Studies in Political Philosophy, at the University of Pavia, Italy. Local logistics were superbly organized by Enrica Ruaro, Michele Bocchiola, Emanuela Ceva, and Ian Carter. We thank them, and the graduate students who helped them, for laying the foundation for a successful workshop. We'd also like to thank all those who attended this event for making the workshop a stimulating and fun event. All of the papers in this volume were reviewed by referees (many of whom serve on the editorial board of Oxford Studies in Political Philosophy) and were typically improved by helpful comments. We very much thank these referees for doing this vital work. Last but not least, we thank the authors of these interesting papers for presenting them at the workshop and having them included in this volume.

Contents

List of Contributors

Kimberley Brownlee, University of Warwick

Johann Frick, Princeton University

Aart van Gils, University of Reading

Nils Holtug, University of Copenhagen

Christian List, London School of Economics

Valeria Ottonelli, University of Genova

Japa Pallikkathayil, University of Pittsburgh

Zofia Stemplowska, University of Oxford

Patrick Tomlin, University of Warwick

Laura Valentini, London School of Economics

PART I
RIGHTS AND WRONGS

1

Getting Rights out of Wrongs

Kimberley Brownlee

Introduction

We have some moral rights to act wrongly. We have moral rights to say mean things, to be wasteful, and to join xenophobic groups, for example. These are not Hohfeldian moral permissions. They are claim-rights against interference which protect us in acting in ways that we shouldn't act (see Waldron 1981; Raz 2009, chs 14–15).

More interestingly, sometimes, we *gain* moral rights *by* acting wrongly and only by acting wrongly. Equally, sometimes, we gain moral rights from other people acting wrongly and only from them acting wrongly. These rights are also claim-rights against interference. They are rights either to continue unencumbered to do wrong or to enjoy the fruits of our own or others' wrongdoing. Some of these rights are uncontentious. Others, however, are both contentious and morally complex, such as the relationship rights that we can sometimes gain after forming social connections we never should have formed.

This chapter presents a typology of the rights that we can get through wrongdoing. It builds up a profile of the contexts in which new wrong-generated rights seem to emerge when we do wrong ourselves (Section 1) and when others do wrong (Section 2). The chapter then analyses why some wrongs change the moral ballgame to give us new rights, and others do not (Section 3). That analysis focuses on (a) how legitimate expectations can sometimes grow out of illegitimate expectations; (b) how personal investments, such as labor, skills, resources, genes, and identity, can make a moral difference; and (c) how we can have rights that piggyback on others' interests even against a backdrop of

Kimberley Brownlee, *Getting Rights out of Wrongs* In: *Oxford Studies in Political Philosophy Volume 6*. Edited by: David Sobel, Peter Vallentyne, and Steven Wall, Oxford University Press (2020). © Kimberley Brownlee.
DOI: 10.1093/oso/9780198852636.003.0001

wrongdoing. Finally, the chapter explores two ultimately unsuccessful strategies to resist this analysis of wrong-generated rights (Section 4). The first strategy focuses on the defeasibility of rights. The second focuses on the conditionality of rights.

1. Getting Rights from Doing Wrong

1.1 Cases of Wrongdoing

Let me demarcate my subject by detailing first the kinds of rights that I'm *not* talking about. I'm not talking about the non-activated rights that we have before we act wrongly, which are triggered only once we act wrongly. We have non-activated due process rights before we act wrongly, which we can assert only once we act wrongly or are suspected of acting wrongly in ways that (properly) interest the law.[1] Similarly, we have non-activated rights to be fed, sheltered, and treated humanely when we are in prison, rights which we can assert only once we are incarcerated for an offence. These moral (and legal) rights compel other people to continue to treat us decently after we act wrongly. These are rights that we should get, or we should be recognized as having, once we act wrongly.

There are also non-codifiable moral rights that we can assert only once we act wrongly. For instance, if we do serious wrongs—wrongs which no claim-right could protect us in doing—then we have a moral right to contribute to public debates about how to treat people who have committed serious wrongs. Among other things, we have, in virtue of our serious wrongdoing, a certain perspective, experiential knowledge and insight into how society should view and respond to wrongdoers' behavior.[2] Once again, these are rights that we have, or should be acknowledged as having, only once we act wrongly.

The rights that I am discussing in this chapter are more complex than this. Sometimes, once and only once we act wrongly, we gain *new* moral rights that did not pre-exist our wrong in some non-activated form.

---

[1] Of course, the law might be mistaken when it says we do wrong. Let's bracket that possibility.

[2] I thank Joseph Raz for this example.

These rights are instead *newly created* by our wrongdoing. Here are several examples, which I offer undefended until Section 3.

Let's begin with a case that relates to rule-breaking as well as property use:

1. *School Building*: A community has no moral right *ex ante* to build a school with scarce public funds which is structurally sound but in breach of the necessary planning regulations. However, the community and the school users have a moral right *ex post* to keep their school once it is built, especially if tearing it down would waste public money or leave the community without a school.[3]

This case is synchronic: the community and school users have moral rights to keep their school as soon as it is built. Their *ex post* rights do not depend on the school having existed for some time.

Whereas *School Building* is a synchronic case, my next property-related case, and many of the other cases I will present, are diachronic, which is a complicating feature, as I explain below:

2. *Treatment-taking*: Sameer has no moral right *ex ante* to steal the first dose in a life-saving course of treatment that he needs, especially if other people need it too, the resource is scarce, and a fair procedure allocates it. But, *ex post*, once he has started the course, he has a moral right to continue, especially if he will die a slow, painful death from withdrawal (where previously he would have died quickly and painlessly) and the remaining treatments in the course cannot be repurposed.

And, here is a third property-related case:

3. *Squatting*: Suppose that Hatti, who already owns a decent home, decides to squat on unoccupied, ecologically fragile land for several years. While some readers might think that Hatti does no wrong in doing this, the common view, I take it, is that she does do wrong and has no moral right *ex ante* to reside on this land that does not belong to her and may be damaged irreparably by her presence. If, however, she squats unimpeded for a long enough time (and we can debate how long that

---

[3] I thank Clare Chambers for this case.

must be), then she has a moral right *ex post* to remain, or at least to be compensated if she is removed.[4]

This kind of case has many variants. For instance, if we migrate to a country illegally and, in time, build up a life there, then we can come to have moral rights to remain. Of all the cases I consider, this kind is the least contentious, I presume. But, it also raises the specter of colonization, which I will address below.

Next comes a synchronic case premised on common views about valuable family relations and dependents' interests:

4. *Big Family*:   Suppose that Jack and Jill, who have easy, legal access to contraception and abortion services and no conscientious opposition to such measures, decide to have a fourteenth child together. In having a fourteenth child, they act wrongly for many reasons. They reduce the time they can devote to their existing children; and they knowingly guarantee that they will have only limited time for this new child, Ramona. What they can offer her is barely minimally adequate. They also put further pressure on the natural environment as well as their society's material resources, pressure that increased with each additional child they chose to have.

Some readers might think that Jack and Jill do no wrong in having a fourteenth child. Other readers might think that they do wrong, but act within their rights because there is no upper limit to the number of children that parents have a right, in principle, to have. Parents have a defeasible right to have as many children as they like, so the thought goes. Still other readers might take the view I take, that there is an upper limit *somewhere* to the number of children that two people have a moral right to have in principle, and they have no right to have the n+1th child after that. Let's stipulate that n+1 is fourteen. This characterization of parents' rights reflects a general truth about all moral rights. At a high level of abstraction, we can speak about a person's right to property and her right to a family. But, when we unpack the content of such rights, we

---

[4] Anna Stilz argues for a presumption in favor of repatriation and return in the first generation of wrongful settlers. She holds that this presumption extends to second and higher generations of settlers in some cases. See Stilz 2017.

see that they are not just defeasible. They are also limited in scope. A person's defeasible right to property does not include, even in principle, a right to own the entire planet. A person's defeasible right to (try to) have a family does not include, even in principle, a right to insert herself into *every* family in the world or a right to knock on any given person's door and announce that she is joining their family. The same truth about scope applies to less content-sensitive rights: they have principled limits too. A person's freedom of movement does not give her a right, even in principle, to enter every space on earth. And, her freedom of religion does not give her a right, even in principle, to engage in human sacrifice.[5]

Given this fact about rights, we have in *Big Family* the kind of morally complex case that drives this chapter:

> Jack and Jill have no moral right *ex ante* to have a fourteenth child. But, if they do have a fourteenth child, then *ex post* both they and their new child, Ramona, immediately and persistently have moral rights to be together as a family.[6]

This is a synchronic case. Jack's, Jill's, and Ramona's rights do not depend on their relationship growing over time. From the start, they can assert familial rights to be together.

Here are three diachronic cases that are also premised on common views about valuable family relations and dependents' interests:

5. *Caring Kidnapping*: Stella has no moral right *ex ante* to kidnap a child, Jenny, and become her caring parent. But, if Stella does kidnap

---

[5] In highlighting this point, I aim to answer an anonymous referee who suggested that none of the cases I present actually involve the generation of new rights, but instead simply describe ordinary, defeasible rights we already have, such as the right to have a family and the right to hold property. My answer in the text stresses the fact that, while we can speak in highly abstract terms about rights to family and property which might seem to capture the cases I present, nevertheless our rights to family and property have limits which *ex ante* do not protect the kinds of wrongdoing I describe. Only *ex post*, once the moral ballgame has changed, can we speak about these wrongs—or their effects—falling within the scope of our rights.

[6] I thank Zofia Stemplowska for this case. My claim that Jack and Jill have no moral right *ex ante* to have a fourteenth child says nothing as such about legal rights, duties, or enforcement. Rather, it means that Jack and Jill cannot appeal to their moral rights to shut down the conversation about their parenting choices; they are legitimately open to censure from their existing children, family, friends, and others for having yet another child.

Jenny and raise her well for many years, then Stella can have a moral right *ex post* to continue to be Jenny's parent, especially if Jenny wishes it and is well-served by it. (See, for instance, Cowan 2015.)[7]

6. *Beauty and the Beast*:   Beast has no moral right *ex ante* to imprison Beauty as his companion. But, if they bond together over time, then he has a moral right *ex post* to remain her companion even if her initial impulse to bond with him stems from psychological stress, provided that (1) being with him is in her general interests and (2) after receiving competent psychiatric treatment, she still wishes to be with him.

7. *Life-generating rape*:   If Brett commits a life-generating rape, he has no moral right *ex ante* to be a parent to the child, Lisa, who results from that rape (even though some legal jurisdictions, including in the US, afford such biological progenitors parental rights by default) (see, for instance, CBS News 2017). But, if Brett raises Lisa well for many years, then he has a moral right *ex post* to continue to be Lisa's parent, despite the severity of his wrong, especially if Lisa wishes it and is well-served by it.

Finally, here's an example that combines common notions of property rights and family connections:

8. *Zygote-stealing*:   Maja has no moral right *ex ante* to break into an IVF clinic to mix her genetic material with that of a donor she admires in order to have a child, Carlos, with those genes. But, if she does have Carlos in this way and raises him well for many years, then *ceteris paribus* she has a right *ex post* to remain Carlos's parent, especially if he wishes it and is well-served by it.

---

[7] In discussions of this chapter at Nuffield College, Oxford, and the Institute of Philosophy in London, I was pressed to consider whether a person who commits a kidnapping could really be a caring parent. Could such a person really be committed to close, supportive, nurturing relations? Could she really have a child's interests at heart, given that she wrenched a child out of a caring relationship (let's suppose)? In reply, we must look at her reasons for committing the kidnapping, which need not be nefarious, and we must look at her conduct in her parenting role to judge whether this concern is warranted. Although, initially, she might fail a test for sincere commitment to caring relationships, she can nonetheless be a competent, attentive parent, and can grow to have a sincere commitment in time.

These various wrong-generated rights do not so much compel other people to treat us decently after we act wrongly as give us new benefits—new claims against people—precisely because we have succeeded in acting wrongly.

The idea that wrongs can generate rights is not contentious when the wrong in question is rights-protected. For instance, a conjoined twin arguably has a right to separate herself from her sibling even if the sibling objects. In doing this wrong, she gets new rights to act independently of her sibling, including rights to bar her sibling from sharing in experiences that she previously could not have barred her from sharing. What makes most of Cases 1–8 contentious is that the wrongdoers have no right to do the things that set in motion the train of events that produce new rights for them.

Put differently, in Cases 1–8, the wrongdoers change either their own interests or other people's interests in ways they have no right to do. And, as a result of changing those interests, new rights emerge including sometimes new rights for the wrongdoers. For instance, in *Treatment-Taking*, although Sameer has the same powerful interest in having the course of treatment before and after he takes the first dose, after he takes that first dose, he eliminates anyone else's interests in getting that course of treatment. Similarly, in most of the relationship cases above, the wrongdoer alters third-parties' interests in a relationship with the victim, while building up the link between his own interests and the victim's interests in a relationship.[8]

1.2 Causal Connections

In Cases 1–8, I describe the causal connections between the wrongs and rights in non-technical terms. Here and below, I speak loosely of rights 'arising as a result of', 'stemming from', and 'flowing from' wrongdoing. Despite the vagueness of these phrases, they pick out tight causal connections. This becomes clear when we consider a contrast case. Suppose that, as a consequence of committing fraud, Tom meets his life partner

---

[8] I thank Patrick Tomlin for highlighting that this interest-eliminating mechanism is what drives many of my cases.

in prison and they have a child together. Although his fraud enabled him get the rights of being a life partner and a parent, the causal connection between his fraud and those rights is tenuous. Tom's fraud plays a contingent role. In principle, he could have met his partner in some other, non-wrongful way.

By contrast, since Jack and Jill have thirteen children already, they have no non-wrongful way to get parental rights over a fourteenth child, Ramona. Their wrong is causally necessary, and central, to gaining parental rights over Ramona. Similarly, Hatti has no non-wrongful way to get rights over land that she neither owns nor may buy. Her wrong is causally necessary, and central, to her getting rights to remain on that land. Likewise, if a doctor won't prescribe the scarce life-saving course of treatment that Sameer needs, he has no non-wrongful way to get it. His wrong is causally necessary, and central, to his gaining the rights to continue the course of treatment. So too, Beast, as a beast, has no non-wrongful way to get Beauty to be his companion. His wrong is causally necessary, and central, to his gaining rights to be her companion. And, Maja has no non-wrongful way to have a child with the person she admires. Her wrong of stealing the genetic material is causally necessary, and central, to her gaining parental rights over Carlos.

Admittedly, some of the wrongs in Cases 1–8 seem more loosely linked, causally, to the rights they can generate. But, that looseness depends on the way we specify the case. For instance, Stella has no non-wrongful way to become a parent to Jenny, but she probably does have a non-wrongful way to become a parent to some child. Similarly, Brett, who commits the life-generating rape, has no non-wrongful way to become a parent to Lisa, but probably does have a non-wrongful way to become a parent to some child. The community has no non-wrongful way to build their new school here and now, but possibly might get planning permission in the near future if they wait. In all these cases, we might say the agents do have non-wrongful ways to achieve what they want, but their success, admittedly, depends on specific conditions being met.

The causal link between the wrongs done and the rights they generate might seem most tenuous in diachronic cases where several, contingent effects of the wrongs seem to play some role in changing the interests that then yield new rights. To show that even in diachronic cases wrongs can be the sole or primary cause of new rights, consider the following:

9. *Lock-Up*:   Raja has no right *ex ante* to lock Marie and herself in a room and throw the key out the window so that she can enjoy various relational benefits with Marie that she couldn't before. But, if Raja does lock herself up together with Marie and throw the key out the window, then *ex post* Raja starts to have new claims upon Marie which eventually solidify as rights. These claims start off small. After a brief period in which Marie might be warranted in shunning Raja, Raja then has a right that Marie engage with her decently. Raja's claims become greater the longer the two of them wait for rescue. She has a right that Marie contribute her brain-power and labor to the task of getting out. She has a right that Marie give some thought to her needs in how Marie behaves within the locked room. In time, Raja even has a right that Marie share any food or water she has with her.

In this case, as in Cases 1–8, Raja gets new rights causally *because* she did wrong. She gets her new rights normatively *in spite of* doing wrong. This is the main contrast between these cases and the non-activated rights cases noted at the outset. Wrongdoers gain due process rights, rights to decent treatment in prison, rights to contribute to public debates about how to treat wrongdoers, and so on, not just *causally* but *normatively* because they acted wrongly. They get the rights *in virtue of* acting wrongly. In the cases I am considering, wrongdoers gain rights normatively *despite* having acted wrongly in ways they had no right to act.

Before tackling the obvious objection that at least some of the wrong-generated-rights in Cases 1–9 are not real rights, let me fill out the profile of the contexts in which wrong-generated rights seem to emerge, by presenting cases in which other people do wrong.

2. Getting Rights from Other People Doing Wrong

As in Section 1, my focus is not on non-activated rights, which we can assert only once other people do wrong. Examples of such non-activated rights include the following. Only once a person does wrong can third-parties assert their moral rights to intervene. Only once someone wrongs us can we assert our rights to compensation and restoration.

Similarly, only once the electorate does wrong by electing an incompetent leader can that leader assert the moral and legal rights of that office. Likewise, only once an employer does wrong by appointing an incompetent person to a post can that person assert the moral and legal rights of that position.

The cases driving this chapter are, once again, more morally complex than this. They concern particular rights that did not pre-exist the wrong in some non-activated form. Instead, once other people do wrong, we can gain new rights that we did not have beforehand in a non-activated form. These wrong-generated rights can come either from other people wronging us (type A) or from other people wronging other people (type B). (We might also gain rights from people doing wrongs that do not directly wrong anyone such as damaging the environment. But, I'll set that possibility aside.)

Here's an example that includes both type A and type B wrongs, premised on common assumptions about family bonds:

10. *Forced marriage*:   Two teenagers, Aneeta and Mak, have no moral right *ex ante* to assert spousal claims over each other. But, suppose that they are forced by their families to marry. (All fifty US states allow underage marriage with parental approval. Twenty-five US states set no minimum age for marriage where there is parental approval and a judge's consent. Sometimes, parental approval amounts to parental pressure. (See van der Zee 2018.[9])) Suppose that, in time, Aneeta and Mak bond together, have kids, and affirm their relationship. Their families have wronged them (type A) and have wronged their spouse (type B). From those wrongs, Aneeta and Mak gain at least some of the moral rights *ex post* that spouses have against each other since their lives now intertwine legally and socially. They also gain at least some moral parental rights in relation to their kids, and some moral rights against third-parties who might interfere. (Their families might also gain moral rights from their relationship, which is another case of people getting new rights by doing wrong.)[10]

---

[9] In most cases of child marriage, the parties are an under-aged girl and an adult man. Those cases look more like abusive versions of *Beauty and the Beast* than like *Forced Marriage*.

[10] As this case shows, we can gain new duties when we are wronged: Aneeta and Mak gain duties both to each other and to their kids.

Here is a case involving discrimination:

11. *University Student*:   A 19-year-old white man, John, has no moral right *ex ante* to be allocated an undergraduate place through a university illegitimately discriminating against better-qualified women or people of color. But, if the administrators' discrimination only comes to light in John's final year, he has a right to keep his place and complete his degree. The university would do an additional wrong if it expelled him as an improperly admitted student.

Here is a property-related case, which turns on accepting the principle of *innocent purchase*:

12. *Innocent cyclist*:   If Jess buys a bicycle from Bruce without knowing or having reason to think that he stole it from someone else, then Jess has a moral right to keep the bicycle. Causally, Jess's right to the bicycle exists because Bruce stole it. (Of course, Jess's right conflicts with the original owner's right, which possibly should take priority.)

Next, here are four of the cases from Section 1, recast to show that the victims gain new moral rights because of the wrong done to them (type A):

13. *Caring Kidnapping*:   Jenny's right to stay with Stella exists as a result of Stella doing the wrong of kidnapping her and raising her undetected for many years.

14. *Beauty and the Beast*:   Beauty's right to remain with Beast follow from Beast imprisoning her.

15. *Life-generating rape*:   Lisa's right to stay with Brett arises, casually, as a result of Brett committing life-generating rape and then raising Lisa for many years. (Indeed, all of Lisa's rights flow from that wrong since her very existence depends on it.)

16. *Zygote-stealing*:   Carlos's rights in relation to his parent, Maja, exist because Maja did the wrong of stealing genetic material. (All of Carlos's rights flow from that wrong since his existence depends on it.)[11]

---

[11] A potential objection against some of my examples of wrong-generated rights is that they trade on our intuitions about dependents and, particularly, children. In reply, cases involving

Finally, here's a case involving both type A and type B wrongs, premised on common views of both property rights and family relations:

17. *Gene-mix-up*: If an IVF clinic either mismatches the genetic material of two couples, or switches the couples' embryos during implantation, then the couples gain new moral rights over, and duties to, each other and the resulting children, rights and duties they only have because of the wrong done by the clinic.

With these various cases on the table, let's analyze the phenomenon of wrong-generated rights.

3. Expectations, Investments, and Piggybacking

Many of the above cases are controversial, including some of Cases 10–17 in which we can get new rights from other people doing wrong. Consider, for instance, *Innocent Cyclist*. Instead of embracing the principle of *innocent purchase*, we might embrace the competing principle that someone's title to some property is only as legitimate as the title of the person from whom she acquired that property. According to that principle, since Bruce doesn't have a right to the bicycle, Jess doesn't get a right to it when she buys it from him.

However, not all the above cases are controversial. Sometimes, justice demands that we get new rights at least when other people do wrong, even in morally complex cases. For instance, consider *Forced Marriage*. Aneeta and Mak's marriage should not exist. Hence, ideally, they should not be able to assert moral rights over each other. Indeed, they arguably do something wrong when they do assert their spousal rights over each other. Nevertheless, *ex post* Aneeta and Mak *must* get some new moral rights (and duties) over each other, third-parties, and any kids they have. The wrongs they endure fundamentally change their interests. We would leave them in a radically morally compromised position, adding insult to injury, if we said that they gain no new rights (other than restitution

children are useful, as they do not invite the knee-jerk intuition that freedom of dissociation should prevail. Also, not all my cases involve children. Beauty, while vulnerable, is not a child. *Forced Marriage* could be recast as a case involving two of-age people who are forced to marry.

rights) from the wrongs done to them. Similarly, justice demands that both Beauty and Jenny gain new rights from their situations. The kidnapping and concealment they endure fundamentally changes their interests. They too would be in a radically morally compromised position if they didn't gain significant, new moral rights from the wrongs done to them.[12]

Cases like these show that there is nothing about morally complex, interest-changing wrongs *as such* that prevents those wrongs from generating rights, even when victims' assertion of those rights is deeply morally problematic. This gives us one plank in the defense of the more contentious claim that we can get new moral rights when we *ourselves* do serious wrong, even in morally complex cases like *Caring Kidnapping* and *Beauty and the Beast*.

The key question is: If the moral ballgame does change sometimes once we or others do wrong, why does it change? Why do we get new rights in those cases despite the serious wrong done? And, why does the moral ballgame clearly stay the same in other cases, like the following:

Poisoning: If Souz starts slowly over time to poison Zak indefensibly, she doesn't then get a moral right to carry on poisoning him until she has killed him. Other people have a duty to stop her.

Inciting: If Bo starts to spew inciting speech that even the broadest notion of free speech cannot protect, and he continues unimpeded for a long time, he doesn't then gain a moral right to continue fomenting violence until he starts a riot. Other people have a duty to stop him.

---

[12] In *Moral Repair*, Margaret Walker makes several observations that align with my view that we must privilege victims' interests. Among other things, she observes that *moral repair* is centrally about putting things right for the victim who suffered the wrong. In cases of shattering harm, no wrong is ever undone. It is at best a sequel to the wrong that either 'does right' by the victim or not. 'It's important to remember that when people behave wrongly and hurt others, we don't always think, or only think, of punishing them. Spouses and lovers are unfaithful, children selfish, associates unfair, friends deceitful; there are slights, insults, lies, acts of indifference, betrayal, aggression, or violence among us, and in some instances these dent or shatter lives. While we do sometimes seek to punish people who wrongfully harm us or others (or wish that we could), there are a lot of alternatives to punishment that in fact are always there, and we often need and use them. Some of these responses exclude each other while others can be combined or deployed in sequence' (p.9); 'what victims seek and deserve…has to do not only with what the victim or society can do to the offender, such as demanding accountability, voluntary or otherwise, but also with what the victim needs the offender or the community to do for her or him' (p.19); and, 'Victims have the power to forgive, releasing themselves from a position of anguish, anger, and protest, and releasing a wrongdoer from continuing reproach and demand' (p.28). See Walker 2006.

Explaining precisely *why* the moral ballgame changes in some cases and not others is difficult. First, we cannot give an exhaustive list of contexts in which the moral ballgame changes. Second, people's intuitions about cases differ. One person might think *Poisoning* is sufficiently morally akin to *Treatment-taking* that neither wrongdoer should get a right to continue in her conduct. But, another person might stress that Sameer, in *Treatment-taking*, doesn't intend to kill anyone and is acting to save his own life. Third, no single factor makes the difference in all cases when the moral ballgame changes.

Nevertheless, we can advance a general explanation for why the moral ballgame changes when it does. Briefly, sometimes, it's morally worse to try to undo a wrong than to accept the situation it produces. Put differently, sometimes, a wrong changes people's interests so radically that we would disrespect or harm them more to ignore that change than to accept it. Other times, such as in *Poisoning* and *Inciting*, it is clearly better to try to abort the wrong than to accept the situation that it is producing. Despite the consequentialist tone, this general explanation is not a consequentialist explanation. Protecting innocent persons' interests and rights, which can change radically once wrongs are done, is what must drive us often to accept a wrong-produced situation.[13]

This general explanation relies on the following premise: In ballgame-changing cases, the fact that the new rights are grounded in interests that are born out of (serious) wrongdoing does not block their generation.[14] Briefly, in defense of this premise, nothing in the Razian interest

---

[13] As this general explanation and the discussion so far make clear, this analysis of wrong-generated rights is rooted in a broadly Razian interest theory of rights, which says that we have a right when an interest or set of interests is sufficiently strong that it grounds duties in others. This is the account of rights that I find most persuasive. Although I won't explore the will theory of rights in this chapter, I suspect that wrong-generated rights operate in a fairly similar way within the will theory with a few modifications. The will theory says that the function of a right is to give a person control over another person's duty (and, one way to read that is that rights protect our particular *interest* in having control to decide whether others have to honour duties or not). Most trivially, in doing serious wrong, I can give other people new powers—new forms of control—over how I should act. I also can give other people new forms of control over how others should act. For instance, in marrying my child to another child, I give them new powers over each other, over third parties, and over me. And, in doing serious wrong, I sometimes give myself new powers over how other people should act. The reasons I can make these normative changes to my own and others' powers are the same reasons that I'll discuss here in relation to interest theory: legitimate expectations, personal investments, and piggybacking (in the sense that it matters not just to you, but to others that you have this new power).

[14] I thank Joseph Raz for pressing me to address this issue.

theory of rights which I deploy here blocks the generation of rights that are grounded in wrong-created interests. Nothing in the theory says that interests that would otherwise be sufficient to ground duties in other people are insufficient to ground those duties when they are the fruit of wrongdoing. Admittedly, the rights they ground could be overridden or could be forfeited. But, those matters are different matters from the idea that the rights *won't come into being in the first place* if rooted in wrong-generated interests. I explore these thoughts further in Section 4.

The analysis I am offering can be challenged from the opposite direction as well. A critic might say that the real issue is that the wrongdoing that features in all of my cases is irrelevant to whether the parties' interests ground rights, in the same way that the white color of a light switch is irrelevant to whether that switch turns on the light.[15] In response, in all of the cases I have described, the wrongdoing is more like the electrical wiring of the switch than its color. Built into the parties' interests in these cases is the fact that they have a corrupt pedigree. With luck, the force of this point will become clearer in the analysis below.

Although no single factor changes the moral ballgame in all game-changing cases, an overlapping set of factors working in different combinations distinguish Cases 1–17 from cases like *Poisoning* and *Inciting*. These factors are: (a) legitimate expectations; (b) personal investments; and (c) rights-piggybacking. Each of these factors highlights a way in which our fundamental interests can change significantly. Let's take them in turn.

3.1 Expectations

Most of Cases 1–17 involve people forming expectations, such as relying on property or relying on other people. In *Squatting*, Hatti relies on the fragile land that she is using unchallenged. In *Treatment-taking*, Sameer relies on the life-saving drugs he is taking, without which he will suffer horribly. In *Caring Kidnapping*, *Life-generating Rape*, and *Zygote-stealing*, both the wrongdoing parent and the child rely on each other in a long-term, mutually supportive, joint narrative. In *University Student*, John

---

[15] I thank David Sobel for this objection and for putting the point with this analogy.

relies on the institution that is educating him. In *School Building*, the city and families rely on the school they have established.

In all these cases, the people's expectations start out as illegitimate. But, legitimacy is neither binary nor fixed. It can grow by degrees. Illegitimate expectations can become increasingly legitimate over time, especially if they are left unchecked and become integral to a person's life well-lived. Legitimacy can also change abruptly. Illegitimate expectations can become legitimate at a stroke when, for example, an authorizing agent gives us permission to do a thing which we can only do legitimately if we have that permission. When people's illegitimate expectations morph into legitimate ones in these ways, their interests become bound up in those expectations.

But, of course, illegitimate expectations cannot always morph into legitimate expectations. The wrongdoers' expectations in *Poisoning* and *Inciting* remain illegitimate as the wrongdoers progress in their nefarious projects. No one can gain a right to continue indefensibly to harm someone else simply because we have failed to stop her before now. In some cases, a party remains unimpeded because it—traditionally a state—is too powerful to be stopped. And sometimes, a party remains unimpeded because we're unaware of what the party is doing. For instance, Ariel Castro held three women captive in his house for over a decade because Cleveland authorities didn't know what he was doing. When powerful parties such as states engage in acquisitive wars or colonialism, they are akin to the person who is slowly poisoning her victim. They gain no new rights simply from the fact they haven't been impeded. However, individual members of an acquisitive state who are prodded to resettle in the conquered territory may indeed, in time, gain new moral rights to remain or to be compensated if removed.

I expand below on this idea that only sometimes can legitimate expectations arise from illegitimate expectations.

3.2 Personal Investments

Most of Cases 1–17 involve people investing parts of themselves, such as their genes, labor, skills, uniqueness, material resources, and personal identity. In *Squatting*, Hattie invests her labor. She also builds up her personal history around persisting in that place. In *School Building*, the city invests scarce resources, and the community families invest in the resulting school. In all the relationship cases, both parties invest their labor, skills, personal identity, and uniqueness into that relationship. In some of the relationship cases, the wrongdoer invests their genes too. In *Innocent Cyclist*, Jess invests her resources. In *Gene Mix-up*, the couples invest their genes, gestational labor, and personal identity.

Some kinds of investment, such as modest amounts of recoverable material resources and our genes, possibly aren't potent enough on their own to give us new rights in cases of serious wrongdoing. But, other kinds of investment, such as caring labor or unique skill, might be. And, combinations of investments—such as genes plus extensive caring labor—probably are potent enough together to give us some rights. This is because making such investments often radically alters our own interests and others' interests, and this, in turn, changes which rights we can assert.

3.3 Piggybacking

Third, some of the above cases involve a variant of the much-discussed phenomenon of piggybacking whereby a right-holder's own interests are insufficient to ground her rights, but others' interests in her having these rights are sufficient to ground them. *Caring Kidnapping, Life-generating Rape, Beauty and the Beast, Zygote-Stealing*, and even *Forced Marriage, School Building*, and *Gene Mix-Up* all have the structure of piggybacking. (On piggybacking, see Raz 1986, 179, 247–8; Raz 1994, 149–51, 274–5; Sreenivasan 2005; and Cruft 2013. On duty-bearing as a ground for holding rights, see Wenar 2013). By contrast, *Squatting, Treatment-taking, University Student*, and *Innocent Cyclist* do not.

Joseph Raz describes the ordinary phenomenon not as *piggybacking*, but as a *double harmony* between the right-holder's interests and others' interests in her having the rights in question. A journalist's rights to access sensitive material, enter dangerous places, protect her sources, be secure against action for libel or breach of privacy, and report freely would lack the weight and importance they have, Raz says, if protecting the journalist's interests did not also serve society's interests in a free press (Raz 1986, 247–8). Similarly, a judge's rights to decide which evidence is admissible, to instruct the jury, to issue judgements, and to determine sentences would lack the weight and importance they have if the judge's rights did not also serve society's interests in a functioning corrective justice process.

Critics of Raz such as Leif Wenar and Frances Kamm point out that it is not so much the *weight* as the very *existence* of the journalist's and judge's rights that depends on society's interests in them having these rights. Their rights are *grounded* at least partly, if not solely, in society's interests.[16] Wenar states:

> Whatever interest a judge has in exercising her right to impose criminal punishments, for example, it cannot be sufficient to justify the dramatic normative effects of her exercise of this right. Raz's response to this difficulty attempts to boost the strength of the judge's interest in exercising her power by drawing attention to the fact that protecting the judge's interest also protects the interests of the public. Yet this attempt to add the interests of the public to the interest of the judge merely highlights the fact that the judge's interest is in itself insufficient to ground this right.   (Wenar 2005, 242)

In other words, there is no double harmony in these cases since the right-holder's own interests play little or no part in grounding her rights. She piggybacks on her society's interests in her holding her official role. In referring to roles, however, Raz offers a potential route to a solution, Wenar says, which is that rights do not attach to individuals. They attach to roles.

Let's remain agnostic about Wenar's claim that all rights attach to roles, but use the two ideas that, first, a right can be grounded in others' interests; and, second, a right can attach specifically to a person's role. Armed with these tools, we can say that, even if the wrongdoers' interests in *Caring Kidnapping*, *Life-generating Rape*, and *Beauty and the Beast* can play no part in generating rights for them (or the part their

---

[16] Kamm observes that 'If the satisfaction of the interests of others is the reason why the journalist gets a right to have his interest protected, his interest is *not sufficient* to give rise to the duty of non-interference with his speech'. Kamm (2002), 485. Cited from Wenar (2005), 242 n.34.

interests would play is outweighed by competing factors), nevertheless these wrongdoers can gain role-related rights out of their wrongdoing when their victims' interests (or others' interests) are sufficient to ground their role-related rights.[17]

In *Caring Kidnapping*, *Life-generating Rape*, and *Beauty and the Beast*, the wrongdoers have significant duties to their victims. Stella has significant duties to care for, nurture, love, respect, and value Jenny, whom she is raising. She has these parental duties both before and after her kidnapping is exposed. Indeed, the longer she delays exposing the kidnapping, the greater her duties become to love and care for Jenny, since the kidnapping has shaped Jenny's life course and radically changed her interests. Similarly, Beast has significant caring duties toward Beauty both before and after he frees her since his wrongdoing alienates her from her community, changes her options, and, consequently, changes her interests.

These caring duties give the wrongdoers duty-based rights to fulfil them. (For an examination of why duties are not rights, but can be protected by rights, see Cruft 2006; and Brownlee (2012) ch. 4, sect. 2.) These duty-based rights derive from the rights of the victim, who has done no wrong and who has a strong claim-right that the wrongdoer remain in this caring relationship provided that (a) the wrongdoer's performance in that caring role is adequate; (b) their continued occupancy of that role is compatible with, or necessary to, the victim's best interests; and (c) the victim has legitimate expectations and wishes that the relationship persist.[18]

---

[17] Gopal Sreenivasan is sceptical of the idea of piggybacking even in ordinary cases involving journalists and judges, arguing that such grounds for rights instrumentalize the person as a right-holder. If a journalist's own interests are insufficiently weighty to defeat others' interests in knowing her sources for example, then 'either she has to reveal her sources or, more plausibly, freedom of the press will have to be regarded as (at least, largely) a matter of net social utility, *rather than* as a matter of individual rights.' See Sreenivasan (2005). I shall set this general worry aside while noting that, in relationship cases, it's hard to say that we protect the wrongdoer's interests purely for instrumental reasons. This is because relationships involve interdependencies. In close relationships, our rights are *intersubjective*. They are rights that we hold together. They're not group rights because, in a relationship, I have claims against you that differ from your claims against me. But, our rights as partners or as parent and child are intertwined: you cannot have your rights against me unless I have my rights against you. This fact scaffolds further the claim that wrongdoers can, and indeed must, have rights in the relationships in which their victims have rights.

[18] One problem with the voluntarist argument (i.e. that a child has a right to stay with the parent she chooses) is that it ignores adaptive preferences, trauma, and vulnerability. Despite

One challenge for this analysis is legitimacy. Ordinary piggybackers such as journalists and judges undoubtedly have their role-related rights because they are legitimate occupants of their legitimate offices and have the right to perform the functions of those offices. By contrast, the (putative) rights-holders in my cases, such as Stella or Beast, seem to be illegitimate role-holders. They seem less like real judges and more like the person who grabs a judge's robe from chambers, sits behind the judge's bench, and dispenses justice competently for many years before being discovered.[19] My cases seem to require us to ignore the value of having correct procedures for legitimate role-occupancy. Correct procedures not only promise quality control, expectation-satisfaction, predictability, uniformity, coordination, and accountability, but also satisfy some demands of justice.

However, as I suggested above, legitimacy comes in degrees and can either change over time or morph abruptly. Stella and Beast start out as illegitimate occupants of their roles. But, they can grow in legitimacy over time, especially if the people most closely affected—their victims—affirm their legitimacy.

Moreover, sometimes, correct procedures matter less than we suppose. People are most likely to enjoy growing legitimacy when their expertise, skill, competence, and other distinguishing features matter more than the correctness of the procedures through which they come to occupy their role.

One context in which correct procedures matter less than unique skills are emergencies. In emergencies, competence is king. If an epidemic breaks out in a war-torn country, someone with medical training but no practicing license has a duty-based claim-right to treat suffering

those worries, Amy Mullin observes that: 'The idea that, in child-custody cases, the preferences of a child should be given consideration, and not just the "best interest" of the child, is beginning to gain acceptance in the U.S., Canada and Europe. "Gregory K," who at age 12 was able to speak rationally and persuasively to support his petition for new adoptive parents, made a good case for recognizing childhood agency in a family court. Less dramatically, in divorce proceedings, older children are routinely consulted for their views about proposed arrangements for their custody' Mullin (2014).

---

[19] In this discussion, I bracket questions about structural injustice which could lead us to say that ordinary judges, police officers, legislators, and executives are illegitimate occupants of their offices in virtue of an unfair distribution of positions of authority within society. I thank Fay Niker for this observation.

people around her. Her moral right to act without a license derives from the needy people's rights to assistance.[20] Similarly, someone with life-guard training, firefighting skills, CPR training, self-defense training, or insider knowledge, who is not formally authorized to act, nonetheless can have duty-based rights to act in emergencies, and those rights derive from others' humanitarian rights to assistance.

Even in some non-emergency contexts, competence matters more for role-occupancy than correct procedures do. Indeed, it is interesting to identify the domains that prioritize competence and those that priori-tize correct procedures. It is notable that, for some of our most morally important roles like parenting, correct procedures are secondary. Admittedly, Stella's rights as a parent are more morally fragile and con-tingent than ordinary parents' rights are because ordinary parents' rights do not depend on their child's wishes or her *best* interests (it's enough that the parents' efforts be adequate). Nevertheless, Stella has competency-related rights despite the procedure through which she became a parent. Her rights are akin to those of a journalist who gains credentials in an unorthodox way. She can lose her credentials if she doesn't do her job well; her rights turn on her competence and unique value in the role, and not on the proper procedure for coming to hold it.

Professions such as journalism are structured to privilege expertise over credentials. Someone without journalistic training could go into the field, get scoops that other journalists miss, become indispensable to a newsroom, and grow to have the legitimacy, and get the credentials, of professional standing. (In doing this, she would become an ordinary piggybacker, as society came to have interests in her having the protec-tions of the formal position.) Other professions such as academia can also privilege expertise over correct procedures. As the films *Good Will Hunting* and *Gifted* show, a talented mathematician with no formal training can get an elite institution's support when society has more interest in him or her being educated than in him or her jumping through all the correct hoops to become a university student.

---

[20] Similarly, in quasi-emergencies where institutional structures are weak, such as in the 18th–19th-century Western frontier, people can gain legitimate role-occupancy when no other people with better credentials are available to perform the requisite functions. For instance, when few preachers could be found to conduct marriages, funerals, and other services, mayors, ship captains, and military leaders became legitimate officiants of these services.

By contrast, in other professions, a person cannot grow into legitimate role-occupancy by squatting in it for a long time. If we have a functioning criminal justice system, then squatting behind a judge's bench will not give someone rights to that office, even if she dispenses justice beautifully. If we have a functioning republic, then hijacking the presidency will not give someone the title to that office, even if he executes its functions competently. If we have a secure legal system, then engaging in vigilante law enforcement will not entitle someone to the formal standing of a police officer, even if she does it well.

Many of Cases 1–17 necessarily privilege skill and uniqueness over correct procedures. In *Forced Marriage*, for instance, Aneeta and Mak are more like unlicensed doctors working in an emergency than like would-be judges. Their situation is akin to a crisis. Despite the illegitimacy of the forced marriage procedure, they get some rights to act, grounded partly in their spouse's and kids' interests and partly in their own interests.

In *Beauty and the Beast*, as noted above, Beast is more like a would-be judge than an unlicensed doctor in an emergency. He should not enjoy the position he has as Beauty's companion even though he becomes a good companion. But, unlike the would-be judge who, in a functioning legal system, does not gain legitimacy over time, Beast does gain legitimacy over time precisely because he has taken away Beauty's functioning social system and replaced it with his own company. Thereby, he sets up the conditions for her other joint narratives to end and his and her lives to intertwine in ways that radically change Beauty's interests. This seems to be doubly problematic: Beast is both holding a role he shouldn't hold and engineering conditions to make his role legitimate. But this result is difficult to resist if we privilege Beauty's interests.

The same is true for Jenny and Stella in *Caring Kidnapping*. Stella should not enjoy the position she has as Jenny's parent even though she is a caring parent. But, the longer Jenny stays with her, the more their lives intertwine and the less Jenny is intertwined with her original family. Jenny's interests change radically, thereby setting up the conditions for Stella to become her legitimate caregiver. Again, this seems doubly problematic but is difficult to resist if we privilege Jenny's interests.

This reality about our relationship-interests is morally tragic. The original parents of Jenny now must compete with Stella for the right to raise her. And, if we prioritize Jenny's psychological and emotional interests, then, in time, Stella will have the stronger claim.

This reality about our relationship-interests not only is tragic, but also has a sting in its tail, because it can be exploited. During custody battles, the parent who has a child in her care has reason to stall proceedings because the longer the child remains in her care, settled in school, and doing well, the stronger her claim is that the child's best interests are served by preserving the status quo. This strategy not only changes our views about the child's best interests. It *actually changes* the child's best interests.

In addition to being exploitable, this reality seems to invite a bad moral precedent. Seemingly, all a person needs to do to get relationship rights is succeed in acting wrongly in a way that alters and then serves another person's interests. Seemingly, all a person needs to do to get parental rights that are potentially stronger that the original parents' rights is kidnap a child and raise her well for long enough that the child comes to have legitimate interests in continuing the relationship. Seemingly, all a person needs to do to get companion rights is kidnap someone and treat her well enough that she then has interests in staying with him.

This worry about bad precedents is particularly acute for women's reproductive rights. History and literature overflow with examples of men violating women, both within marriage and outside marriage, precisely to gain the parental rights that can arise from rape. In *The Forsyte Saga*, Soames desperately wants a son. He rapes his wife Irene to try to get one. In the film *The Duchess*, the Duke of Devonshire is desperate for an heir. He rapes his wife in the hope of getting one. Most legal jurisdictions have historically granted men a legal right to sexual relations with their wife. Many jurisdictions still allow marital rape.

This worry about bad precedents is problematic more generally. Rights are supposed to end the argument and tell us what to do. But, some of the wrong-generated rights I have identified are highly unpalatable. Ideally, we want to avoid a moral framework for the general regulation of our behavior that entails these kinds of rights. Acknowledging these rights seems to leave us without good action-guidance.

In reply, first, morality is complex, tragic, pluralistic, and demanding. Many a correct moral conclusion is simply the least bad option of a bad bunch.

Second, we can neutralize part of the sting of some wrong-generated rights by rejecting exclusivity. We need not assume that Beast's rights, Stella's rights, or even Jess's rights are *exclusive*. Someone can have a right to be a parent, or a companion, or an owner without having an *exclusive* right to be that thing.[21] While helpful, non-exclusivity removes only part of the sting since these rights remain unpalatable regardless of whether they are exclusive.

Third, although we cannot entirely avoid the undesirable result that people can gain new rights when they successfully do serious wrongs which alter others' core interests, nevertheless we can highlight that the rights they gain are part of the *ex post* analysis which we undertake only after the moral ballgame has changed. We can insist that *ex ante* people have no right to do wrongs that can generate these benefits. People have no right to reshape others' interests in these ways. We should intervene if people attempt such wrongs. And, failing that, we should intervene as quickly as possible after they do such wrongs to prevent victims' interests, or others' interests, from changing too much. Moreover, we should insist that, even once victims' or others' interests have changed, wrongdoers have duties to compensate, apologize, repair, and restore as well as possible when that is consistent with respecting those changed interests.

All that said, we might still hanker for strategies to resist the above analysis of wrong-generated rights. One potential strategy appeals to the defeasibility of rights. A second appeals to the conditionality of rights. Let's take each in turn.

4. Possible Solutions?

4.1 Defeasibility

Rights have special normative force. They are often described as conversation-stoppers, argument-thresholds, and trumps. They are special, weighty reasons that tend to override competing considerations to pursue other social goals. They are a check on straightforward conse-quentialist reasoning. In virtue of these special properties, rights secure

---

[21] I thank Clare Chambers for this point.

for us a basic level of equal treatment, protection, and freedom. Such equal protections are only genuine if rights cannot be easily defeated. As Peter Jones puts it:

> If rights can be removed or overridden when they come up against competing considerations, that may seem to imperil their very character as rights…[For example,] what sort of guarantees would we possess if the right to a fair trial or the right not to be tortured were not absolute [i.e. indefeasible]?   (Jones 1994, 190)

But, of course, despite their normative force, rights are not absolute. They are sometimes defeasible. First, some rights are more important than other rights. When more important rights conflict with less important rights, the more important rights should usually defeat the less important rights. Second, sometimes, a projected bad outcome is so horrific that the argumentative threshold posed by the rights at stake is surmounted, at least when those rights are less important (Dworkin 1984, 153–67). In slightly stronger terms, Jones states that 'For virtually every right that one might assert it is possible to think of circumstances in which there is a plausible case for setting that right aside' (Jones 1994, 192).

The defeasibility of rights offers a possible strategy to resist the full implications of morally complex wrong-generated rights. This strategy says that at least the most problematic wrong-generated rights are invariably defeated by competing considerations. To test this possibility, let's return to *Caring Kidnapping*. Jenny's right to remain in this caring parent-child relationship is defeasible (by hypothesis). So too then is Stella's right, which derives from Jenny's interests and rights. If Jenny's right is actually defeated by her original family's prior claim, then so too is Stella's derivative, duty-based right to raise her.

Which factors are salient to determining whose rights prevail in this case? Would it matter if Jenny's original family includes brothers and sisters whom she doesn't know and who don't know her, as well as a mother, a father, and some grandparents? These people all have legitimate rights-claims. Do their claims collectively defeat hers (and with hers, Stella's)? Would it matter that, whereas the members of this larger family all have each other, Stella has no other family? Do Jenny's expectations and wishes defeat the claims of whichever parents she does not want to raise her? Do her best interests and no one else's trump all other considerations? These questions illustrate the complexity of the project of untangling the competing claims to determine which rights should triumph.

The problem with the defeasibility strategy is that a right is not much of a right if it is *always* defeated by competing considerations. And, to avoid wrong-generated rights like Stella's, we would have to say that all rights like Jenny's from which Stella's rights could derive are always defeated by competing considerations. If intersubjective rights like Jenny's are so easily defeated that they fall to any counter-pressure, then they are not much of an argumentative threshold. They do not trump anything. They have no special normative force. They're not really rights.[22]

One way forward might be to unpack *defeasibility* in terms of a proportionality test: Is the interference with a given undisputed right proportionate and, hence, justified (i.e. an infringement)? Such a proportionality test would have at least four conditions. First, the interference with the right must have a legitimate aim. Second, a rational connection must exist between that aim and the interference. Third, no less restrictive means will suffice to achieve the legitimate aim. In other words, the interference is necessary. Fourth, the legitimate aim must be weightier than the right at stake.[23] This approach would give us a set of tools to combat some of the questions that the above cases raise. However, this approach is unlikely to fend off all complex wrong-generated rights, since those rights, and the rights and duties that can produce them, will sometimes pass this proportionality test.

4.2 Conditionality

Whereas defeasibility and absoluteness pertain to the moral *weight* of rights, conditionality pertains to their *nature*. Most, if not all, rights are conditional in some respect. Consider, for example, contractual rights.

---

[22] In contrast with my line of thought here, Benedict Rumbold argues that a right may still be considered a right even when it fails to present decisive reasons for action against competing considerations. See Rumbold (2018).

[23] Alasdair Cochrane summarized the proportionality test along these lines in a lecture at All Souls College, Oxford (2016).

If you hire me to paint your house for £500, my right to the £500 is conditional on my painting your house. Similarly, a medical professional's moral right to treat people suffering in a war-torn area is conditional at least on her having the requisite medical expertise. But are rights conditional on anything else, like not coming about through *egregious* wrongdoing?

Addressing this question returns us to the premise noted at the beginning of Section 3: the fact that these rights arise from wrongdoing is not a reason to reject these rights. A critic of the above analysis might ask why (serious) wrongdoing does not block the generation of rights, at least for the wrongdoer.

In reply, first, it is true that egregious wrongdoing can be a deal-breaker for many rights. But, it is not a deal-breaker for *all* rights. Some of our rights are secure, which means that we have these rights regardless of whether we (or others) meet certain standards of good behavior and good standing. We cannot forfeit these secure rights through bad behavior. James Nickel holds that, at the most basic level, we have four secure claims:

(1) a secure claim to have a life;
(2) a secure claim to lead a life;
(3) a secure claim from excessively unfair treatment; and
(4) a secure claim from degradation and cruelty (Nickel 2005 385–402, 391ff and Nickel 2006, 62ff).

If we flesh out the details of these secure claims, we will find that they cover many of the morally complex cases that generate rights, including intimate relations of interdependency, emergencies, and core-service provision. Consequently, conditionality does not enable us to avoid the conclusion that morally complex wrongs can generate rights in troubling cases.

Second, when egregious wrongdoing is a deal-breaker, what that means is that we *forfeit* our rights. That is quite a different matter from saying that, in light of our wrongdoing, we do *not get the rights in the first place*. A reader who is skeptical of the above analysis must explain why, when we act wrongly in potentially game-changing ways, we do not even get the rights in the first place that would ensue from our wrongdoing. I noted in Section 3 that there is nothing in the Razian interest theory as such that says wrong-generated interests cannot be sufficiently strong to ground duties in others.

If the defeasibility strategy and conditionality strategy offer the best prospects to avoid the analysis of this chapter, then we must conclude that, sometimes, doing serious wrong gives us significant new rights despite the morally tainted pedigree of the interests that produce these rights. In a nutshell, we shouldn't assume that the interests which underpin rights are necessarily morally clean. As this chapter shows, often they are not.[24]

References

Brownlee, Kimberley (2012), *Conscience and Conviction: The Case for Civil Disobedience*. Oxford: Oxford University Press.

CBS News (2017), 'Judge Rescinds Order Granting Rapist Joint Legal Custody of Victim's Child', CBS News, 17 October 2017: https://www.cbsnews.com/news/judge-rescinds-order-granting-rapist-joint-legal-custody-of-victims-child/

Cowan, Jill (2015), 'Dickson County Couple Drops Sonya Custody Battle', *The Tennessean*, 25 August 2015: https://www.tennessean.com/story/news/local/dickson/2015/08/24/dickson-county-couple-drops-sonya-custody-battle/32290381/

Cruft, Rowan (2006), 'What Aren't Duties Rights?' in *The Philosophical Quarterly* 56: 223, 175–92.

Cruft, Rowan (2013), 'Why is it Disrespectful to Violate Rights?' in *Proceedings of the Aristotelian Society* 113: 2 pt2, 201–24.

---

[24] For helpful written comments, I thank Helen Brown Coverdale, Clare Chambers, Luís Duarte d'Almeida, Simon Gansinger, Simon Palmer, Alice Pinheiro Walla, Patrick Tomlin, Leif Wenar, and an anonymous referee. I also thank the editors, David Sobel, Peter Vallentyne, and Steven Wall, for valuable suggestions to improve the chapter. For helpful discussions, I thank the participants of the University of Edinburgh Foundations of Normativity Conference, June 2016; the Nuffield College Political Theory Workshop, Oxford, February 2018; the Institute of Philosophy's Practical, Political, and Ethical Seminar, London, May 2018, the Oxford Studies in Political Philosophy Conference, Pavia, June 2018, the Cambridge Moral Sciences Club, November 2018; the York Political Theory Seminar, April 2019; and the ANU Philosophy Department Seminar, Canberra, August 2019. For helpful feedback on related work, I thank the participants of the *Being Sure of Each Other* manuscript workshop at the University of Warwick, September 2016.

Dworkin, Ronald (1984), 'Rights as Trumps', *Theories of Rights*, ed. Jeremy Waldron. Oxford: Oxford University Press.

Jones, Peter (1994), *Rights*. Palgrave.

Kamm, Frances (2002), 'Rights', *Oxford Handbook of Jurisprudence and Philosophy of Law*, ed. Jules L. Coleman, Kenneth Einar Himma, and Scott J. Shapiro. Oxford: Oxford University Press.

Mullin, Amy (2014), 'Philosophy of Childhood', in *The Stanford Encyclopedia of Philosophy*, ed. Ed Zalta: https://plato.stanford.edu/entries/childhood/

Nickel, James (2005), 'Poverty and Human Rights', *The Philosophical Quarterly* 55 (2005), 385–402.

Nickel, James (2006), *Making Sense of Human Rights*, 2nd edition. Oxford: Blackwell.

Sreenivasan, Gopal (2005), 'A Hybrid Theory of Claim Rights' in *Oxford Journal of Legal Studies* 25: 2, 257–74.

Stilz, Anna (2017), 'Settlement, Expulsion, and Return', *Politics, Philosophy & Economics* 16: 4, 351–74.

Raz, Joseph (1986), *The Morality of Freedom*. Oxford: Oxford University Press.

Raz, Joseph (1994), *Ethics in the Public Domain*. Oxford: Oxford University Press.

Raz, Joseph (2009 [1979]), *The Authority of Law*. Oxford: Oxford University Press, chs. 14–15.

Rumbold, Benedict (2018), 'Towards a More Particularist View of Rights' Stringency', in *Res Publica*: doi: 10.1007/s11158-018-9396-3

van der Zee, Renate (2018), "It Put an End to My Childhood": The Hidden Scandal of US Child Marriage', *The Guardian*, 6 February 2018: https://www.theguardian.com/inequality/2018/feb/06/it-put-an-end-to-my-childhood-the-hidden-scandal-of-us-child-marriage

Waldron, Jeremy (1981), 'A Right to Do Wrong', *Ethics*, 92: 1, Special Issue on Rights, 21–39.

Walker, Margaret (2006), *Moral Repair*. Cambridge University Press.

Wenar, Leif (2005), 'The Nature of Rights', *Philosophy & Public Affairs* 33: 3, 242.

Wenar, Leif (2013), 'The Nature of Claim-Rights', *Ethics*, Symposium on Rights and the Direction of Duties, 123: 2, 202–29.

2

Duties to the Dead

Is Posthumous Mitigation of Injustice Possible?

Zofia Stemplowska

1. Introduction

Is it ever possible to mitigate any of the past injustice that was done to the living but who are no longer alive? Or should we rather think that, as Horkheimer put it, '[p]ast injuries took place in the past and the matter ended there. The slain are truly slain'?[1] I will argue that matters did not end with the death of the victims; it is possible to mitigate some injustice done to those who are no longer alive. As a result, the living will sometimes have duties to the dead to mitigate some of the injustice they suffered.

Much valuable ink has now been expended on arguing about what might be owed to the living on account of past injustices.[2] Much less focus has been paid to the question of what might be owed at the bar of justice to the dead.[3] One such strategy of establishing that mitigation of past injustice is possible, despite the fact that the victims are no longer alive, would be to deny that one's well-being can only be affected during one's biological life and argue that since we can benefit or harm people posthumously we may mitigate (or exacerbate) injustice when we do so. And while I think that we can harm or benefit people posthumously, in

[1] Transl. and quoted in Meyer (2015).
[2] See for example Sher (1981), Thompson (2002), Boxill (2003), Lu (2007), Butt (2009), and Spinner-Halev (2012).
[3] Either because some, like Scheffler (2013), seem to be skeptical that mitigation of injustice is possible or because they side step the topic of posthumous justice entirely (cf. Kagan, 2012) or because, while they assume the existence of duties to the dead they, explicitly, do not set out to justify their existence since their focus lies elsewhere (cf. Ridge, 2003). Others, like Meyer (2004), offer such a justification but in this chapter I focus on a distinctive strategy.

Zofia Stemplowska, *Duties to the Dead: Is Posthumous Mitigation of Injustice Possible?* In: *Oxford Studies in Political Philosophy Volume 6*. Edited by: David Sobel, Peter Vallentyne, and Steven Wall, Oxford University Press (2020). © Zofia Stemplowska.
DOI: 10.1093/oso/9780198852636.003.0002

this chapter I explore a complementary strategy that is not directly concerned with establishing the possibility of posthumous benefit and harm.[4] Although some of my arguments bear on the possibility of posthumous well-being, I want to show that justice should be concerned with the distribution of opportunities people have for the fulfillment of their preferences, including their preferences over outcomes that stretch beyond their well-being and biological lives. Since we can affect such outcomes even though the people whose preferences are at stake are no longer alive, we can curtail, advance, and mitigate (in)justice.

I will have the space here to establish only one element of this picture: that death of the victims of injustice does not make mitigation of the injustice impossible. I will simply assume that, in general, bystanders can have duties to mitigate injustice that they did not perpetrate themselves. I will also assume (and return to briefly in section 5) that if posthumous mitigation of injustice is possible then sometimes the bystanders will have duties to do so rather than always needing to attend only to the interests of the living. As I will understand it here, an injustice occurs when people are not treated by others as others have a duty to treat them.[5] An injustice is understood here as 'past' or 'historic', even if it is still ongoing just as long as many of its victims are no longer alive, since this fact poses a unique problem for mitigation of the injustice. Mitigation is understood as anything that reduces the extent of the injustice suffered by the victim, however limited the reduction may be. Through the initial sections of the chapter, I will work without a discussion of what we should mean by mitigation. In section 4, I will distinguish between a narrow view of mitigation where mitigation requires something akin to direct rectification and a permissive view where simply improving the position of the victim overall will qualify as mitigation. Whichever reasonable version of the view, or a mix of views, we adopt, posthumous

---

[4] I pursue the other strategy in 'Descendants', a working paper.

[5] This is a sufficient condition only that suffices for my purposes here (I do not take a stance in the chapter on whether injustice may also consist in something else). 'Treatment by others' here is meant to encompass both treatment by individuals and by collectives. In saying that a person has a duty to treat another in a certain way I am merely saying that she is required to deliver such treatment, even if she has some discretion about how to achieve it, not that the recipient necessarily has a right to it.

mitigation of past injustice is possible, though there are many more opportunities for it on the more permissive understanding of mitigation.

There are what we might call two problems of injustice. The first problem of injustice is that it amounts to a particular mistreatment (and often loss) for the victims. That is, injustice deprives victims of something particular that they are due from others in a given instance (e.g. bodily integrity, property, particular opportunities, an appropriate reaction, etc.). The second problem of injustice is that the mistreatment by others is a violation of the moral status of people as beings to whom the particular mistreatment should not happen. We address this second problem of injustice, at least partially, when we affirm the moral status of the victim of injustice. Some may consider such mitigation of injustice through the affirmation of the value of the person as, at best, symbolic.[6] In what follows, however, I focus on the mitigation of the first problem of injustice: the fact that injustice consists in a particular mistreatment that often results in a tangible loss.

I begin, in section 2, by setting out in general terms why I think it is possible to mitigate injustice even if its victims are no longer alive. As already signaled, the idea appeals to the fact that people have preferences concerning posthumous outcomes. In section 3, I defend the idea that justice should care about such preferences even if these are impersonal preferences. In section 4, I say more about what needs to be the case about people's preferences that fulfilling them posthumously can qualify as posthumous injustice mitigation. In section 5, I consider the

---

[6] I do not think it is merely symbolic and I think it too is possible. We affirm the moral status of a person when we guide or are prepared to guide our actions in light of the fact that the people are sources or repositories of value. (I put aside the role perpetrators must play in this.) We can, for example, observe their wishes (as long as these wishes themselves did not reflect the person's inaccurate idea that they lacked the required moral status). Someone's death is no obstacle to us being able to nonetheless guide our actions in light of her being a source of value. To be clear, for our action to count as affirmation of the moral status of the relevant person, we must be motivated by the fact that the person herself is the source of value. For example, when we fulfill her wishes we must do it because they were *her* wishes. If, by contrast, we fulfill them merely because we independently want to act this way, we may show respect for the victim's judgement, but we do not thereby affirm the person's moral status as someone who is of such value as to affect or constrain how we act. However, if we are at least in part motivated by the fact that these were their wishes, then we thereby respect the dead as sources of value that guide our actions.

implications of my claims given the enormity of past injustice we face today. Section 6 concludes.

Of course, the presence of injustice and dead victims does not only give rise to considerations of what duties of mitigation, if any, we may owe the dead. We have duties with respect to the dead that we owe the living. We also have duties to the dead, if my argument is successful, that we have on account of injustices done to them once they were no longer alive. And, of course, we have a host of reasons that have nothing to do with past justice to the dead to set requirements regarding how we remember, commemorate, or forget the dead. But my focus here is on the duties we owe to the dead on account of the fact that they had suffered injustice while alive and whose construction does not presuppose that we must be able to benefit or harm them now that they are no longer alive.

2. The Possibility of Posthumous Mitigation of Injustice

Let us begin with a case of someone having a project. Suppose I would like to become a published novelist. My opportunity for it to happen depends on what I do as well as what others do. Suppose a barrier to the success of my project has been erected during my lifetime—although I do not know about it, the manuscript of my novel has been stolen from the publisher. Clearly, it would remove this barrier to my success as a novelist to retrieve it and return it to the publisher. But if it would remove this barrier to the publication of my novel to return it to the publisher while I am still alive, it would also remove this barrier to do so after I am already dead. In essence, just as long as our opportunities for X—for example, to achieve things and to have things happen to us—span more than our biological lifetimes, they can be posthumously advanced and curtailed. And it is undeniable that some of our projects span more than our lifetimes. Some of our projects may even require our death. For example, Chopin's opportunity to have his heart buried in Warsaw depended on him no longer being alive.[7]

---

[7] The heart traveled from Paris and was smuggled into partitioned Poland by his sister and is buried in the Holy Cross Church in Warsaw (then part of the Russian partition).

Justice, as I argue below, cares[8] about the distribution of the conditions for the fulfillment of at least some of people's projects, goals, what they value and their preferences (while distinct, I will use these terms interchangeably unless otherwise stated).[9] Or, to offer a simpler phrasing, justice cares about the distribution of opportunities to have one's preferences fulfilled.[10] And, as the aspiring novelist story shows, biological death does not put an end to our capacity to advance or curtail opportunities for preference fulfillment. If advancing or curtailing opportunities of preference fulfillment when a person is alive can mitigate (or exacerbate) injustice, it can also, I will argue, do so posthumously. This is, in a nut shell, the core of my case. It thus rests on the following key moves: that justice cares about opportunities for preference fulfillment; and that there is nothing about preferences that were once those of a living person but which survived her that would disqualify them from being the concern of justice. I focus on the first of those moves in subsection 2.1 and on the second in subsection 2.2 and section 3.

2.1 Justice and Preferences

Why might people have duties of justice to one another with respect to their projects and preferences? There is a simple story to be told here

---

[8] For example, for justice to care about X means that it is a matter of justice what happens vis-à-vis X where justice may, among other things, maximize, minimize, weigh X, or have X as a constraint.

[9] The distinctions matter to what exactly mitigation would require, but the overall shape of my case can be stated without highlighting them.

[10] What this means, given the stipulation above about how to understand justice, is that people will have duties towards others with respect to these conditions, that is with respect to the likelihood of success of such projects and preferences. These duties will sometimes call for specific actions and sometimes, qua imperfect duties, will leave duty-bearers with a choice of how to discharge them. Although shortfalls in justice are here assumed to correspond to some failing to perform their duties, for simplicity, I will usually talk only about victims' projects or preferences being unfulfilled or people lacking opportunities for preference fulfillment, rather than about the perpetrators failing to advance the fulfillment of the preferences or failing to preserve or deliver conditions for their fulfillment. Admittedly, there is a certain linguistic oddness to saying that justice may care about posthumous opportunities, since we often think of opportunities as opportunities to do something and the dead cannot do anything. But opportunities need not be merely or only opportunities to act. Think back to the example of publishing a novel. We may say that writing and getting a novel published means accessing the opportunity to become a novelist. This opportunity involves acting by the person whose opportunity it is (writing the novel) but also the novel getting published by a publisher that need not involve the writer doing anything. The opportunity is thus advanced when the manuscript is sent to the publisher following the death of the writer and is curtailed if it is burnt.

according to which justice is concerned only with opportunities for preference fulfillment (or with preferences for short) where this is the fundamental currency of justice. This is not the story I wish to advance. As I see it, the content of our duties of justice is set by a variety of considerations, one of them is what people care about (and how much), but people's well-being, interests, ability to control, autonomy, what might demean people also matter.[11] These are, of course, not mutually exclusive categories—for example, getting something may be in my interest only when and because I care about it; or fulfilling my preferences may sometimes matter only because doing so protects my autonomy or well-being.[12] This means that preferences may matter to justice for a variety of reasons. This variety is no obstacle to the possibility of mitigation of injustice through preference fulfillment, but, to clarify, I do think that justice must care that there are at least some opportunities to fulfill one's preferences even when these do not serve one's well-being or autonomy; it is the fact that they are one's preferences that matters.

Why should we accept that justice should at least to some extent care about what people care about? Since there may be various reasons for justice to care about preferences, there may be many rationales here but a general rationale is also available that captures why preferences would matter in their own right. Justice that is sensitive to what people care about is justice that, in the words of Tom Parr (2018: 307), 'consults, rather than usurps'.[13] Why should justice consult?[14] We may think, following

---

[11] For a particularly illuminating discussion of various grounds for wrongful and non-wrongful actions, see Tadros (2017).

[12] There are good reasons to think that justice should care about what people care about not only when and because it bears on their well-being. There is also the issue of whether well-being should be understood as preference fulfillment. On this other issue see, for example, Richard B. Brandt (1979), Derek Parfit (1984), and David Sobel (1994). My own view is that a plausible account of well-being cannot be a mere preference satisfaction account (on this see also note 27). But whether I am right about this does not, in fact, matter for the purposes of establishing the possibility of posthumous injustice mitigation; it matters only for the purposes of establishing the less interesting fact that my argument from the importance of surviving preferences to justice offers a distinctive way for establishing the possibility of posthumous injustice mitigation than an argument that appeals only to the importance of posthumous benefit and harm would.

[13] Parr uses this idea to argue for a specific way in which justice should be sensitive to people's views: not just their views about what matters but their valuation of their own comparative standing vis-à-vis others. He goes on to explain how justice having this shape helps it avoid three objections: the usurpation, disrespect, and burdens objections. I draw on some of his claims here but my task is less ambitious. All I need for my argument to go through is that justice displays some (reasonably extensive) sensitivity to people's views about what matters.

[14] One obvious reason is that it may tend better to people's well-being this way. But this is only one reason and often not consulting would bear better fruit.

Rawls and others, that this is what is required by thinking of people as self-authenticating sources of valid claims. It is, inescapably, each person's task to take a stance on what is of value in this world and it would therefore be disrespectful not to allow justice to be sensitive to such decisions.[15]

Is it possible that justice should not care about preferences fulfillment at all? Perhaps, with Dworkin and Rawls, we should think that justice requires that people get a fair share of resources or primary goods. Notice, however, that the justification offered by Rawls (2001: 57–61) for justice distributing primary goods is that such goods let people achieve whatever else they wish to achieve. Similarly, Dworkin (2002: ch. 2) is concerned with giving people resources such that their ambition is not unfairly constrained. It is a complicated question how preference satisfaction relates to autonomy, welfare, or respect on these accounts and, clearly, the two theorists do not postulate equal preference satisfaction as their measure of justice. I return below (subsection 3.2) to the problem of accommodating some preferences in a Dworkinian account but my point here is that opportunities for preference satisfaction have to come somewhere into the story of what justice requires. This is because a just society is a society that must leave reasonable amounts of space for people to select their own ends.[16]

All this leaves open how many people have to care about something for that something to become a concern of justice. The answer likely depends on the nature of the good they care about, the intensity with which they care, and the expense of providing it. For some goods merely one person caring about it should be enough for justice to also care—for example, if Andrew cares about being present at the birth of his child then, barring opposing considerations, justice should deliver this. For some goods (religions), a certain number of people must care but once they do, all should have access to it (e.g. access to a temple, as compatible with that religion's rules). In this case, if some people care, all must have access to it to protect their autonomy; in other cases, all may need to

---

[15] Cf. John Rawls (2001: 23–4), Ronald Dworkin (2011). Dworkin argues that we value 'each individual's responsibility to determine for herself what it means to live well' (Parr, 2018: 309). We may also think that deciding for people would display, as Tom Parr (2018: 309) summarizes Jonathan Quong's view, 'a negative attitude concerning the individual's ability effectively to judge and to advance her own interests in a given situation'. See also Quong (2011: 100–6).

[16] See also Parr (2018).

have access because when some people care about it, they produce something that is valuable for all (democracy) or desired by (almost) all (the internet). And this is compatible with it being the case that for some goods there is only an injustice when those who care about it cannot have it (holidays).

Of course, what people care about, or at least care about deeply, is hardly the only determinant of the content of justice and indeed leaves wide open how the sensitivity should be achieved. In any case, any claim that justice should be sensitive to what people care about needs to be subject to caveats. Let me list four (while in subsection 3.2 I concede a further one).

(1) For justice to care about what people care about it must be the case that advancing the fulfillment of what they care about, and placing people under a duty to advance it, is appropriate in light of other considerations of justice.[17] I am not going to specify here in full what the 'other considerations of justice' might consist in but even this vaguely stated caveat should be understandable. The content of what people care about may be such that in light of other considerations of justice, people may have a duty not to have the preference, or not to act on it, or for others not to advance its fulfillment. For example, simply because some people would like to advance racist projects, this does not make the advancement of racist projects a concern of distributive justice: we have a duty not treat each other in a racist way. And even if the content of the preference is innocuous—for example, when they are adults, I would like my daughters to speak to me every week—there may be no duty on anyone to advance its fulfillment because of what it would cost them, in autonomy, to do so. True, if their speaking to me every week would mitigate an injustice they would have a reason of justice to visit me though still not necessarily a duty (Stemplowska 2018a). I will return to the problem of whether the preference to be remembered can meet this caveat in subsection 4.3 below.

---

[17] This means that advancing the fulfillment of what people care about requires that the fulfillment of all the preferences be compatible with each other as well as the remaining considerations of justice or that we have a hierarchy of the advancement of the preferences and the remaining considerations.

(2) Advancing the fulfillment of what people care about must appropriately reflect the value of what people care about. This means that advancing the fulfillment of the preferences does not make a mockery of the value the preference expresses. For example, if I have a preference for being a master judge of the number of people present in a seminar room and believe that there are a hundred people present while there are in fact eleven, it would fulfill my preference to be correct if someone were to usher an extra eighty-nine people into the room but I would not thereby display masterful judgement.[18]

(3) I am also prepared to grant for the sake of the argument that for justice to care about people's preferences, these preferences need to be authentic in two senses. First, what people care about should not itself be a mere product of injustice (Parr, 2018: 308). Second, the preferences must be appropriately attributable to people: they should not be stray preferences they themselves wished they did not have.

(4) It may be the case that for justice to care about what people care about, what people care about should not be too irrational. Perhaps preferences over success at grass counting or access to unlimited sauerkraut or to erect a statue to Hitler in one's garden (even if permissible) need not concern justice. But a just society also needs to allow people secure access to a range of projects the rationality of which may be in question (as the firm atheists and devout religious people who nonetheless believe in liberal freedoms will attest).

Since I leave it open how justice should achieve sensitivity to preferences, let me make what I say more concrete by pointing out that there are three main ways in which what people care about will matter for mitigation. First, justice may care about the distribution of opportunities for the fulfillment of specific preferences, for example, to avoid

---

[18] I thank Tom Parr for assisting me with this difficult maths here (and drafting an early version of this footnote). I am grateful to Victor Tadros for a version of this example. I am also grateful to Hillel Steiner for pointing out the important political resonance of this example in light of Trump's inflated inauguration attendance figures.

hunger or to have children. Of course, when justice cares about these opportunities it may be because they are rights or something else normatively fundamental, but the language of preferences serves a purpose here since, following death, that is the currency in which we will deal when it comes to mitigation. When justice cares about the distribution of opportunities for the fulfillment of specific preferences then, clearly, depriving people of the requisite opportunities amounts to an injustice (in need of mitigation).

Second, there are also other cases when it is accurate to say that justice cares about the distribution of our opportunities for the fulfillment of given preferences, even if it is not in itself unjust to deprive someone of the opportunity for the fulfillment of these preferences. This is the case when a person suffers some independently identifiable injustice (e.g. an assault) that affects her opportunity to fulfill the preference and this loss of opportunity must be taken into account when calculating how much injustice a person has suffered due to the original and independently identifiable wrongdoing. For example, it may not be unjust to stop a person from getting a job by competing with her fairly, but, if one wrongs a person by assaulting her, the fact that the assault also stops her getting a job she wanted counts in the calculus of injustice the person has suffered.[19] The idea here is that some shortfalls in opportunities to fulfill one's preferences count as injustice in need of mitigation if they are due to an independently identifiable injustice (as in the case of murder here).[20]

Third, even if justice did not care about the distribution of opportunities for preference fulfillment, it may still care about preferences as a matter of corrective justice.[21] That is, even though the injustice of an assault a person suffers is not exacerbated by the fact that the assault stopped her from obtaining the last signed copy of a book, if (implausibly in most cases) the only thing we could do for the victim is not get her a signed copy, justice may require this to be done.

---

[19] There was an injustice in the actual sequence of events, which I take is sufficient (e.g. this is not a counterfactual view).
[20] I defend the view that injustice can be compounded this way further in Stemplowska (2018a).
[21] I am grateful to Tom Parr for this point.

2.2 Surviving Preferences

Following Feinberg (1984), I will refer to preferences that were the preferences of the now dead person and that were about outcomes that can in principle be realized even or only after one's death, as her surviving preferences. The pertinent question, then, is whether justice should care about the fulfillment of *surviving* preferences and projects, and thus opportunities that can be advanced *posthumously*, or whether access to these opportunities matters only while people are alive. And the answer is that justice should concern itself with the fulfillment of surviving preferences and projects because people themselves, while alive, have strong preferences about posthumous states of affairs and take steps to block or bring them about. Since justice must be sensitive to what people care about, it should take a stance on the distribution of opportunities for the fulfillment of surviving preferences, especially (though not exclusively) when this would allow us to mitigate injustice. For us not to do so, we would need to argue that surviving preferences exhibit some feature that disqualifies them. I argue below that they do not.

Right away, some may object that the surviving preferences, and the corresponding opportunities to have them fulfilled, are disqualified because they cannot survive as victim's preferences. This is because, being dead, they cannot have any preferences or projects; a person's projects *were* her projects rather than *are* her projects. I have no quarrel with the linguistic move requesting the use of the past tense in the attribution of preferences to the dead. But such a linguistic move does not settle the normative question of whether justice ought to care merely about the opportunities for the fulfillment of the preferences of the living or also the preferences that survive our death.

Can surviving preferences meet caveat 4 (subsection 2.1 above), according to which for justice to care about preferences they cannot be too irrational? Luckily, I do not need to take a stance on the precise content of this caveat to show that it can. This is because, at worst, preferences over posthumous outcomes will qualify as acceptable irrational preferences (on a par with self-regarding preferences relating to homeopathy, say). But even this worst case scenario is unlikely. More likely, as Scheffler (2013) has suggested, is that preferences over posthumous outcomes are preferences over matters that genuinely give meaning to our lives. Posthumous preference satisfaction should not strike us as a weird superstition but, rather, something towards which it is reasonable and not uncommon to orient much of one's life, deriving meaning from projects that span more than one's lifetime (think here, e.g., of one's children or other projects that are meant to transcend a single lifetime).[22] In any case, preferences over posthumous states of affairs should not be deemed so irrational as to fall short of this caveat.

In what follows I will look at a different strategy that may disqualify surviving preferences from being the object of justice: not because they are preferences that were held by those who are no longer alive but because they must be impersonal preferences and, so the argument goes, justice need not be concerned with our opportunities to advance our impersonal preferences.

3. The Importance of Impersonal Preferences (Though Not All Surviving Preferences Are Impersonal Anyway)

Following the literature, let me call preferences that affect the person, one's personal preferences. Impersonal preferences are all the remaining preferences a person has. People clearly have strongly held impersonal preferences and many of my own surviving preferences are impersonal. I care that no one needlessly harms kids now or ever; or, less crucially, that even if I do not, one day humanity learns whether John Stuart Mill and/or Harriet Taylor burnt Thomas Carlyle's sole draft of his 'History of the French Revolution' book manuscript on purpose or whether it was genuinely an accident.

Dworkin (2002: 27–8) captures the skepticism about the importance of impersonal preferences to justice in the context of outlining his egalitarian theory of justice:

> [o]f course people do care, and often care very deeply, about their...impersonal preferences. But it does not seem callous to say that insofar as government has either the right or the duty to make people equal, it has the right or the duty to make them equal in their personal

---

[22] Scheffler suggests that it is not possible to mitigate posthumous injustice, but here I am referencing his argument to the effect that for our lives to be as meaningful as we imagine them to be, there must be future generations that will preserve/respect/carry on some of what we do now.

situation or circumstances, including their political power, rather than…in the degree to which their differing visions of an ideal world are realized. On the contrary, that more limited aim of equality seems the proper aim for a liberal state, though it remains to see what making people equal in their personal circumstances could mean.

I will argue below (in subsection 3.2) that justice should care about impersonal preferences just as it cares about personal ones. First, however, let me point out that, in any case, at least some surviving preferences can be personal preferences.

3.1 Must Surviving Preferences Be Impersonal Preferences?

There are going to be difficult cases considering the classification of preferences into personal and impersonal, just on the basis of what it means for a person to be affected.[23] If a person invests herself fully into a preference—orients her life around a project—for example, follows the trials the tribulations of a football team, it becomes unclear whether her preference that the team wins is personal or impersonal.[24] Similarly, any parent who loves her children will have preferences about their well-being that seem personal even if the child's well-being has no impact on the experience of the parents. For example, suppose that children were taken from a loving parent (say, through a mistake made by the social services). It seems the parent benefits, not just the children, when the children find alternative happy homes.[25]

---

[23] There is a further difficulty I leave aside regarding the classification of preferences about being respected. I am grateful for Victor Tadros for pointing this out.

[24] I discuss this in greater detail in Stemplowska (2018b).

[25] This can be contrasted with a case, similar to one initially offered by Parfit (1984: 494) in support of the thesis that not all preference satisfaction bears on one's well-being. Consider a person who chats with a stranger on the train and in the course of the brief encounter (that is never to be repeated) develops a preference that the stranger gets the job she has applied for. Suppose the stranger goes on to get the job. Although her preference is satisfied, it is counterintuitive to think that this bears on the person. The difference between this and the case of the parent mentioned in the main text resides in the fact that in the parent case the parent does not merely have a preference regarding the well-being of her children but—we would standardly assume—invests the preference with meaning for her life and shapes her identity round it.

But even if we are careful to keep the category of personal preferences narrow, we will find it difficult to classify all surviving preferences as outside this category. This is at least if we grant—seemingly unadventurously—that the preferences a person has about her achieving things herself are her personal preferences. Given the complexity of our causal involvement in the world some of our surviving preferences will turn out to be personal rather than impersonal preferences on this view. This is, for one, because a person can achieve things collectively with others. That is, we can see a project as someone's achievement (together with others) if this person was appropriately involved in bringing it about. For example, if she raised the funds for a forest, the forest is one of her (collective) accomplishments, even if she did not plant all or even any of the trees herself. For notice that if we want to appropriately describe what the person has achieved, we must say that the forest is her partial achievement, not merely that 'fundraising' was. We may get away with saying that she achieved 'fundraising for the forest' but the implication even here is that she is partially responsible for the forest itself, not just the fundraising—the fundraising had an object. Similarly, the violinist who plays a concerto in her orchestra is not merely playing her violin; the player who plays defense in a football game is not merely stopping the other team from scoring; he is winning or losing the whole game; the men stabbing Julius Caesar are not merely wounding him but killing him.

All this, of course, raises the famous problem of under which conditions we can attribute part of the collective outcome to the individual. My point here is not to offer a solution to this problem but only to point out that on any plausible view of agency, a person has to be seen as partially responsible for outcomes that go beyond what her physical reach has been. That is, inevitably, there will be outcomes that can be (partially) attributed to the person even if the person was not causally involved in them all the way to the finish line. But this means, of course, that one can, non-metaphorically, achieve outcomes that happen to arise only following one's death. So if, as I assumed, preferences about achieving things oneself are one's personal preferences some of such preferences may also become surviving preferences that concern posthumous outcomes.

3.2   Must Justice Be Sensitive Only to Personal Preferences?

In any case, we should not grant the claim that justice should be sensitive only to personal preferences. Granting this would not make posthumous mitigation of injustice impossible, but it would certainly restrict the opportunity for it. The quoted passage from Dworkin at the start of this section contained a mere assertion or an appeal to an intuition. But one thought animating it that appears elsewhere in his work is that we may thereby give more weight to some people than others and not enough to some (Dworkin, 2002: 23–4). Altruists, for example, may discount their own personal preferences and ask only that others fare well. People whose welfare matters to more people might end up with more.

One obvious response, then, is to grant that the impersonal preferences that count should not be preferences about other people's welfare or access to resources; in other words, they need to be doubly impersonal. This would rule out, importantly, justice taking into account preferences of ancestors over the welfare of their descendants thus reducing scope for mitigation of injustice, but it would still leave other avenues for its pursuit, for example through completing the victim's projects and commemorating them. A self-abnegating altruist, however, may pose a further challenge. Even if their care of others would not be permitted to translate into requirements of justice, they may simply self-abnegate such that justice cannot serve their welfare. But, if so, allowing impersonal preferences as a concern of justice seems to be a move that at least allows justice to serve their impersonal preferences and so we have less of a reason to worry, putting adaptive preferences aside, that they are inappropriately discounted in the calculus of justice. In any case, even if we allow only doubly-impersonal preferences and even if we bestow on any self-abnegators inalienable rights to some level of welfare (or against suffering specific kinds of harm), we would be left with a range of impersonal preferences that could be the concern of justice without invoking any of the worries about double or undercounting of people.

In any case, note that on Dworkin's vision of a just society—as already flagged up in (2) above—a just society would offer opportunities to pursue one's impersonal preferences. Although people's share of resources would be ascertained without reference to what they might need to advance their impersonal preferences, they would be permitted to pursue all permissible impersonal preferences. Indeed, the rules of liberty in a just society would ensure that there would be space for the pursuit of such preferences.[26]

To bolster the last thought, suppose that all people have a range of preferences: some deeply-held personal and impersonal preferences, and some weakly-held personal and impersonal preferences. If a policy was passed that would prevent people from realizing all of their deeply-held impersonal preferences there would be a *prima facie* (or even *pro tanto*) injustice, even if this did not manifest in any harm to the persons. Such a policy would be in need of a special justification. What would make the policy *prima facie* (or *pro tanto*) unjust would be precisely the fact that the person did not get to advance any of the impersonal preferences she was invested in. We should accept that the fulfilment of at least some of one's (deeply-held) impersonal preferences should matter to justice in its own right.

There is a positive reason that explains the intuition that justice must care about impersonal preferences and accord them the treatment it accords personal preferences.[27] As Lippert-Rasmussen (2016: 101), who—almost uniquely among egalitarians—thinks that justice should care about impersonal preferences, puts it, '[t]aking account of people's … [impersonal] concerns is a way of respecting them.'[28] Lippert-Rasmussen does not elaborate on this, but I take it that the idea is along the following lines. It is respectful to people to take into account what matters to them, and the fact that people may care as much, or even more, about the fulfilment of their impersonal preferences as their personal ones makes it hard for us to insist that only the fulfilment of personal preferences should matter to justice. Such a move would be

---

[26] There is more to be said here to explain the implications of this view for how we might count what is a fair share of resources for Dworkinians or primary goods for Rawlsians. My view is that these metrics must themselves to some extent track people's preferences (including impersonal ones) to be plausible. I am grateful to Tom Parr for pressing me to clarify my position here (even if not my argument).

[27] At least *qua* preferences; it may treat preferences that bear on a range of things it cares about as more fundamental—for example, autonomy—differently depending on how these preferences interact with that more fundamental category.

[28] Grammatically, it might be that it is the concerns (not their bearers) that are respected but this would amount to a restatement rather than an explanation, so I opt for the more natural interpretation.

arbitrary. To avoid such arbitrariness, we should see justice as concerned with impersonal preferences (at least those that are equally strongly held as the personal ones that we accept justice should care about). To construct a full theory of justice we would need to know how to construct a comparative measure of the importance of fulfillment of each person's impersonal preferences and what counts as a fair opportunity to fulfill them.[29] But we do not need to do that to establish that advancing the surviving impersonal preferences of persons could in some cases mitigate some of the injustice done to her.

3.3 The Importance of People's Lives

I think that the argument just advanced explains why impersonal preferences must matter to justice but for those who are uneasy about incorporating into justice a full spectrum of impersonal preferences (of sufficient strength and quality), here is an argument designed to harness the intuition that justice would be amiss if it did not care at all about at least a specific subset of impersonal preferences: those concerning people's lives.

Here I follow Kagan (1994) and Glannon (2001) in drawing a distinction between a person and her life. Suppose we grant that, for the purposes of this argument, a *person* is understood as a unified body and mind. On a widespread understanding of a unified body and mind, this would make a person an embodied collection of connected psychological mental states.[30] By contrast, when we think of a person's *life* we more intuitively reach for a broader category than that of a person: a life is composed of a sequence of events that together add up to a story, in which the person features as the central character (Glannon, 2001: 129, 140). A life so understood is the history of the person rather than just one's biological life. And it is easy to see why posthumous events can

---

[29] Dworkin (2002), Lippert-Rasmussen (2016), Stemplowska (2019).

[30] And, incidentally, on such an understanding of personhood, according to Glannon (2001: 140), 'if a person is nothing more than a body and mind, then it is difficult to see how facts that do not either directly or indirectly affect the body or mind and cause adverse changes in the person [since they happen posthumously] can harm him.'

affect one's life, since posthumous events bear on the story in which the person features as the central character.

For example, if a great project is dismantled, the lives of the architects of the projects amount to less as a result. If *Sagrada Família* is never finished, Gaudí's life amounts to less. If Trump fully dismantles 'Obamacare', Obama's life amounts to less, whether or not Obama is alive to witness it, because he would no longer be the architect of lasting healthcare reform. Or consider the fact that Trump becoming elected has cheapened the honor of achieving the presidency for all who had achieved it before him (even if merely by revealing the presidency as something that a person with no virtues can get). The other presidents need not be alive for this fact to affect the story of their lives. Similarly, many accept that bringing health and well-founded joy to the lives of others does make for a better *life*. For example, Maria Skłodowska-Curie's life is better (in that it amounts to more) on account of the fact that she discovered radium that led to a technology that saves lives. And van Gogh's life is better on account of the fact that his paintings bring well-founded joy to millions. If we accept that lives can go better when they positively affect others and accept that lives stretch beyond one's biological existence, then we must accept that lives can become even better on account of how they affect others including after the biological person is no longer alive.

Are preferences about lives impersonal? By definition, lives are distinct from personhood. They also do not fully overlap with one's well-being or even what people can achieve themselves. On the account of impersonal preferences adopted here, then, at least some preferences of people about their lives will be *im*personal . And the reason to think that justice should care about the shape of people's lives is, as above, that people care about their lives not just the harm and benefit to themselves.[31] But note that this general appeal to the importance for justice of what people care about is here enhanced by the fact that it is intuitively

---

[31] We may even think that—independently of whether people care about their lives—lives are the type of thing that justice should care about. Just as justice should care about harm and benefit to persons even if all they care about is glory in the eyes of God (at least in so far as the two don't conflict), justice should care about lives even if all people care about is pain and pleasure. If so, it would seem that improving someone's life posthumously may mitigate injustice. But see subsection 4.2 for my argument that mitigation requires that we fulfill the preferences that the victims of injustice actually had.

easy to see why caring about one's life is a reasonable and meaningful preoccupation. Indeed, there would be an odd dogmatism in saying that justice is insensitive to people's preferences concerning their lives when we readily accept that it should be sensitive to their preferences concerning their personhood. We will need to set conditions on at which cost such impersonal preferences should be given a chance of fulfillment but it would be a philistine notion of justice that held that the only thing worth fighting for was the person and never anything beyond her that she may care about. People see themselves as parts of the world and the universe, and justice should reflect that.

I think we have conclusive reasons to accept that justice should concern itself with the opportunities people have to fulfill their preferences including their surviving preferences. It should do so even in a world in which there is no injustice. However, even if I am wrong and justice should not directly care about the opportunities for the fulfillment of people's deeply-held impersonal preferences, this does not entail that, as a matter of *corrective* justice it should not care about them. That is, if we accept a permissive view of mitigation, it may be that the advancement of impersonal preferences is the only (or best) way to mitigate the injustice done to people whose welfare was violated while they were alive.

4. The Possibility of Mitigation

4.1 Permissive and Narrow Mitigation

Suppose then a young woman has been murdered. If her parents set up a university scholarship in her honor, do they thereby mitigate any of the injustice? Not necessarily. The murdered young woman may not have cared about university education. But suppose she wanted to be noticed (and perhaps even posthumously remembered) and so the scholarship does fulfill a surviving preference of hers. The discussion so far proceeded with an intuitive notion of mitigation. Mitigation is something that reduces the extent of the injustice suffered by the victim, however insignificant that reduction may be in the context of the injustice. Of course, nothing can undo the original injustice but anything that responds to the injustice in a way that is focused on the position of the victim can potentially qualify as mitigation.[32] At this point, however, we can distinguish between a permissive and a narrow view. On a permissive view, to mitigate is to improve the position of the victim. We can do so by fulfilling the dead woman's surviving preferences.

Should we be guided by the preferences a person held at the end of her life or the preferences the person had the longest during her lifetime? I do not know the answer to that. Luckily, in many cases many preferences a person has remain stable so we can simply focus on those. We cannot always be sure that fulfilling given preferences meets all the conditions. But the balance of probability may be enough to command us to act.

On a narrow view, to mitigate is to engage in direct rectification where the particular loss suffered by the victim is addressed. On this view, that is, the improvement must take the form of direct (even if partial) rectification. We must in some sense advance the opportunities that the injustice took away from the victims. Clearly, we cannot rectify what is the most important loss: one's life. Is there anything we can rectify? We need to understand what it means to, in some sense, rectify the loss of an opportunity to fulfill the victim's preferences.

Consider the case of an activist who was murdered and thus was unable to donate money to a forest fund. We may wonder whether it really counts as rectification of the lost opportunity—for example, to donate to the forest fund—when we deliver the outcome (a donation) rather than restore the person's opportunity to donate herself? Of course, if all the person wanted was to achieve the outcome singlehandedly, then it does not. But suppose she cared independently about the outcome being achieved. We cannot now restore the opportunity for her to pursue it, but we can still deliver the outcome (or a chance of/opportunity for the outcome being realized). It mitigates the injustice of the loss of the opportunity to have at least some of the outcome for which this was an opportunity brought about.

Does this prove too much? Does it imply that we would also mitigate an injustice if we delivered the outcomes that the dead took steps to avoid but for which they lost opportunities due to the initial injustice? For example, murdering the forest enthusiast also deprived her of the

---

[32] I am grateful to Rainer Forst for making me clarify my position.

opportunity to donate to the oil industry. And, after all, with the living we are not standardly concerned with their preferences when mitigating an injustice. For example, we mitigate an injustice for the living owner of her car if we return the stolen car to her, even if she dislikes the car and would rather not have it.

But the car analogy is misleading because in the car case the person was entitled to the car while in the case of the donation to the oil company the forest lover was not entitled to such a donation. Moreover, with the living we normally assume that they can dispose of any unwanted returns. If it really were the case that the car owner did not want the car, but returning it, for some reason, would deprive her of the possibility to get rid of it that she had before the car was stolen, we may not see such a return as required or even permissible. It is only when the victims would have wanted the specific outcomes we deliver to transpire that we mitigate injustice that took the opportunity for those outcomes away.

On both the narrow as well as the permissive view of mitigation, then, we need to have a sense of the surviving preferences of the dead victims of injustice. In some cases we will know them. In others, we can make reasonable guesses. Even when we know nothing about the victims other than the most general facts about them, we can make such guesses. It is my conjecture, for example, that most typical people currently alive in numerous cultures (whether in Africa, Asia, Europe, Latin America, or elsewhere) share the preference to be remembered. If in doubt, therefore, we can always try to mitigate injustice by learning more about the public persona of the dead person,[33] taking into account that victims of injustice may have wanted to be remembered (also) as they were before they were wronged (Stemplowska, 2014). Think here, for example, of memorials, such as the Vietnam War Memorial in Ho Chi Minh City that contains stories by parents about their murdered children's lives; or Yad Vashem that, as far as possible, contains histories of the victims. And if we know more about the people, our guesses can improve. Journalists will have typically wanted their work to be read, architects their work to be built, football supporters their teams to be well-funded, etc.

---

[33] I say 'public' since people may not want their private lives to be known. By 'public' I do not mean 'the public life' of the person but what the person herself was projecting into the world, even if the world itself was, say, that of the neighborhood shop.

4.2 Is Consent Not Needed?

My claim that we may in some cases know, or reasonably guess, which surviving preferences to fulfill invites an objection. Suppose that you are alive and well, and, say, spend every day painting a long fence round the local park that you got permission from the local government to repaint. While you are asleep, your painting is vandalized and I (a person whom you never met before) repair the painting while you are still asleep. My action may not count as mitigation of injustice. I repaired a wrong but might have committed another wrong of making it the case that the final coat of paint of the fence was not placed with your hand. Since you were asleep, we could not be sure if you wanted the fence painted or if, in particular, you wanted to be the person who painted the fence. But even if we knew you merely wanted the fence painted, it still does not seem that justice necessarily calls for me to repaint the fence while you are asleep. Rather, I should ask you what you would wish. I need your consent.

But if consent is needed before the fulfillment of one's preferences counts as mitigation of injustice, then posthumous mitigation is doomed (except in the rare cases where such consent had been granted). So is consent always needed? Notice that the reason why we must ask for consent while people are alive (other than to ascertain if they wish an outcome or to bring the outcome about) is that we thereby recognize that those who set themselves goals might also change their mind. More precisely, it is not the probability of them changing their mind that is decisive but the recognition that they have a mind to change. But the dead do not have a mind to change so if a goal was theirs before they died, it remains theirs posthumously. Of course, goals only make sense within their context and so as the context changes, our ability to say what the goal would be like in the new context erodes until it evaporates entirely. This will mean that there will be instances when we can no longer respect people by advancing their goals but such crippling uncertainty about people's surviving preferences is not always our fate.

Is this too hasty? Why not say that it is precisely because the dead have no minds to change that the goals they once had are no longer theirs: there are no goals we can ascribe to people once they have died. The idea here is not that they cannot have goals merely because they do not exist—the idea of surviving preferences does not require existence—but that they cannot have them because as contexts change so do goals and since they cannot endorse any new goals, there are no goals that survive them.

I accept that as circumstances change, it will become increasingly uncertain which preferences the now dead would have in the new circumstances. But it is epistemically unwarranted to say that death alone makes it radically uncertain what preferences a person would have on any issue. Most parents who cared about their children while they were alive, for example, would still care that their descendants fare well, even if, eventually, we may be unsure what they would have seen as such. And not all goals are as context sensitive as others. We can be pretty sure, for example, that those who wanted to be remembered would want to be remembered even by people who are very different to them. Or think of the practice of completing and performing works of art. As I type, musicians are practicing for a concert in Warsaw at which they will perform Beethoven's Ode to Joy with the words in Hebrew based on a translation begun in the Warsaw Ghetto during the German occupation despite the German ban on Jews performing non-Jewish music. Even if the authors of the original translation would have wanted the symphony performed by a different orchestra and choir, preparing performance music and texts means expecting that it would be performed by a variety of authors. Moreover, the costs of getting their surviving preferences wrong is relatively small.[34] Even if the performance did not mitigate any of the injustice it is unlikely to compound it.

4.3 Is Mitigation Through Remembrance Permissible?

At this point, however, we may worry whether the surviving preferences to be remembered or for one's work to be commemorated meet the condition of permissibility (caveat 1 in subsection 2.1 above). If one's surviving preference is that one's novel gets published or a forest gets planted this seems innocuous enough. But for most people the surviving preferences we are most likely to know about will be over the welfare of

---

[34] This is not to deny that there may be cases where specific performers—perhaps the perpetrators—should not perform a given piece of art.

their children; which we may be unable permissibly to fulfill if such welfare would come at the expense of other people's children; over political projects, which would need to be accommodated to make room for the democratic decisions of the living;[35] and to be remembered.

What shall we say about the permissibility of fulfilling the preference to be remembered? Clearly, preferences whose fulfillment dictates states of mind or actions of others may exhibit lack of respect for others. Is wanting to be remembered by numerous strangers—rather than wanting to merit remembering or just wanting to be remembered by one's family and friends—a preference that exhibits lack of respect for others? It may be, even if we understand remembering in a way that aligns with our current practices of remembrance: we are not required to constantly ruminate on those we are asked to, or want to, remember but occasionally to recall them or allow ourselves to be reminded of them. Still, it seems clear to me that if I wanted to be remembered by everyone for generations to come, this preference would exhibit lack of respect, most likely both for those who merit or are entitled to remembrance ahead of me and for those who would do the remembering. My preference to be remembered should be for no more than my fair share of memory.

That said, however, it may still be permissible—and even required—to advance the fulfillment of such a disrespectful preference.[36] In this instance, even if the rememberee is asking for more than her fair share of the world's attention, delivering it to her need not amount to a recognition that she really is more important than others but only, as the case may be, that doing so would fulfill her surviving preference and thereby mitigate some of the injustice she had suffered. In this respect, fulfilling the preference for remembrance is different to fulfilling the preference of a racist for a racist statue to be erected: fulfilling such a preference would normally remain impermissible given what the fulfillment

---

[35] There is no reason to think that this cannot be done; I just cannot outline it here. For a discussion of how not to do it, see the vignette offered by Hillel Steiner (1994: 2050) of corrupt Chicago politics where the dead would remain on the electoral roll.

[36] But even if remembrance may be a required form of mitigation of injustice (even when it fulfills over-bloated and disrespectful surviving preferences), it still seems appropriate to privilege the fulfillment of permissible over impermissible preferences. This means, for example, that we would be privileging the preference to be remembered by one's family and kin over one to be remembered by all as well as privileging the preference to be remembered together with other victims of the same or similar injustice over a preference to be remembered as, say, the symbol of that injustice.

communicated about people with different skin color. This means that even if some victims of injustice are owed remembrance this does not mean that they are owed remembrance in any form they would welcome. But it allows for the fulfillment of some preferences for remembrance to count as mitigation.

5. All the Victims Who Have Ever Lived?

The history of the world is a history of injustice. Is there no expiration date on the injustices whose presence triggers the duty to mitigate? I think that the passage of time does not matter in its own right for lessening the concern of (corrective) justice with the injustice that initially took place (Butt 2007: 152; 2013: 265–6). I do not have the space to argue for this here but can help myself to the assumption since it makes my case harder rather than easier. Clearly, that seems to leave us with quite a lot of injustice to mitigate.

That the problem is so enormous alone does not reveal the analysis to be wrong, however. It just means we need tools for deciding which parts of the injustice we face we must tackle first. But for those who would like our duties of mitigation to conservatively resemble what we currently tend to imagine them to be there is some good news. First, the mitigation we can offer to the living is far greater than the one we can offer to the dead, let alone the prevention we can offer the living. This means that, on reasonable assumptions that the effectiveness of our efforts bears on the requirements to engage in them, we have good reasons to privilege focusing our justice advancement measures on the living. But we should not expect the duty to mitigate the injustice done to the living to colonize entirely our efforts here. This is because the effort needed to mitigate injustice for the living may call on a different set of resources than that needed to mitigate injustice for the dead. On a plausible view of our duties, even after we campaigned, voted, and transferred resources to mitigate the injustice done to the living, we will have time left to remember the dead.

All this is compatible with us thinking that there may be unusual cases when the living do not even get priority at all. Imagine a very unlikely case in which two people's reputations have been unjustly tarnished and we can only repair one of them. Suppose also that one person is already dead while the other alive but that they and their situations are identical in all other respects, and, moreover, the person who is alive will never get to experience or be otherwise affected by our actions in ways other than whatever we can do for the dead person.[37] In such a case, when deciding what we owe the victims, the living victim does not get priority as victims to whom mitigation is owed.

There is another reason why we may expect conservative results: as time passes our knowledge of who suffered injustice, of what type, and which surviving preferences they might have had, fades dramatically. This means that we cannot help but tend to focus on the more recent injustices rather than the more distant ones.

What to say about cases where our knowledge of the surviving preferences of individual victims is equal? Should we prioritize, say, the injustice suffered by someone murdered in the 21st century or the 11th? If the (whole life) injustice they suffered were of similar magnitude, our efforts likely to be similarly effective and our confidence about them equal, and we discount considerations about relatives and education effects, etc., then the case for privileging mitigation of the more recent injustice over the more distant one is hard to make. We may have a greater reason to act on injustices that we are more closely involved in—as a community— or more likely to have benefited from and this would give us a reason to privilege the recent injustice over the more distant one. Absent such considerations, however, we might be engaging in a form of 'presentism' that is akin to 'speciesism' should we privilege things that are closer to us in time than those that are more distant.

6. Conclusion

I argued that it is possible to mitigate injustice posthumously provided we know—or can make a reasonable guess—about the dead person's preferences and projects. I also think that such knowledge is not scant on the ground. This leaves many elements of the picture still missing. For example, I said nothing or next to nothing about the problem of

---

[37] I am grateful to Daniel Elstein for this example.

how to weigh the importance of such posthumous mitigation versus mitigation of ongoing injustice or how to maximize whom we can collectively remember. Nor did I say on whom the duty may fall, whether it is over-demanding to require people to remember horrific injustice, which of our actions may unacceptably compound injustice to the dead, or how to select whose injustice to mitigate given the countless (equally mistreated) victims. But there is plenty we can all be doing to mitigate past injustice even before we have answers to all these questions.[38]

References

Boxill, B.R. (2003). "A Lockean Argument for Black Reparations," *The Journal of Ethics* 7: 63–91.

Brandt, R.B. (1979). *A Theory of the Right and the Good*. Oxford: Oxford University Press.

Butt, D. (2007). "On Benefiting from Injustice," *Canadian Journal of Philosophy* 37: 129–52.

Butt, D. (2009). *Rectifying International Injustice: Principles of Compensation and Restitution between Nations*. Oxford: Oxford University Press.

Butt, D. (2013). "Inheriting Rights to Reparation: Compensatory Justice and the Passage of Time, *Ethical Perspectives* 20: 245–69.

Dworkin, R. (2002). *Sovereign Virtue*. Cambridge, MA: Harvard University Press.

Dworkin, R. (2011). *Justice for Hedgehogs*. Cambridge, MA: Harvard University Press.

Feinberg, J. (1984). *Harm to Others: The Moral Limits of the Criminal Law*. Oxford: Oxford University Press.

---

[38] I am grateful for outstanding research assistance to Henrik Dahlquist and for written comments to Ben Jackson, Kieran Oberman, Tom Parr, Hillel Steiner, Ronen Shnayderman, and the editors of this volume, as well as for comments to the audience at the Annual OSPP conference in Pavia (2018), the Leeds philosophy workshop (2018), the Frankfurt Normative Orders seminar (2019), the UCL and Institute of Philosophy seminar (2019), and the Edinburgh political theory seminar (2019). I am also grateful for written comments on previous, sometimes very distant versions of this chapter to Simon Caney, Matthew Clayton, Jonathan Quong, and Andrew Williams as well as to the audiences of the Warwick Graduate conference (2013), the Aarhus workshop (2013), the Oxford Moral Philosophy seminar (2017), the Reading Graduate and Early Career conference (2017), the Oxford CSSJ Seminar (2018), and the Essex political theory workshop (2018).

Glannon, W. (2001). "Persons, Lives and Posthumous Harms," *Journal of Social Philosophy* 32: 127–42.

Kagan, S. (1994). "Me and My Life," *Proceedings of the Aristotelian Society* 94: 309–24.

Kagan, S. (2012). *Death*. New Haven: Yale University Press.

Lippert-Rasmussen, K. (2016). *Luck Egalitarianism*. London: Bloomsbury.

Lu, C. (2007). *Justice and Reconciliation in World Politics*. Cambridge: Cambridge University Press.

Meyer, L.H. (2004). "Surviving Duties and Symbolic Compensation," *Justice in Time: Responding to Historical Injustice*, L.H. Meyer (ed.). Baden-Baden: Nomos Verslagsgesellschaft, 173–84.

Meyer, L.H. (2015). "Intergenerational Justice," *Stanford Encyclopedia of Philosophy*, section 5.3. Available at: https://plato.stanford.edu/entries/justice-intergenerational

Parfit, D. (1984). *Reasons and Persons*. Oxford: Oxford University Press.

Parr, T. (2018). "How to Identify Disadvantage: Taking the Envy Test Seriously," *Political Studies* 66: 306–22.

Quong, J. (2011). *Liberalism without Perfection*. Oxford: Oxford University Press.

Rawls, J. (2001). *Justice as Fairness: A Restatement*. Cambridge, MA: The Belknap Press of Harvard University Press.

Ridge, M. (2003). "Giving the Dead Their Due," *Ethics* 114: 38–59.

Scheffler, S. (2013). *Death and the Afterlife*, N. Kolodny (ed.). Oxford: Oxford University Press.

Sher, G. (1981). "Ancient Wrongs and Modern Rights," *Philosophy & Public Affairs* 10: 3–17.

Sobel, D. (1994). "Full Information Accounts of Well-Being," *Ethics* 104: 784–810.

Spinner-Halev, J. (2012). *Enduring Injustice*. Cambridge: Cambridge University Press.

Steiner, H. (1994). *An Essay on Rights*. Cambridge, MA: Blackwell.

Stemplowska, Z. (2014). "*Polin*: A Wish to be Remembered; The Museum of the History of the Polish Jews", *Times Literary Supplement*, 19 November.

Stemplowska, Z. (2018a). "Should Coercive Neurointerventions Target the Victims of Wrongdoing?," *Treatment for Crime*, D. Birks and T. Douglas (eds.). Oxford: Oxford University Press, 338–50.

Stemplowska, Z. (2018b). "Should I be Proud of Liberalism with Excellence?," *The American Journal of Jurisprudence* **63**: 1–11.

Stemplowska, Z. (2019). "How Generous Should Egalitarians Be?," *Critical Review of International Social and Political Philosophy* **22**: 269–83.

Tadros, V. (2017). *Wrongs and Crimes*. Oxford: Oxford University Press.

Thompson, J. (2002). *Taking Responsibility for the Past: Reparation and Historical Injustice*. Cambridge: Polity.

3

Free Speech and the Embodied Self

Japa Pallikkathayil

Democratic theories of free speech hold that the right to free speech is grounded in the nature of collective self-governance.[1] As Ronald Dworkin puts it, "The majority has no right to impose its will on someone who is forbidden to raise a voice in protest or argument or objection before the decision is taken" (Dworkin 2009, p. vii).[2] Views of this kind might be thought to be in tension with hate speech regulation. Dworkin argues that when we attempt to put in place laws protecting members of minority groups from various kinds of discrimination, we must not forbid "any expression of attitudes or prejudices that we think nourish such unfairness or inequality, because if we intervene too soon in the process through which collective opinion is formed, we spoil the only democratic justification we have for insisting that everyone obey these laws, even those who hate them" (Dworkin 2009, p. viii).

My aim in this chapter is to diffuse the tension Dworkin sees between a democratic justification of the right to free speech and hate speech regulation. I do this by developing an account of how our bodily rights constrain the right to free speech. These constraints suggest two grounds for regulating certain kinds of hate speech. The first reflects the way in which hate speech can be threatening. The second reflects the way in which hate speech involves a problematic intrusion into our mental lives. These arguments, however, will leave open the possibility that some hate speech is immune to regulation, and thus the possibility that Dworkin's argument contains a grain of truth.

---

[1] For a classic statement of this kind of view, see Meiklejohn (1948). For recent treatments of hate speech informed by this kind of view, see Post (1991) and Weinstein (2009).

[2] Dworkin also suggests a more abstract version of this argument that would justify a right to free speech in authoritarian regimes as well. See Dworkin (2009), p. ix. But the details of that argument will not concern me here.

Japa Pallikkathayil, *Free Speech and the Embodied Self* In: *Oxford Studies in Political Philosophy Volume 6*. Edited by: David Sobel, Peter Vallentyne, and Steven Wall, Oxford University Press (2020). © Japa Pallikkathayil. DOI: 10.1093/oso/9780198852636.003.0003

I. Hate Speech as Intimidation

This section does not reflect directly on messages of hate, but rather on the way in which messages of hate are often intimately bound up with messages of violence. My aim in this section will be to defend The Argument from Intimidation:

(1) Threats to violate legally-recognized bodily rights are an appropriate object of legal regulation.

(2) Communicative acts doing one or more of the following in a manner that gives individuals reasonable cause to fear for their physical safety constitute threats to violate their legally-recognized bodily rights: (a) advocating or endorsing violence against members of a group in virtue of their group membership; (b) using symbols strongly associated with violence against members of a group.

(3) Therefore, communicative acts of these kinds are an appropriate object of legal regulation.

Let us begin by considering premise (1). I take the basic idea behind premise (1) to be largely uncontroversial. When Dworkin suggests that we must not forbid "any expression of attitudes or prejudices" we should interpret this in a way that is consistent with the following observation. The right to speak is constrained by the legally-recognized rights of others. I may not, for example, graffiti someone else's house with my manifesto. Likewise, my right to speak is properly constrained by your right to your own body. So, of course, I also may not tattoo my manifesto on you without your consent.

Threatening a person is a similar though less direct way of taking control of her body without her consent. Threats aimed at inducing action are perhaps the most familiar kind of threat. Consider, for example, a mugger's threat to kill you if you do not hand over your wallet. The mugger here illicitly uses your life as a bargaining chip even though your life is not hers to control. She thereby prevents you from deliberating in terms of all the options to which you are entitled, namely keeping both your money and your life. In doing so, she defeats an important part of the point of your rights.

Threats need not be aimed at inducing action in order to have this feature. Suppose we have a disagreement and as we part ways I say, "You better watch your back." This threat aims at intimidation rather than inducement. Here I convey something along the lines of: "I intend to physically harm you in a way that would violate your bodily rights." Given this gloss, the effect of my statement on the options about which you may deliberate is much like that of the mugger's threat. You may now, for example, no longer take for granted your physical safety when walking through my neighborhood. In this way, you are no longer free to deliberate about your choices in the way in your right entitles you.

Although I do not take the argument I am developing to be beholden to First Amendment jurisprudence, it may be helpful to observe the affinity between the grounds for prohibiting threats I have just given and the U.S. Supreme Court's 'true threats' doctrine:

> "True threats" encompass those statements where the speaker means to communicate a serious expression of an intent to commit an act of unlawful violence to a particular individual or group of individuals.... The speaker need not actually intend to carry out the threat. Rather, a prohibition on true threats "protect[s] individuals from the fear of violence" and "from the disruption that fear engenders," in addition to protecting people "from the possibility that the threatened violence will occur."[3]

I have emphasized the way in which threats prevent people from relying on their rights and thus the disruptive effect of threats. Although criminalizing threats may also help to protect people from the threatened violence, I take the disruptive effect of threats to be sufficient grounds for prohibition. As we have seen, this effect already constitutes a way of undermining an important part of the point of people's rights.

We will have occasion to further consider what constitutes a threat as we turn to premise (2). Recall that premise (2) identifies two kinds of communicative acts: (a) advocating or endorsing violence against members of a group in virtue of their group membership; and (b) using

---

[3] Justice O'Conner, writing for the majority, in *Virginia v. Black*, 538 U.S. 343 (2003) and quoting from the ruling in *R.A.V. v. City of St. Paul*, 505 U.S. 377 (1992).

symbols strongly associated with violence against members of a group. The premise holds that when these acts are done in a manner that gives individuals reasonable cause to fear for their physical safety they constitute threats to violate their legally-recognized bodily rights.

I am going to begin by considering communicative acts of type (b). Here I will argue for two claims. First, although we generally think of threats as undertaken with the intent to induce or intimidate, one may also negligently cause another to fear for her physical safety. And that too should be regarded as threatening. Second, given this, a much wider range of acts of type (b) may be appropriately subject to legal regulation than has been previously observed.

The Supreme Court's ruling in *Virginia v. Black* will helpfully bring out the issues I want to consider. In that case, the Court held that the government may prohibit cross burning with the intent to intimidate but may not treat cross burning as itself evidence of the intent to intimidate. The Court observes that "a burning cross is not always intended to intimidate. Rather, sometimes the cross burning is a statement of ideology, a symbol of group solidarity. It is a ritual used at Klan gatherings, and it is used to represent the Klan itself" (*Virginia v. Black* 2003). For this reason, the Court holds that the *prima facie* evidence provision of the statute under consideration blurs the line between constitutionally proscribable intimidation and "political speech at the core of what the First Amendment is designed to protect" (*Virginia v. Black* 2003).

The Court also indicates that the *prima facie* evidence provision involved a problematic shifting of the burden of proof from the prosecution to the defendant. That may well be the case and for that reason I am not arguing that the Court erred with respect the statute before it. But I want to examine whether there are grounds for prohibiting speech even if we grant that it is not made with the intent to intimidate so long as it would be reasonable to interpret it as giving those exposed to it reasonable cause to fear for their physical safety.

The Court claims: "It may be true that a cross burning, even at a political rally, arouses a sense of anger or hatred among the vast majority of citizens who see a burning cross. But this sense of anger or hatred is not sufficient to ban all cross burnings" (*Virginia v. Black* 2003). It is curious, however, that the Court focuses here on anger and hatred rather than fear. Given the close association between cross burning and violent acts, it would not be unreasonable for those viewing such a public display and who are members of groups that have been historically targeted by the Klan to fear for their physical safety. Of course, a cross burning at a rally does not target a specific person in the way that cross burnings that involve trespass on private property do. But the Court has already acknowledged that one might act so as to intimidate the members of a large group. There seems to be no reason, then, why one could not unintentionally accomplish the same kind of intimidation.

The Court also emphasizes the political value of cross burning as a form of expression. It symbolizes an ideology and the Klan itself. But recall that I may not tattoo my manifesto on your body without your consent no matter how clearly political my message is. Likewise, why think that I should be allowed to make you reasonably fear for your physical safety in order to make a political point? After all, in doing so I prevent you from relying on your rights.

Notice that this position does not suggest that cross burning be completely prohibited. Klan members might still use a burning cross as part of their own private rituals if they take due care to ensure that those for whom such displays would be a reasonable cause for fear are not subjected to them. It is also potentially possible for public cross-burning displays not to reasonably inspire fear if adequate care is taken to present them as having non-threatening aims—say in the context of a historical reenactment. It is however doubtful whether the Klan itself could ever distance itself sufficiently from its violent past to be able to use cross burning publicly in a non-threatening manner. And that suggests a potential worry about this position. It is straightforward how I could express the content of my manifesto without tattooing it on you. But Klan members lose some expressive power if they are unable to use the symbols associated with the Klan's history. And this invites Dworkin's challenge: if the legitimacy of imposing democratically enacted laws on dissenters requires free public discussion of those laws, constraining the expression of Klan members' viewpoints will undermine the legitimacy of the laws on which those viewpoints bear.

I take this challenge to be unsuccessful with respect to the kind of expression under consideration because it fails to appreciate the priority of the kind of bodily rights in question in a properly ordered democratic constitution. To see why, it will be helpful to begin by considering more closely the grounds for Dworkin's position. The aspect of the democratic case for free speech that is most relevant to the argument of this section turns on a conception of citizen equality. Dworkin argues:

> It is essential to democratic partnership that citizens be free, in principle, to express any relevant opinion they have no matter how much those opinions are rejected or hated or feared by other citizens. Much of the pressure for censorship in contemporary democracies is generated not by any official attempt to keep secrets from the people, but by the desire of a majority of citizens to silence others whose opinions they despise. That is the ambition of groups, for example, who want laws preventing neo-Nazis from marching or racists from parading in white sheets. But such laws disfigure democracy, because if a majority of citizens has the power to refuse a fellow citizen the right to speak whenever it deems his ideas dangerous or offensive, then he is not an equal in the argumentative competition for power. We must permit every citizen whom we claim bound by our laws an equal voice in the process that produces those laws, even when we rightly detest his convictions.   (Dworkin, 2000, pp. 365–6)

Here Dworkin runs together two rather different grounds for restricting speech—opposition to its message and fear engendered by its message. But as far as citizen equality is concerned, the latter ground differs significantly from the former. One cannot be thought to be free to participate as an equal in democratic decision making if one's body is not at least in some core respects one's own to control. But that is precisely the situation brought about by threatening speech, which renders one unable to rely on one's rights.

To appreciate the connection between secure bodily rights and citizen equality, notice that in order to treat you as an equal in 'the argumentative competition for power' I must not treat you as already subject to my command. But since your body is the basic site of your agency in the world, taking control of your body is a way of treating you as if you were subject to my command. As I will note in the next section, there are more direct and less direct ways of taking control of your body. And whether less direct forms of control violate your bodily rights is something that may be the appropriate subject of democratic decision making. But if you are to be able to participate in democratic decision making as an equal, you at the very least need a secure vantage point from which to deliberate. And that requires an effective right against private persons damaging or destroying your body for non-defensive purposes. For this reason, I take the right to this kind of bodily integrity to be constitutionally prior to the right to free speech.

It is worth distinguishing this argument from another that Dworkin considers, namely that the expressions of derogatory opinions about a race, gender, or ethnic group "itself injures citizen equality because it not only offends the citizens who are its targets but damages their own ability to participate in politics as equals. Racist speech, for example, is said to 'silence' the racial minorities who are its target." Dworkin expresses uncertainty about the empirical claim that minorities are in fact silenced by the expression of derogatory opinions. And he argues, "We could not possibly generalize a right to such protection—a fundamentalist Christian, for example, could not be protected that way—without banning speech or the expression of opinion altogether" (Dworkin 2000, p. 366). But it is important to recall that in this section I am not focusing on hate speech as such but rather the way in which hate speech may be threatening. And my concern about threatening speech is not that it silences its targets, although it may do that too. Rather, my concern is that threatening speech prevents its targets from participating in democratic decision making as equals. If I must deliberate as if my very life is at your disposal, I am not deliberating as your equal. And that will be so even if it turns out that your threats do not deter me from speaking my mind. Thus the concern about neo-Nazis marching and racists 'parading in white sheets' is not that their views are despicable, although of course they are. Rather the concern is that their expression gives the targets of their hate reasonable cause to fear for their physical safety.

Given this, as I indicated above, a much wider range of acts of type (b) may be appropriately subject to legal regulation than has been previously observed. Displays of the swastika are a good example. Consider the famous case of the neo-Nazis who wanted to march in Skokie, Illinois, home to a significant Jewish population, many of whom were survivors of the Holocaust. The neo-Nazis challenged in court Skokie's attempt to prevent them from marching. When the case was finally returned to the Illinois Supreme Court after a series of appeals, that court ruled in favor of the neo-Nazis. Of particular note was their claim that displaying a swastika is a constitutionally protected expression because it does not constitute 'fighting words', that is, words that are likely to incite to violence those who are exposed to it.[4] But this was the wrong ground on which to seek to exclude those displays from constitutional protection. Whether or not displaying a swastika is likely to incite violence, it is an act of intimidation. And it is so regardless of whether the neo-Nazis actually intend it as such.

With this in mind we can turn our attention to communicative acts of type (a), in which one advocates or endorses violence against members of a group in virtue of their group membership. I take the following example to be instructive. In 2015, Jack Eugene Turner, a resident of Virginia, hung a life-size black mannequin from a noose in a tree in his front yard. He was convicted of violating a Virginia law prohibiting the display of nooses in public places "in a manner having a direct tendency to place another person in reasonable fear or apprehension of death or bodily injury."[5] This law correctly acknowledges that an act of type (b), namely displaying a noose, may be appropriately treated as a threat.[6] While awaiting sentencing for displaying the noose, Turner "placed a handmade cardboard sign against his house that read, 'Black n----- lives don't matter, got rope'" (Moyer 2016).[7] This is an instance of act type (a). Turner is clearly endorsing violence against black people. Turner's sign is also clearly a political message addressed to the public. But this sign conveys roughly the same message as his original display and is problematic for the same reason. This kind of speech gives those who are its subject reasonable cause to fear for their physical safety. For this reason, I take the Virginia law not to go far enough insofar as it fails to prohibit this kind of speech.[8] Likewise, suppose the neo-Nazis who wanted to march in Skokie agreed not to display swastikas but

---

[4] *Village of Skokie v. Nat'l Socialist Party of America*, 69 Ill. 2d 605 (1978).

[5] Va. Code Ann §18.2–423.2 (2009).

[6] The law also requires that the individual displaying the noose act with the intent to intimidate. For the reasons given earlier, I take this aspect of the law to be misguided.

[7] To be clear, Turner spelled out the slur on his sign. *The Washington Post* declined to follow him in this, and I have as well.

[8] Turner was actually arrested for displaying the cardboard sign as well, but only because it was a condition of his release while awaiting sentencing for displaying the noose that he not display any further symbols or messages in his yard (Harvey 2015).

instead carried signs saying, "Death to Jews!".[9] That would of course be no less an act of intimidation.

One might worry that taking acts of type (a) to be the appropriate object of legal regulation may make it impossible to express a position that ought to be expressible. This position involves advocating a change in the laws while maintaining fidelity to the law as it stands. The Klan might insist, for example, that although they think we should return to a legal circumstance in which black people's bodily rights are not legally protected, the Klan will nonetheless not violate the present laws on this matter.

Taken at face-value, speech expressing this message is not subject to the argument for regulating acts of type (a). That argument focuses on speech that gives people reasonable cause to fear the violation of their legally-recognized bodily rights. But it does not extend to speech that gives people reasonable cause to fear only that the law governing bodily rights will change. So, regulating acts of type (a) in principle leaves open the possibility of expressing nuanced messages of the kind described above.

Note, however, that the meaning of one's words depends heavily on context. Although it may in principle be possible to express the nuanced message without giving people reasonable cause to fear the violation of their legally-recognized bodily rights, one might be unable to do so if one has a history of engaging in unlawful violence. It may be difficult to credibly express fidelity to the law if one's actions have not borne that out. Consider a convicted murderer attempting to 'just joke' about who his next victims will be. Such a person's history makes it very difficult to pull off such a speech act. Something similar is true of individuals who affiliate with organizations that have a history of unlawful violence. It may be very difficult for them to convey the kind of nuanced message that would not be proscribable. But bearing that kind of expressive burden is just the price of a history of violence.

---

[9] Consider a disturbing example from a recent soccer match in Utrecht, Netherlands: " 'Hamas, Hamas, Jews to the gas,' sang a section of home supporters towards the fans visiting from Amsterdam, a city historic in part for its Jewish community. 'My father was in the commandos, my mother was in the SS, together they burned the Jews, because Jews burn the best!' " (Miller 2015).

Before turning to the next section, three features of The Argument from Intimidation merit further attention. First, although I have argued that negligent acts of intimidation are an appropriate object of legal regulation, that is consistent with taking intentional acts of intimidation to constitute more serious crimes. And indeed, it seems entirely appropriate to do so. Thus, the intentions of speakers may still be of significant legal consequence.

Second, suppose it is common knowledge between you and I that I am in no position to carry out an attack.[10] Then nothing I do could constitute even negligently threatening you. In such a circumstance, The Argument from Intimidation does not provide a reason for prohibiting me from advocating or endorsing violence toward you. But this kind of common knowledge rarely if ever obtains. To know that I could not violate your bodily rights you would have to know quite a lot about me. Even the severely disabled can, after all, conspire with or hire others to do their dirty work. Nonetheless, showing this kind of common knowledge obtained would be an appropriate defense to a charge of negligent intimidation.

Finally, one might wonder whether adequate police protection could deprive the kind of speech I have identified as threatening of its credibility. And if so, why not focus on trying to provide such protection rather than regulating the speech?[11] In reply, let me begin by acknowledging that it is of course very important to try to improve police protection, especially for historically underserved populations. But note what an extraordinary level of police protection would be needed to deprive these threats of their credibility. It is difficult to even envision what it would take for a sign like Turner's not to be reasonably intimidating. And it is even more unclear how that could be accomplished consistently with other important constitutional protections, like rights to due process. But if we were actually in a circumstance in which the state's enforcement of our rights were so complete as to deprive threats of violence of their credibility, premise (2) of The Argument from Intimidation would no longer be true. This, I think, just reflects the familiar point that the same words uttered in very different contexts may mean very different things.

---

[10] I am indebted to an anonymous reviewer for prompting me to consider this issue.

[11] I'm indebted to Steven Wall for prompting me to consider this issue, and to David Estlund for helpful discussion of it.

Proscribing the kind of speech identified by The Argument from Intimidation would constitute a radical change in the United States given the state of First Amendment interpretation. And I have not attempted to show that The Argument from Intimidation would pass constitutional muster in the United States.[12] But as I have tried to emphasize, this is an argument about the necessary conditions on legitimate democratic rule that is not beholden to First Amendment interpretation.

II. Hate Speech as Intrusion

In Section I, I focused on a feature of a certain kind of hate speech that may be shared with other kinds of speech, namely, being threatening. In this section, I consider whether speech may be proscribable simply because it expresses antipathy toward individuals in virtue of their possession of certain attributes, like their race or sex. This argument will have two parts. First, I will defend the following premises:

The Argument from Intrusion

(1) 'Public speech' is speech addressed to individuals in their capacity as citizens, government officials, or members of the public at large. 'Private speech' is speech addressed to individuals in any other capacity.
(2) Public speech merits constitutional protection even if it is addressed to an unwilling audience.
(3) Private speech merits constitutional protection only if it is addressed to a willing audience.

I will then turn to giving a positive argument for regulating private speech when it expresses antipathy toward an unwilling audience in virtue of their possession of a certain kind of characteristic.

---

[12] It is worth noting a case that is suggestive of a more expansive conception of what constitutes a true threat than First Amendment rulings have generally countenanced. *Planned Parenthood of the Columbia/Willamette Inc. v. American Coalition of Life Activists* 290 F.3d 1058, 1088 (9th Cir. 2002) upheld the finding against American Coalition of Life Activists for publishing 'wanted posters' of abortion providers in a manner that was deemed to constitute a true threat even though the posters themselves did not explicitly contain any threats. The Ninth Circuit held that the context of the posters' publication was important for understanding their meaning.

Let us begin by considering premise (1), which defines public and private speech in terms of who is addressed. Consider an example. Suppose Arthur is standing on the street corner handing out pamphlets about a new ballot initiative. His pamphlet is addressed to the public at large.[13] Beatrice takes a pamphlet and begins to ask Arthur questions about it. Here Beatrice and Arthur address one another as fellow citizens. So, both Arthur's pamphlet and his ensuing conversation with Beatrice are examples of what I am calling public speech. They are contributions to public discourse. In contrast, consider your conversation with the waiter from whom you are ordering lunch. You do not address him in his capacity as a citizen, but instead as the employee of the establishment at which you are dining. Or consider your conversation with your friends about which movie to watch tonight. Here again you do not address your friends in their capacity as fellow citizens, but rather as people who stand in a certain relationship with you.

Premises (2) and (3) refer to willing and unwilling audiences. I take a willing audience to be one that prefers to be addressed or is indifferent to it. And I take an unwilling audience to be one that prefers not to be addressed. The idea of an unwilling audience bears some similarity to the idea of a captive audience, which has a home in First Amendment interpretation. But the idea of an unwilling audience is primarily tracking one's attitude toward being addressed rather than the ease with which one could avoid being addressed.

Premise (2) makes use of one of the categories marked out by premise (1) and claims that public speech merits constitutional protection even if it is addressed to an unwilling audience. Premise (2) thus aims to address a potential objection to the constitutional protection of public speech. In what follows, I begin by demonstrating the inadequacy of one potential defense of premise (2), and the failure of this defense will clarify why one might be concerned about speech addressed to an unwilling audience. I will then develop a democratic justification of premise (2) that responds to this concern.

---

[13] In general, I take it to be sufficient for being addressed to the public that the speech in question be offered to the public. So, for example, a movie distributed for public consumption in the usual ways counts as being addressed to the public.

A helpful articulation of the inadequate defense of premise (2) is given by Kant, who holds that we have an innate right

> to do to others anything that does not in itself diminish what is theirs, so long as they do not want to accept it—such things as merely communicating his thoughts to them, telling or promising them something, whether what he says is true and sincere or untrue and insincere (*veriloquium aut falsiloquium*); for it is entirely up to them whether they want to believe him or not.   (Kant 1996, pp. 393–4)

Understanding this claim requires some articulation of what would 'in itself diminish what is theirs'. Kant provides an example: "the false allegation that a contract has been concluded with someone, made in order to deprive him of what is his" (Kant 1996, p. 394). Given that Kant also holds that we have some kind of innate right to our own bodies, we might also add that threats to violate rights of the sort described in Section I also might be plausibly thought to in itself diminish what belongs to another. These potentially proscribable forms of speech notwithstanding, the right to speak described is quite capacious. Merely communicating my thoughts to another or telling them something are both described as not in themselves diminishing what belongs to another.

Helga Varden helpfully explains the reasoning behind this part of Kant's view:

> The utterance of words in space and time does not have the power to hinder anyone else's external freedom, including depriving him of his means. Since words as such cannot exert physical power over people, it is impossible to use them as a means of coercion against another.
>
> (Varden 2010, p. 42)

Of course, as Varden acknowledges, words can physically affect people— one might be startled or deafened by yelling. But in such cases, "it is not the words or their content that constitutes my wrongdoing, but the noise" (Varden 2010, p. 43).

This suggests the following defense of premise (2). Merely addressing you does not really do anything to you. You may after all simply ignore me. So, even if you would prefer not to be addressed, you have no grounds for complaint if I do.

But this defense of premise (2) overlooks the way in which hearing speech in a language one understands inevitably affects one's thinking. And given one's embodiment, this effect on one's thinking proceeds by way of affecting one's body. To appreciate this point, it may be helpful to begin by first observing the physiological effects particular kinds of speech may have. If I tell you something disturbing, even if you do not believe me, simply hearing what I said might cause your heart to race, leave you with a lingering sense of disquiet, or result in nightmares that disturb your sleep. These are all ways in which the operation of your body is impacted by what I say in virtue of its content rather than its status as mere noise.

To say that speech *can* have physiological consequences is not yet to say that it *always* does. But once one appreciates the former claim, I think it requires very little to move to the latter. Suppose I say, "It's raining." And suppose we grant Kant that it is up to you whether to believe me or not.[14] Still, it is not up to you to whether or not to hear my words as meaningful.[15] When I tell you it is raining, I put that proposition before your mind. I capture your attention and make the proposition I uttered salient to you. And I do that by affecting your brain. Addressing you is thus a way of acting on your body. Of course, in this case unlike in those above, it is not plausible to think that I have in any way harmed you.[16] But I take it that merely taking control of something that is yours is a way of wronging you whether or not that also harms you. Consider by way of analogy cases of harmless trespass.

What we see, then, is that, contra Varden, words as such can 'exert physical power over people'. This is not yet to say that the kind of

---

[14] I think Kant overstates this point. You may have some choice about whether to trust me. And in the absence of trust, you may have some discretion about how my statement figures into your total body of evidence about the matter. But you are not epistemically free to simply ignore my statement unless you have some good reason for doing so. My statement constrains how you may think about the matter even if it does not compel belief. This is not a constraint that one can shake off at will. But the point I make in the main text holds whether or not one accepts this objection.

[15] Christine M. Korsgaard makes a similar point in a rather different argumentative context (Korsgaard 1996, p. 140).

[16] For a helpful overview of the ways in which speech can harm, see Delgado (1993), pp. 89–110.

physical power that speech exerts over people deprives them of anything to which they have a right. Whether or not that is so depends on whether we take their rights to their bodies to include the right to be free from this way of being acted on. This is not a kind of control that you need in order to be able to participate in democratic decision making, which as we will see shortly actually presupposes that others must have some right to address you even if you would prefer that they not. But since your body is uncontroversially yours, I suggest we need some compelling reason for taking others to be permitted to act on your body when you would prefer that they not, as they do when you are the unwilling object of address.

A compelling reason for protecting speech addressed to an unwilling audience can be provided if we restrict our attention to public speech and consider its role in democratic governance. States inevitably impose laws on some people who disagree with them. Democratic governance seeks to address the complaint of such individuals by giving them an equal right to participate in the process by which such decisions are made. But this process is not exhausted by voting. One votes on a given slate of proposals or candidates for public office. The development of that slate is itself part of the political process. And voting does not close the political process. The conclusion of a vote settles merely what will happen until the next vote and marks the beginning of a new process of agenda setting. Thus the right to political participation must include not only the right to vote, but also the right to participate in the public discourse that shapes the questions that formal political decision making will eventually take up. If we suppose, then, that we have some compelling reason to subject people to some form of governance and that the right to participation just described is necessary to address the objections of dissenters, we arrive at a compelling reason for treating public speech as constitutionally protected even if it is addressed to an unwilling audience.

But this line of argument might be thought to suggest a worry about premise (3), which holds that private speech merits constitutional protection only if it is addressed to a willing audience. Private speech may also contribute to shaping the questions that formal political decision making will eventually take up. So why take the right to political participation to be limited to the right to participate in public discourse?

Notice that just about everything I do may contribute in some small way to setting the political agenda. So this line of thought does not suggest a unique ground for protecting speech. And it would be implausible to hold that the way any action of mine might contribute to setting the political agenda suffices to justify constitutional protection of my actions in the face of the objections of those who do not want to interact with me. Even noise ordinances would be constitutionally suspect if that were the case.

The distinction between public and private speech enables us to accommodate the following feature of our situation. Because we must govern together, you must have some ability to address me whether I like it or not. But we are not always 'conducting the business of the state' when we interact. And when we are not, it matters whether I want to hear what you have to say.

One might agree with this sentiment but worry about whether I have drawn the distinction between public and private speech in the right way. Consider two alternative possibilities. The first focuses on the content of the speech and treats as public only speech that clearly engages with political questions. But much that goes into shaping the political agenda is not overtly political. So this characterization would be too narrow. Alternatively, consider focusing on the venue of speech, namely whether the speech occurs in a public or private place. But taking place in public is neither necessary nor sufficient to capture what it means to participate in the political process of agenda setting. One may do this privately, as for example when one debates the merits of a candidate for office around the dinner table. One may also speak with others publicly but still not be participating in the political process of agenda setting, as when I draw your attention to the wallet you dropped on the sidewalk.

Nonetheless, I take it that there will be many cases in which it is not transparent whether one addresses another in her capacity as a fellow citizen or something else. In these cases, considerations about the content and venue of one's speech may be helpful in providing interpretative context. Given the importance of the right to participate in securing the legitimacy of democratic governance, when in doubt we will generally have good reason to err on the side of classifying speech as public. But just because there are hard cases does not mean that there are no easy cases.

The most straightforward kind of private speech is speech that address you in virtue of some specific feature of you or your circumstances, as when I point out your dropped wallet.

With this in mind, let us return to considering premise (3). Once we have the distinction between public and private speech in view, the case for protecting private speech cannot be based on the right to political participation required for democratic legitimacy. But a case for constitutional protection for private speech might still be made by reflecting on the proper scope of the state's authority to regulate interactions between consenting adults. The freedom to interact with others in mutually agreeable ways is quite plausibly a pre-political right that only compelling state interests may constrain. And this is no less true of willing communication. Still, I have formulated premise (3) as giving only a necessary condition for constitutional protection of private speech because I will not attempt here to characterize what kind of compelling state interests might be relevant to the regulation of private speech addressed to a willing audience. There are undoubtedly some, as when willing communication would constitute a conspiracy to commit a crime.

Note one final feature of premise (3). Taking private speech directed at an unwilling audience not to merit constitutional protection does not yet establish that such speech should be prohibited. Rather it simply indicates that the regulation of such speech is the appropriate subject of democratic decision making. The comparison with noise ordinances is instructive here again. Just because making noise is not a constitutionally protected activity does not mean that there are no good reasons for sometimes allowing people to make noise even if it bothers others or imposes costs on them if they want to avoid being bothered in this way. Similarly, the argument thus far leaves open whether and how private speech addressed to an unwilling audience should be regulated.

With all this in mind, we can turn to the second part of The Argument from Intrusion, which articulates a reason for regulating a particular kind of private speech. With respect to a great deal of abusive or insulting speech, I think we face a genuinely open question about how civil we want people to be legally required to be in private speech. We might take a 'sticks and stones' approach to abusive or insulting speech. Or we might decide that some such speech constitutes some kind of minor civil or criminal wrong. I suggest, however, that there is a kind of abusive private speech we have strong reason to prohibit:

(4) 'Injustice-inflected disparagement' is speech that may be reasonably taken to express antipathy toward individuals in virtue of their possession of the kind of characteristic that has been a common basis for unjust treatment.

(5) When injustice-inflected disparagement is addressed to individuals as possessors of the relevant characteristics, it is private speech.

(6) Injustice-inflected disparagement addressed to an unwilling audience involves the use of illicit expressive power to shape the addressee's thinking.

(7) We have strong reason to protect unwilling audiences from having their mental lives intruded upon in this way by private speech.

(8) Therefore, we have strong reason to prohibit injustice-inflected disparagement when it is private speech addressed to an unwilling audience.

Let us consider each of these premises. Premise (4) focuses on expressions of antipathy toward individuals in virtue of their possession of the kind of characteristic that has been a common basis for unjust treatment. I will not attempt an exhaustive list of the relevant kinds of characteristics. But I take race, ethnicity, sex, gender, religion, and sexual orientation to be prime examples of the kinds of characteristics that have historically been the basis for unjust treatment. Note that this does not mean that, say, all racial groups have been historically subjected to unjust treatment. The claim is rather that race is a common basis for unjust treatment.

In a wide range of cases, addressing someone with a slur may reasonably be taken to express antipathy toward that person in virtue of their possession of the relevant kind of characteristic.[17] This kind of speech is typically addressed to an unwilling audience. I take these to be paradigmatic cases of injustice-inflected disparagement. But this category is not

---

[17] I leave open here the possibility of friendly, intra-group uses of slurs.

limited to these uses of slurs. Consider, as addressed to a black person, the statement: "Do you want some bananas? Go back to the jungle."[18]

Premise (5) applies the conception of private speech articulated in premise (1). When injustice-inflected disparagement is addressed to individuals as possessors of certain characteristics, it is private speech. Note that in light of premise (3), when injustice-inflected disparagement is private speech addressed to an unwilling audience, it does not merit constitutional protection.

Premise (6) holds that injustice-inflected disparagement involves the use of illicit expressive power to shape the addressee's thinking. To see why, consider the difference between expressing antipathy toward a person in virtue of her race and expressing antipathy toward a person in virtue of her large ears. These are both unchosen features. So race's status as unchosen cannot explain why the former expression of antipathy seems so much more concerning. Perhaps the difference lies in the way in which race may constitute a core element of one's identity. But one's profession might likewise constitute a core element of one's identity. And yet antipathy expressed toward a person in virtue of being, say, a philosopher also seems to lack the distinctively concerning character of antipathy expressed toward a person in virtue of her race. Notice, however, that if one's ear size or profession came to be treated as a common basis for unjust treatment, antipathy expressed in virtue of these features would seem much like expressing antipathy toward a person in virtue of her race. For this reason, I take premise (6) to identify a feature of certain types of expression that is already implicit in our thinking about these matters.

Injustice-inflected disparagement relies on characteristics that have the significance they do in virtue of their association with injustice. And although addressees may take steps to avoid being addressed and may ignore what is said when they are addressed, they cannot fail to hear speech in a language they understand as meaningful. Such speech thus makes salient to them a feature of themselves the meaning of which is bound up with injustice. Injustice-inflected disparagement thus involves exercising illicit power over their minds.

---

[18] I draw this from a real case involving a slur. I take the message to be problematic even when the slur is omitted. For a description of the original case, see Cohen (1993), p. 207.

This account also explains why injustice-inflected disparagement seems more problematic when addressed to the recently oppressed than to other groups. The relationship between the specific characteristics of the recently oppressed and injustice is extremely salient. Nonetheless, even if one's race, say, has not been recently subjected to injustice, the category of race has the social significance it does in virtue of its association with injustice.

Premise (7) holds that we have strong reason to protect unwilling audiences from having their mental lives intruded upon in this way by private speech. I take the characterization of the speech in premise (6) as exercising illicit expressive power to already make that reason apparent. We have reason to protect people from such exercises of power. But it is worth addressing two considerations that might be thought to mitigate the force of that reason. First, perhaps one might think that people should develop 'thick skins' with respect to disparaging speech and thereby blunt its force. But notice that even if one could condition oneself in ways that would mitigate the downstream effects on one's thinking of being addressed, the problem begins as soon as the speech is understood. Injustice-inflected speech draws attention to one's possession of characteristics that are associated with injustice. And that is an effect on one's thinking that speakers of the relevant language cannot avoid. Try as I might, I cannot hear what you are saying as mere noise.

Second, perhaps one might think that it is incumbent upon potential addressees to avoid being addressed. Given that private speech can take place in public, I think this suggestion overlooks how incredibly burdensome that would be. But the more fundamental response to both this suggestion and the previous one is to ask why I should have to take steps to avoid your use of illicit expressive power—a power that you have only in virtue of the legacy of injustice.

This question, however, raises another. Why take the reason we have to protect people from this kind of illicit expressive power to apply only when the speech in question is private speech? Political protests may, for example, also use slurs and the like. Why should we not also protect passersby from having their mental lives shaped by injustice?

A state's laws and institutions may involve a commitment to not using some characteristics as the basis of the distribution of rights or of benefits and burdens because doing so would be unjust. When we are not conducting the business of the state together, our interactions may be appropriately regulated in keeping with this commitment. But democratic legitimacy requires allowing people who object to this commitment to express their opposition in public speech. Employing a conception of justice to restrict public speech would involve begging the question against those who are opposed to the present public understanding of justice because what constitutes justice and injustice is precisely what is at issue in that context.

For this reason, I do not think that The Argument from Intrusion can do more than justify prohibiting injustice-inflected disparagement when it is private speech addressed to an unwilling audience. Premise (7) reflects this. And this suggests that reflection on our bodily rights leaves non-threatening public hate speech immune to regulation. My argument thus leaves open the possibility that Dworkin's argument contains a grain of truth: that enduring leaflets, protest signs, and public lectures involving slurs and the like is an unavoidable cost of respecting the right to participation of prejudiced citizens.

Note, however, that I have not ruled out the possibility of arguments that close this space. We have already observed one such alternative in passing, namely, that hate speech silences its targets in a way that undermines citizen equality. Or perhaps hate speech constitutes a kind of defamation that sullies its targets' reputations in a constitutionally proscribable way.[19] These arguments may well provide a path to a more thoroughgoing rejection of Dworkin's challenge. But whether or not they succeed, I take the above reflection on bodily rights to blunt the force of that challenge. As I argued in Section I, a democratic theory of free speech affords no constitutional protection to speech that threatens our legally recognized bodily rights, even when it is public speech. And hate speech has a threatening character more often than has been recognized. The argument of this section suggests that the democratic settlement of the scope of those bodily rights that do not merit constitutional protection ought to be responsive to the strong reason we have to protect people from the intrusion into their mental lives that private

---

[19] For a helpful discussion of the distinction between individual and group defamation, and some skepticism about the viability of prohibiting hate speech as group defamation, see Weinstein (2009), pp. 58–60.

speech involving injustice-inflected disparagement constitutes. In these ways, our bodily rights constrain the right to free speech in a way that diffuses the tension between a democratic theory of free speech and hate speech regulation.[20]

Works Cited

Cohen, Joshua. "Freedom of Expression," *Philosophy & Public Affairs*, Vol. 22, No. 3 (1993).

Delgado, Richard. "Words that Wound: A Tort Action for Racial Insults, Epithets, and Name Calling," in *Words that Wound: Critical Race Theory, Assaultive Speech, and the First Amendment*, M. Matsuda et. al., eds. (Westview Press, 1993) 89–110.

Dworkin, Ronald. "Free Speech, Politics, and the Dimensions of Democracy," *Sovereign Virtue* (Harvard University Press, 2000).

Dworkin, Ronald. "Forward," in *Extreme Speech and Democracy*, Ivan Hare and James Weinstein, eds. (Oxford University Press, 2009) v–xi.

Harvey, Neil. "Rocky Mount Man Guilty of Hanging a Noose Is Jailed over New Yard Sign," *The Roanoke Times*, Dec. 2, 2015. https://www.roanoke.com/news/crime/franklin_county/rocky-mount-man-guilty-of-hanging-a-noose-is-jailed/article_0389b2b6-291c-50d3-8b5a-3b2db67e786d.html

Kant, Immanuel. *Practical Philosophy*, Mary J. Gregor, ed. and trans. (Cambridge University Press, 1996).

Korsgaard, Christine M. *The Sources of Normativity* (Cambridge University Press, 1996).

Meiklejohn, Alexander. *Free Speech and Its Relation to Self-Government* (Harper Brothers Publishers, 1948).

Miller, Michael E. "Nazi Chants at Dutch Soccer Game Expose an Ugly Blot on 'The Beautiful Game,'" *The Washington Post*, April 10, 2015. https://www.washingtonpost.com/news/morning-mix/wp/2015/04/10/nazi-chants-at-dutch-soccer-game-expose-an-ugly-blot-on-the-beautiful-game/?utm_term=.f0cc6f550f07

---

[20] I am indebted to Keith Hyams, Meica Magnani, two anonymous reviewers, and the editors of this volume for helpful comments on earlier drafts of this chapter. I am also grateful for questions from audiences at the Workshop for Oxford Studies in Political Philosophy; the Philosophy of Right conference at the University of Leipzig; the University of Georgia; UC Berkley; UCLA; and the Stanford University Political Theory Workshop.

Moyer, Justin Wm. "Virginia Man Who Displayed Noose after Charleston Shooting Loses Court Appeal," *The Washington Post*, Nov. 22, 2016. https://www.washingtonpost.com/local/public-safety/virginia-man-who-displayed-noose-after-charleston-shooting-loses-court-appeal/2016/11/22/4567f15c-b0f3-11e6-8616-52b15787add0_story.html?utm_term=.917ef11841c8

Planned Parenthood of the Columbia/Willamette Inc. v. American Coalition of Life Activists 290 F.3d 1058, 1088 (9th Cir. 2002).

Post, Robert C. "Racist Speech, Democracy, and the First Amendment," *William and Mary Law Review*, Vol. 32, No. 2 (1991) 267–327.

R.A.V. v. City of St. Paul, 505 U.S. 377 (1992).

Va. Code Ann §18.2–423.2 (2009).

Varden, Helga. "A Kantian Conception of Free Speech," in *Free Speech in a Diverse World*, D. Golash, ed. (Springer, 2010) 39–55

Virginia v. Black, 538 U.S. 343 (2003).

Weinstein, James. "Extreme Speech, Public Order, and Democracy: Lessons From *The Masses*," in *Extreme Speech and Democracy*, Ivan Hare and James Weinstein, eds. (Oxford University Press, 2009) 62–80.

PART II
IMMIGRATION AND BORDERS

4

The Right to Stay as a Control Right

Valeria Ottonelli

Do we have a right to stay in the place where we live? Consider the following stories.

Fausto Limon used to own a small farm in the region of Veracruz, Mexico. After the NAFTA agreement came into effect, a big North American company, Granjas Carroll, established pig breeding and pork processing plants in the region. In consequence, many small farmers such as Fausto Limon were driven out of business. Because of the waste produced by the plants, the area became dangerously contaminated. Some nights, Fausto Limon would drive for miles to find a place where his children could sleep safely without getting sick from the smell. Fausto Limon and his family eventually decided to leave their home and migrate to the US border (Bacon 2013: 31–4).

Domenica Raja was born at the beginning of the last century in a small village of Sicily. Right after turning 16, she escaped two kidnapping attempts by a member of the local mafia. Her family realized that if she stayed in the village, she would be in serious danger. They found her a husband in Turin, far in the North of Italy. She packed her few things and left forever.[1]

Faez al Sharaa used to live in Daraa, Syria, with his family. After the civil war started, he witnessed the killings, torturing, and kidnappings taking place every day in his formerly peaceful town. One day he was arrested and accused of being a terrorist. Although he was eventually released, his life and his family were no longer safe. The day after Faez was released, they started the long journey that eventually led to their resettlement in the United States (Altman 2018).

---

[1] Personal recollection.

Valeria Ottonelli, *The Right to Stay as a Control Right* In: *Oxford Studies in Political Philosophy Volume 6.*
Edited by: David Sobel, Peter Vallentyne, and Steven Wall, Oxford University Press (2020). © Valeria Ottonelli.
DOI: 10.1093/oso/9780198852636.003.0004

These stories have something in common: the people involved had little choice but to leave the place where they were born and had long lived. It can be argued that this fact, in and by itself, adds a significant wrong to the violence, threats, persecution, and deprivations they suffered before departing from their lands, and to the wrongs they might have suffered afterwards as immigrants or refugees. In other words, we may believe that those who are forced to leave their place of residence suffer the violation of a specific individual right not to be displaced— that is, a "right to stay." Although at first sight it might seem obvious that people have such a right, international law does not encompass it among fundamental human rights and indeed it is very controversial that such a right should be recognized.

In this chapter, I side with those who believe a right to stay should be counted among fundamental human rights. However, I also acknowledge that there are good reasons for objecting to the ways in which the right to stay is currently defended and accounted for. In response to these objections, I argue that the best way to make sense of the right to stay is to conceive it as protecting control over one's body and personal space, which is an essential condition for personhood and human dignity. This account of the right to stay can overcome the most pressing objections to its recognition as a fundamental human right.

In the first part of the chapter (sections 1 and 2), I present a fundamental problem in the structure of current justifications of the right to stay. In sections 3 and 4, I argue that the right to stay should be conceived as one of the fundamental civil rights that protect the control we are entitled to have over our own bodies and our personal space, and I show that this conception of the right to stay is immune to the problems presented in the first part of the chapter. In section 5, I draw some implications of this conception of the right to stay and defend it against some possible objections.

1. The Problem with the Right to Stay

In the current literature on immigration, emigration, and territorial rights, we often find appeals to an individual right to stay. Such a right is central in discussions on the plight of internally displaced people, refugees, and all who are forced to move from their dwellings because of persecution, war, environmental catastrophes, mass relocations and development plans.[2] A right to stay is also advocated for immigrants, who are claimed to acquire it because of the ties they develop with the receiving society (Carens 2010; Buckinxy and Filindraz 2015; Ochoa Espejo 2016; Savino 2016). Moreover, the right to remain, understood as a right of individual occupancy, is a cornerstone in many of the theories aiming to justify the right of people to their territory (Stilz 2011; Lefkowitz 2015; Moore 2015), although by itself it does not bear all the justificatory burden of full, communal territorial rights (Stilz 2011; Miller 2012; Moore 2015: 37).[3] Such a right, understood as a right of individual occupancy, is a cornerstone in many of the theories aiming to justify the right of people to their territory (Stilz 2011; Lefkowitz 2015; Moore 2015).

Notwithstanding its prominent role in the normative literature on migration and territory, and its apparent obviousness, the right to stay is not recognized as a basic right in international law and its relevance and grounds are very controversial.[4] A main source of resistance comes from the fear that insisting on the right to stay of the people who are potential claimants of the status of refugees can detract from the right to be admitted to foreign countries (Hathaway 1995, 2007a; Barutciski 1998, 2002; Zetter 2015). However, a second, more substantial, objection concerns the very content of the right, rather than its possible misuses. In fact, some authors remark that in the most dramatic cases in which people flee from home, what they need is not "a right to stay," but the fulfilment of basic rights and necessities, such as shelter, food, protection from violence, legal status, or healthcare. Or, if there is any protection that people need *before* displacement takes place, this is the protection against the circumstances that compel them to leave, rather than the protection of a right to stay per se. Indeed, the UN *Guiding Principles on Internal Displacement* (Deng 1999; Entwisle 2005), which represents the most important, although not binding (Pitarokoili 2014), legal document in which the right not to be arbitrarily displaced is

---

[2] See, for example,Waldron 2004; Oberman 2011; Stilz 2013; Nine 2016; Huber and Wolkenstein forthcoming.

[3] But, *contra*, see Angell 2017.

[4] For some recent discussions in relation to forced displacement, see Morel, Stavropoulou, and Durieux 2012; Adeola 2016; Katselli Proukaki 2018.

explicitly appealed to, does not seem to reserve to displaced people any further rights than those usually needed when humanitarian intervention is in order (Cohen 2002; Hathaway 2007b). In short, recognizing a "right to stay" does not make any significant addition to the rights whose violation causes displacement, or the duties of assistance that are activated after displacement. A specific "right to stay" appears to be redundant.

Behind the redundancy objection to the right to stay we can devise a deeper conceptual problem, which becomes evident once we pay attention to the justifications of the right that have been offered in the philosophical literature on the topic. We can find two main families of arguments for the right to stay: attachment-based and life-plan-based.

Attachment-based arguments hold that people have a right to stay in the place where they were born or have long lived because of the attachments and ties they have developed to the territories or the communities that reside there. By living in the midst of a given political community, these arguments claim, one develops valuable and significant ties to its culture, social norms, and institutions, so that when people are uprooted they suffer an important existential, sentimental, and social loss. These ties also extend to the territory where one lives, not only because the territory's physiognomy is shaped by and becomes an integral part of the culture of the community that resides there, but also because the very natural geography of a territory becomes part of the social landscape of its inhabitants. On these grounds, Joseph Carens advocates a "right to stay" for those foreigners who have resided enough years in the host country (Carens 2010: 17).

Life-plan-based arguments for the right to stay hold that uprooting people from their habitual environment implies dispossessing them "of the place that is central to their life-plans." (Stilz 2013: 349). Relationships, commitments, work, career goals, and many other components of people's life projects are *located*—that is, they are built in a specific place and depend on geographical stability to be carried out. These arguments can also be framed in reference to an opportunity conception of freedom—that is, as relating to the external conditions that make it possible for people to do what they want with their lives. Kieran Oberman, for example, argues that the right to stay follows as an *a fortiori* implication of freedom of movement, which protects the "interest that people have in freely being able to make personal decisions without restriction on their range of options"; in fact, "the options that are most important to us are normally situated in our home state" (Oberman 2011: 259; see also 2015: 246).

However plausible these arguments may look at first sight, they provide poor grounds for a right to stay. Both kinds of argument, in fact, seem to rely on a *sedentary bias* by assuming that for all human beings the best options in life and most valuable attachments are to be found in the place where they already reside.[5] In the case of those who are forced to move, this assumption is especially problematic. The fundamental problem with the arguments that ground a right to stay in the value of the opportunities and ties people have in their place of residence, in fact, is that they seem to be the least effective exactly in those cases in which the right to stay is threatened the most—that is, when people are forced to leave because the place where they are staying is literally unliveable. Think of places that have been destroyed by long-lasting civil wars, are poisoned by polluting industries or atomic disasters, or have been dried up by decades of drought. We may feel that there is something very sad in the fate of the people who are fleeing from these disasters, but certainly we do not perceive that there is a great loss for them in not being able to stay in *those* territories. However, these should be the central cases of concern for those who are interested in explaining what is wrong with displacement. Or think of those people who leave their place of residence because of religious persecution or their sexual orientation, or who escape from an environment that is economically and socially strangled by a violent mafia cartel. It is very likely that these forms of hardship are supported and made possible by a web of social customs, practices, discourses, and relations. In these cases, it is not just the immediate causes of one's fleeing one's country that should be dreaded, but the whole social environment that feeds them. To pick an extreme example, consider those Jewish people who fled Germany under the Nazi regime; after such a treatment, many of them had no feelings left for their "home country."[6] In these cases, the idea that the

---

[5] For a powerful criticism of the "botanical metaphors" by which "people are often thought of, and think of themselves, as being rooted in place and as deriving their identity from that rootedness," see Malkki 1992: 27; 1995. On the sedentary bias, see also Bakewell 2008.

[6] See Laqueur 2001: 263–4.

right to stay is grounded in the valuable ties that people have to their community is utterly implausible.

I am not suggesting that all those who migrate are leaving doomed territories, wicked societies, and valueless social relations. Rather, I am claiming that in the most painful and obvious instances of a violation of the right to stay, the relationship between those who leave and their society or territory of origin is often far from being idyllic. Therefore, the right to stay cannot be grounded on the special value of the ties people have to their place of residence.

The same also holds for the justifications grounded in the value of the life plans or of freedom of movement as an opportunity concept. Here the right to stay is conceived as an instrumental good that is valuable because of the opportunities it provides. This kind of justification fails for exactly the same reasons as the justifications grounded in social ties and attachments. The appeal to life plans and opportunities works well when we need to justify the right to *leave* places that are underdeveloped, crime ridden, or devastated by civil war or foreign bombing. It works poorly when we need to justify the right to *stay* of those who are forced to move elsewhere exactly because the place where they reside offers them no acceptable life options.

A related, but more subtle line of reasoning points to the importance of staying put for preserving the functions that allow people to develop and carry out plans. Cara Nine (2018) has argued that people need stability and a fixed and safe home in order to preserve everyday routines and the established meanings attached to the space where they live, which in turn are essential preconditions of good cognitive and psychological functioning. This argument, unlike the standard accounts based on located life plans, does not place any special weight on the opportunities people have where they reside. However, it still unduly assumes that staying put best ensures valuable conditions for pursuing a life plan, which is definitely not the case in the most painful cases in which people are forced to leave. The routine of avoiding snipers while going to school in a place devastated by a civil war, or the routine of walking for miles every day to collect water or food, is not an enabling condition for fully functioning as a planner. In fact, the very feeling of insecurity and inability to plan that people experience in some places is among the reasons why they feel compelled to leave.

There is an additional problem with the stress on attachments or life plans to justify a right to stay. Not only do they build the weakest case where such right is threatened the most, but they also afford the least protection to those who most need it. Think of a city of the Global South. Of all its residents, those who are most likely affected by the conditions that compel emigration are the most destitute ones, those who live in its degraded and dreadful slums.[7] Those, presumably, are the people who have enjoyed the least of the few amenities that can be found in such places. If they eventually manage to emigrate, it is difficult to argue that what they are losing by leaving are the conditions for a meaningful life plan or valuable opportunities.

It is worth noting that the same considerations also extend to immigrants' right to stay in destination countries. Here again, appealing to the ties and attachments they have developed with the host community, or to the importance of the opportunities they have there, risks over-romanticizing the reality of many migration stories, and, what is worse, offers very poor grounds for the claims of those migrants who are most disadvantaged in the receiving society. Victims of trafficking, live-in domestic workers, and unskilled economic migrants—especially if undocumented—who are subject to all sorts of abuses, exploitative work relations, and lead a secluded and impoverished social life cannot claim to have deep and valuable relations with the host society. Even when they are better off than they would have been in their country of origin, grounding their right to stay in the value of such miserable life conditions is implausible.[8] Again, this does not mean that migrants always lead miserable lives in the receiving country. It means, instead, that grounding immigrants' right to stay in the valuable ties that immigrants establish within the host society pulls the rug out from under the most disadvantaged and vulnerable among them—that is, those who are very unlikely to have established valuable ties with the host society or to be offered valuable opportunities. Conversely, to the extent that such

[7] Kieran Oberman (2015) has convincingly argued against the popular assumption that the poorest do not emigrate. I add that such an assumption is most clearly invalidated if we take into account intraregional and short-distance migration.

[8] In their argument against deportation, Buckinxy and Filindraz (2015) explicitly draw this conclusion about those who have not gained significant ties to the host society.

justification succeeds, it is at the price of a hypocritical disregard for the actual treatment and conditions of the migrants involved.

In sum, the shortcomings of the life-plan- and attachment-based accounts seem to point to something deeply and inherently puzzling about the idea of a right to stay: the cases in which it is most threatened are also those in which there does not seem to be much to lose. This paradoxical conclusion corroborates the redundancy objection against recognizing the right to stay as a fundamental right. In fact, if the right to stay is grounded in the attachments and opportunities that people have where they reside, whenever those attachments or opportunities are no longer there (or have never been there) we cannot see any further interest in staying. The right to stay then appears a redundant and misleading addition to the more basic rights that protect people from the disruption of their social, economic, or political environment.

2. The Crux of the Matter

It might be objected that this is how all rights that protect valuable things work: when they are violated, the people who are wronged are left with little or no value in their hands. If I am in jail and my fellow prisoners steal my meal, I am left with an empty stomach and a poor diet. At that point, I can only beg for another meal at the refectory; however, this does not mean that I did not have a right to the original meal, or that there is nothing to regret. However, note how different this case is from those in which people have to leave their home because it is an unliveable place. In the latter, the reason they cannot enjoy their supposed right to stay in that place is the quality of the very object of that right. A more appropriate analogy with the food example, then, would be if today I had been served an inedible lunch, like a piece of stale, mouldy bread. I could claim that I should have received a better lunch, but I could not really regret that I had to separate myself from *that* piece of stale bread. The right to stay, in fact, contains an inescapable element of indexicality: it is not the right to a generic service or kind of good, but to the enjoyment of a *specific* place. When one complains that her right not to be displaced has been violated, what the complaint is about, specifically, is not the quality of the living conditions before departing, or the fact that the place where she was living was spoiled or made unliveable, but the fact that she was compelled to separate from *that* specific place. If we want to justify a universal and fundamental right to stay, then, we need to account for the loss incurred when one is forced to leave the specific place where one resides, and do it in a way that also applies to places that have long been or have become the topographical analogue of a piece of stale and mouldy bread.

In response to this puzzle, one might suggest that the right to stay is grounded not in the present value of the place that people are forced to leave, but in the counterfactual value that the place *would have had*, had it not been spoiled. But this does not really address the fundamental problem. In fact, there are two scenarios to which we can apply this suggestion. The first is the case in which someone is born and resides in a place that has been long deteriorated or unliveable. In this scenario, we are asked to imagine a counterfactual attachment to, or life planning in, a hypothetical land that would be the same as the one the person is leaving, except that it would be completely different, to the point that life there would be agreeable. In the most dramatic cases—those we are concerned with here—it is hard to even understand what this thought experiment asks us to imagine; but even if we succeeded in such an imaginative effort, we would still be left to wonder how the hypothetical attachments and life plans developed in that counterfactual scenario could ground a right to stay in a place that looks, and indeed is, completely different. The second scenario is one in which a place is perfectly adequate to an agreeable life, and then some exogenous catastrophic event—such as a war waged by a foreign country—happens that spoils everything and makes people leave. In this scenario, it is easy to conceive that those who are forced to move have developed strong attachments to their land and may deeply resent the fact that so much value is spoiled. However, in such circumstances the real damage, what spoils people's lives, seems to consist in what is done to those places, rather than in the fact that people must leave as a consequence of such damage. In other words, this scenario makes us focus our attention on the wrong target. The right to stay should concern the wrong people suffer *as* they are forced to leave, rather than the one they suffer because of what is done to the land they are attached to.

Another way we might want to respond to the conundrum is by pointing out that no matter how dismal, corrupted, dangerous, and poor a place might be, its inhabitants *do* develop ties and attachments to it and *do* develop life plans that are located there. It can be argued, in fact, that the source of the value of some of our relationships to people, places, or things does not reside in the intrinsic or instrumental merits of such objects of affection, but in those very relationships. For example, we have reason to keep alive a friendship even if our friend has changed through the years and many of the qualities that made us first become friends are no longer there. However, these considerations can hardly function as grounds for a right not to be displaced in the most dramatic cases we are considering. A special tie or attachment can ground a right only to the extent that it is valuable, at least in the sense that it involves no serious wrong or disvalue. Consider an analogy with battered women. Many of them are deeply attached to their partners and make plans around the very miserable conditions they find themselves in, sometimes with the intent to keep alive a relation that originally was not abusive. However, we do not feel that what makes us sad when they finally leave the relationship is the fact that they leave *that* relationship, no matter how much pain and sense of loss they may experience because of their ingrained attachments and ties. The same can be said about the ties we develop to the place where we are born and live. They can constitute the ground of a right only to the extent that they are actually valuable, whereas the circumstances that make people leave in the most dramatic cases of forced displacement—think again of civil wars, extreme pollution, or racist persecution—can be likened to abusive relationships.

Once we have thus clarified the crux of the matter, it might seem legitimate to conclude that there is no such thing as a right to stay. We might conjecture that the real tragedy for those who are forced to leave their homes does not consist in the fact that they must leave, but in the fact that they have been living in terrible conditions or are facing life-threatening circumstances. Alternatively, it might consist in the adverse conditions many people must face after they have left, as is the case not only with most refugees, but also with many economic migrants. Finally, we can feel pity because some of those who are forced to move were living in formerly agreeable and valuable places, which have been destroyed or spoiled.

However, we should resist this conclusion. Those who are forced to leave do suffer a specific harm and wrong that is not reducible to those they suffer before or after leaving. A wrong is done to them *as* they are forced to separate from their place of residence even if that place was never hospitable to them. Or, if that place was once hospitable to them, but then has become unliveable, the harm of their displacement *adds* to the serious wrong they suffer because their beloved place is now destroyed or spoiled. In other words, they suffer the violation of a specific right not to be displaced—that is, a right to stay. But what is the substance of such a right? Which specific good does it protect, if it is not the value that the place of residence has for its inhabitants in terms of opportunities or attachments?

I suggest that to make sense of the right to stay we need to construe its substance as a freedom, but of a different kind than the instrumental freedom we considered in the last section, whose value consists in making valuable options and opportunities available. More specifically, I suggest that we should conceive the right to stay and the freedom it protects as akin to a broad but very specific category of other personal freedoms, to which the liberty from physical coercion, the integrity of our body, the freedom from sexual aggressions, the right to refuse medical treatment, and many privacy rights also belong. We may call the rights that protect these fundamental freedoms "control rights"; they are rights to control what happens to our body and our most personal space. Before examining in which sense the right to stay belongs to the same family as these rights, in the next section I will pause to better characterize the common features of control rights and the central role they have in protecting the very conditions of personhood.

3. The Right to Control One's Body and Personal Space

What I have termed "control rights" are a broad family of fundamental civil rights; the core element they share is that they all protect our control over our own body and our personal space. The value of this control is not simply instrumental to the protection against damages or interferences that might impair our capacity to pursue our ends. In fact, these rights comprise an irreducible non-instrumental component. Consider for example the right to personal freedom and security, which protects against detention and physical coercion. If I am put in a straitjacket or locked into a small space, there is little I can do and therefore little I can achieve or procure for myself. However, besides this loss in instrumental terms, there is something excruciating in the very fact of being physically constrained in this way, independently of what I miss by being constrained. The fundamental good that is lost in this case is not the health of my body or its function as a means to pursue my ends; rather, it is my very control over my own body.

Another relevant example is the feeling of insufferable loss and wretchedness experienced by victims of rape whose bodies have been violated while they were unconscious. In some cases, they suffer no permanent or even detectable damage to their bodies, and they cannot recollect any hurtful memory of the event. The atrocious harm they suffer, then, cannot be accounted for by the consequences of the violation or its impact on the pursuing of some further goal; rather, it consists in the very fact of having lost control over their bodies, because their bodies have been invaded without their consent and authorization (Archard 2007; Heyes 2016).

Finally, consider the unauthorized trespassing into someone's home or the unconsented inspection or use of someone's personal belongings by a stranger. Even if nothing is stolen or damaged, the person feels violated and deeply wronged; the harm consists in the very fact that someone has accessed her belongings and intimate space without her consent or authorization. In other words, it consists in her loss of control over her most immediate personal space.[9]

Of course, control is an essential component of all liberty rights. For example, freedom of religion implies that I can choose what gods to worship, or to worship no gods. However, the importance of control, in the case of many rights, is mostly derivative: it is important that we can choose our religious beliefs because religious beliefs are important in our lives. Control rights are special in that the control they protect has an independent value; in fact, losing control over what happens to our bodies or personal space is *per se* a highly frustrating and humiliating

---

[9] On the centrality of control in the definition of privacy, see Moore 2008.

experience that undermines our status as persons and indeed the very constitutive conditions of our personhood.

In a seminal article on the foundations of the right to privacy, Jeffrey Reiman has appealed to our control over our own bodies and personal space as what allows us to conceive ourselves as separate individuals with an independent personality. In fact, "a self is at least in part a human being who regards his existence—his thoughts, his body, his actions—as his own," and control over one's own body and personal space is essential to the appropriation of one's actions (Reiman 1976: 39).

In Reiman's account, the importance of control over one's body and personal space depends on the way human beings learn to see themselves as separate and independent individuals as they grow up. We become, or are constituted as, individuals to the extent that rituals of separation and boundedness are enacted around our bodies and our personal belongings. Thus, such rituals, which define privacy and what counts as pertaining to our selves as separate from other people's, are "an essential ingredient in the process by which 'persons' are created out of prepersonal infants" (Reiman 1976: 39). In fact, traumatizing experiences of bodily trespass, such as rape, can seriously challenge the process of individuation in children and adolescents.[10] Also in adults, they may undermine the very sense of being a separate self. Control over one's body and personal space, therefore, should not be conceived as essential to personhood simply because we need control over our actions to do things we want to do; such control, instead, should be seen as *constitutive* of our very personhood. We are constituted as separate individuals via the establishment of boundaries that circumscribe a domain over which we have exclusive control; the domain comprises not only our body, but also our personal belongings, our intimate thoughts, and what can be recognized as our personal, private space.[11]

Of course, what counts as private space or personal belongings, what is socially perceived as the most intimate parts of people's bodies, and the rituals of individuation through which this domain is constituted display wide variations across cultures; also, there are impressive

---

[10] See for example Springer 1997.

[11] On the contrast between the instrumental and the constitutive view of control of the body from a feminist perspective, see Patosalmi 2009.

variations in how the boundaries of privacy are used to prevent, define, and allow intimacy (Moore 2017). However, the importance of the body and personal space is a cultural constant among human beings, and indeed it can even be argued that the unwanted invasion or manipulation of the body and personal space is a highly distressing and traumatizing experience for mammals in general.[12]

This is painfully proven in those circumstances in which loss of control over one's body and personal space is artfully staged to mortify the self. As recalled by Reiman, in his famous analysis of total institutions and of their practices of annihilation of inmates' personality, Ervin Goffman clearly pinpoints control over one's body and personal space as the crucial element in these practices of spoliation:

> On the outside, the individual can hold objects of self-feeling—such as his body, his immediate actions, his thoughts, and some of his possessions—clear of contact with alien and contaminating things. But in total institutions these territories of the self are violated.
>
> (Goffman 1961: 23)

Because of the constitutive role of control over our bodies and personal space in forming and preserving us as separate persons, losing such control can be deeply demeaning and humiliating. In fact, such loss of control, according to Avishai Margalit, is the quintessence of humiliation as the experience of being dehumanized and treated as mere objects or tools (Margalit 1996: ch. 7 and 12), especially when such loss of control happens in the presence of bystanders or is purposely made public. The exposure of the annihilation of the authority we have over our bodies and intimate, personal space dissolves what is acknowledged as constitutive of our personality as separate human beings.

This means that control over our bodies and personal space has an important social and relational dimension, in two senses. First, the significance and source of such control depends on our development as social beings; by acquiring control over our bodies and personal space

---

[12] Richard D. Ryder describes how animals dread and resist loss of control over their own bodies, even when it is not induced by violent physical restraining, but simply by anaesthetics (Ryder 1978).

we get to conceive ourselves as, and are acknowledged as, separate and independent agents. Second, since such control constitutes us as persons, losing it is a humiliating experience that undermines our social standing (Kahn 2003).

It is important to stress that the good that control rights protect is not the exclusive enjoyment and use of our body and personal space. In fact, there are many valuable forms of intimacy and sharing of our most personal space that imply the obliteration of the physical boundaries between us and others. The good protected by control rights, instead, is the control or authority we have over how and when such boundaries can be trespassed. This specification points to a defining feature of control rights: whether such rights are violated crucially depends on whether what happens to our bodies and our personal space is something we have voluntarily done or voluntarily consented to. Sexual intercourse, surgical operations, body massages, piercing and tattooing, sleeping in the same bed with other people, and many kinds of dancing involve physical contact, manipulation, occupation of the space around our body, and other forms of invasion of our close environment. However, to the extent that we have voluntarily consented to these activities, they do not count as violations of our control rights. When such consent is not given, or is not given voluntarily, by definition we lose control over our bodies and our personal space.

Control so conceived is a negative right that prevents other people from performing or making us perform unwanted actions over our bodies and personal space. Therefore, control should not be conflated with agency as the active ability to direct and execute actions. Agency involves the first-personal and direct exercise of our skills and energies, and it realizes independence and autonomy, rather than control. Control, instead, is a form of veto authority over what happens to our bodies and our personal space, which a subject retains even when not acting—for example, when we undergo fully consented medical treatment or hire someone to cut our hair.

Thus understood, control does not imply an absolute liberty to do whatever we want with our bodies and personal space. For example, the right to control my body protects me against unwanted sexual intercourse, but it does not imply that I can force myself on someone else. Likewise, the fact that my personal and most intimate belongings are protected from interference does not imply that I can do whatever I want with them; nobody can rip off the brooch I am wearing on my jacket, but this does not imply that I can throw it at other people.

Further, I cannot decide arbitrarily what counts as "my personal space" just by calling it so. The bag in which I carry my driver's license, my medications, and my notebook definitely is part of my most intimate and personal belongings, so that any unconsented inspection or appropriation of that bag counts as a serious violation of my personal space. This holds even if I bought the bag yesterday and have no special attachment to it. However, I cannot simply declare that the bag I just stole from a store is part of my most personal belongings, thus making it immune to external interferences. This obvious example illustrates that I cannot make something belong to my personal space just by fiat. Rather, I make it so by enacting those practices and behaviours that bring it under the sphere of my intimacy: my bed is the bed where I sleep; my bag is the bag where I carry my belongings; my journal is the journal where I write my thoughts.

These distinctions and qualifications are especially important in view of the claim that the right to stay can be conceived as a control right that protects the sphere of our personal space, to which we now turn.

4. The Right to Stay as a Control Right

The right to stay is not the same as the right to personal freedom and security, the right not to suffer unwanted sexual intercourse, or the right not to have one's privacy invaded; however, it can be conceived as a right that belongs to the same family of control rights—that is, the rights that protect our control over our body and personal space. If we are displaced or separated from our place of residence, we lose control over the space we have made part of our personal, intimate domain by inhabiting it. This happens when we are taken away by some overpowering force, as when people are abducted or deported, but also when we must move because of threats, violence, starvation, fear, and other coercive circumstances, or when we suddenly lose access to our domicile, for example because we are locked out by force or prevented from approaching our area of residence.

In fact, in his analysis of the most common forms of personality annihilation in total institutions, Goffman mentions the constant moving of inmates from one cell to another (Goffman 1961: 19). The wrong inflicted upon people by these repeated relocations can be taken as a paradigmatic example of the distinctive loss incurred when forced displacement occurs. We intuitively perceive that being forcefully and abruptly removed from the physical site one was assigned as living space is a way to undermine dignity and sense of personal security. The harm done through this act is similar to the one incurred in other circumstances in which one loses control over one's body and personal space, such as rape, unwanted medical treatments, and unconsented inspections of personal belongings. This wrong does not necessarily involve material or psychological damages. In fact, it might be imagined that inmates do not develop valuable sentimental attachments to the specific cell they are assigned, nor do they possess so many personal belongings that moving them from one cell to another is especially burdensome. It is also implausible that such a movement can disrupt their life plans. The wrong done by these forced displacements consists instead in the very fact that a person's personal space has been violated and she has lost control over it. By being violently eradicated, one suffers a patent humiliation as someone whose personal and intimate space can be overstepped and erased.

It is important to note that the control that is lost in these circumstances is control over a physical space identified by its spatial coordinates. If I am forcefully moved from one cell to another, presumably very similar to the previous one, the main difference between before and after is essentially topographical. My belongings may be moved to the new cell. I do not lose control over them, but over the site where they were formerly placed, which had become part of my personal space. This topographical dimension also explains why distance matters; the further I am pushed away, the stronger is the violation of my control over the place I made part of my personal space by inhabiting it.

As mentioned, we can try to make sense of this loss by arguing that when people are forcefully displaced they lose their routines and familiar landscapes, on which human beings rely for their basic cognitive functioning (Nine 2018). However, this does not explain why the same loss is not suffered when we move voluntarily to a new apartment or go on a long vacation. Instead, we can easily explain the loss if we point out that when someone is coercively removed from her designated place of residence, she loses control over the spatial coordinates she had made her own as constitutive of her personal space.

As previously remarked, the specific signs and rituals through which we draw the boundaries around the sphere of our personal space are defined by social rules. This also applies to the physical space we inhabit. If I am coerced to leave from a temporary encampment I built while on vacation, I do not feel displaced and deprived of my home; in contrast, if I am coerced to leave my apartment (or the tent where I have established my residence on the street), I feel seriously wronged. The loss does not depend on the value of my belongings, the value of the site, or the length of my stay; rather, it depends on whether that specific site can be recognized as included in the personal spatial sphere over which I should have control. Normally, the place where we usually sleep, cook, keep our personal belongings, and designate as home, or in common parlance the place where we "live," is such a space, while other sites where we occasionally place ourselves do not count as such. The relevant social rules, then, in the case of the right to stay, are those that guide us in recognizing a specific place as where one "lives."

It might be objected that the difference between a place where I am just camping and a place "where I live" may be contested. For example, this is the case with squatters and those who live on the street, whose place of residence can fail to be recognized as such because of its substandard conditions or lack of a legal title for occupying it in the first place. However, note that even in these cases the central claim for resisting displacement from a site, no matter how dismal such a site is, or how unlawful was the way it came to be occupied, is that it is the place where one lives.[13] Most often, what is contested in these cases is not what "living" in a place means, but whether the people involved are actually living in the place where they claim to live. And the proof of such a claim, typically, is that it is where one regularly sleeps, keeps one's belongings and takes care of one's person and intimacy. It is also important to note that, although there may be contested cases in which we may be unsure whether a given person actually lives in a certain place, in the

---

[13] For an exemplary story, see Holland 2014.

large majority of the circumstances of displacement it is pretty clear and uncontested that the people involved are forcefully moved from the place where they used to live.

The right to stay is violated every time people are made to move coercively or non-voluntarily from their place of residence. Forced exodus and relocation are indeed common acts of violence against enemies in armed conflicts and civil wars (Simons 2002; Abebe 2017: 156ff), and one of the forms in which ethnic cleansing is perpetrated and perceived as a form of massive violence and humiliation. The same right to stay is also infringed in the case of internally displaced people, refugees, victims of environmental catastrophes, and people who are fleeing wars and life-threatening conditions. Moreover, it is violated in the case of many "economic" migrants who are forced to move because at home they would not be able to enjoy basic rights to shelter, food, education, and health, to the extent that these constitute coercive circumstances.[14] The fact that longer distances are involved than in other circumstances in which people are forced to move does not make their predicament any different; it just makes it worse. Those forced to migrate end up in a physical and social environment where they had never intended to be, and as a consequence of their displacement they often suffer serious deprivations of their most fundamental rights. But even before then, they suffer a serious harm because they are chased from the space they were inhabiting, and this constitutes an infringement of their right to control their bodies and their personal space.

In all these forms of displacement, those forced to leave feel deeply wronged and diminished even if they were enjoying no special amenity where they were staying. Forced displacement is perceived as a traumatizing and humiliating experience that may deeply challenge people's identity and safety, because it wrecks the control over their own personal space, which is constitutive of their personhood. This explains why forced displacement is a significantly different experience than voluntary migration, even if they both involve moving away from one's attachments and located life plans; the former damages people's sense of their own integrity and dignity while the second, as challenging as it can be, does

---

[14] For an insightful discussion of the coercive nature of extreme poverty, see Meyers 2014. For a definition of voluntary migration, see Ottonelli and Torresi 2013.

not. This also explains why even people who are forcefully relocated in familiar environments where they can keep their communal ties alive, like the Greek-Cypriot refugees, develop such a longing for the place they have relinquished and a sense of identity loss (Zetter 1999; Loizos 2009). In fact, it is reported that even nomadic people experience forced relocations as violent uprootings that disrupt their sense of identity, and develop a longing for return to the place where they last freely resided (Kibreab 1999).

It might be objected that people forced to leave lose control over their personal space only at the moment when they leave, but they may regain control of a new space afterwards. This claim is certainly true. However, this does not make the wrong any less serious or harmful. We can see this by analogy with other infringements of one's control over one's body, such as rape or unconsented medical treatments. These violations of the relevant rights happen at a specific moment in time, and sometimes the victims recover promptly or do not suffer long-lasting physical or psychological damages; however, this does not make such violations any less serious.

We can now go back to our original conundrum. If we conceive the right to stay as a control right, then we are able to overcome the problems reviewed in the first sections of this essay. First, this way of conceiving the right to stay explains its indexicality—that is, the fact that the right is violated when people are made to move from a specific place: the place where they live. However, it also makes it independent of the value of that place; this overcomes the difficulty of explaining how the harsher violations of the right to stay can occur in circumstances in which the place people are forced to leave is literally unliveable and therefore very little value can be attached to it. The wrong of displacement, in such circumstances, does not depend on the specific value of the site from which people are displaced; rather, it depends on the special violence and overpowering force that causes the displacement, which makes fleeing an obvious instance of loss of control. This is made evident, for example, in the case of the forced removal of the inhabitants of slums in the course of urban regeneration and gentrification (du Plessis 2005). Often such interventions are defended by insisting that the affected areas are crime infested, dangerous, unsanitary, do not provide essential services, and are highly inhospitable to their inhabitants. Still, residents resist displacement, even when they agree with such evaluations and in fact are vocal about the need for a radical improvement of their living conditions (Winkler 2009). If we conceive the right to stay as a control right, we can make sense of this apparent paradox; we can conjecture that the reason for resisting displacement is not the protection of the opportunities and ties that the residents can currently enjoy, but rather the protection of their control over the specific site that they inhabit. In fact, the recognition of their living space as inviolable amounts to the recognition of their very personhood and dignity.

For a parallel example in a context of international forced emigration, consider the case of the people who are fleeing by the thousands from their home towns in Honduras as a consequence of unbearable levels of violence, crime, poverty, corruption, and lack of basic rights (Medecins sans frontières 2017). These living conditions are not the product of a sudden and recent change. In fact, many young people were born in these deprived contexts and never experienced better times. Especially for the young members of the most marginalized and vulnerable groups, such as the LGBTI+ community, it would be hard to argue that by leaving the country there is a loss in terms of valuable social ties and opportunities; some of them, in fact, explicitly proclaim that they have no reason to be attached to their home (Taracena 2018: 236). However, they still deeply resent the precipitating events that eventually forced them to leave home and run away. We may feel that in fact their forced emigration adds a significant wrong to the ones they have already suffered in their home country. Again, conceiving the right to stay as a control right help us see where this additional wrong lies.

Conceiving the right to stay as a control right, then, also allows us to overcome the apparent redundancy of such a right. If we conceptualize forced displacement as a loss of control over one's personal space, then we are able to see that the right to stay cannot be simply conceived as a redundant addition to the rights people have to the protection of their social environment *before* displacement becomes a necessary move, or to the humanitarian rights of assistance arising *after* displacement, but needs to be added to the latter as a separate right that is violated *as* people are forced to move.

5. Scope and Implications of the
Right to Stay as a Control Right

What are the normative implications of construing the right to stay as a control right? If the right to stay is added to the list of control rights that protect basic personal, civil freedoms such as the right not to suffer unconsented medical treatments or the right to bodily security, then the forced displacement of people constitutes the infringement of a fundamental human right. This imposes moral and political duties at the national and international level. At the very least, state institutions and other relevant agents have the duty not to coercively remove people from their place of residence. If we also consider the side effects of institutional decisions, then such responsibility will extend for example to military interventions that result in massive displacements, and trade agreements that will predictably cause the sudden ruin of entire regions and the consequent forced emigration of their inhabitants.[15]

These implications simply flow from recognizing the right to stay as a fundamental human right. The special contribution that a control-based approach provides consists in a firmer grounding of such a right, which avoids the conundrums originated by seeing the right to stay as derivative from people's located attachments or plans. However, there are also other, more distinguishing implications of the control-based approach, which are worth discussing in some detail, especially because they can originate qualms that need to be dispelled.

The control-based approach, as we have seen, makes the right to stay independent of the intrinsic or instrumental merits of the place we inhabit. This allows us to claim that people suffer a wrong also when they are compelled to leave disrupted social or physical environments and severely substandard dwellings. This feature of the right to stay as a control right might appear to generate too expansive consequences. It might be thought that once the right is detached from the social ties and opportunities that can only come from the lengthy and lawful presence in a given social environment, then anybody can claim the right not to be removed from any place she happens to stand, be that a bench in a

---

[15] According to some reports, this is what happened in the case of the NAFTA agreements. See Hartman 2010.

city park, someone's garage, or even the apartment where someone else is living. However, this would be a wrong conclusion, for two reasons. First, recall that the right to stay is not the right to stay wherever one simply happens to stand, but the right not to be displaced from the place where one lives. Second, recall that control rights protect against the interference with our bodies, personal space, and belongings, but do not give us the power to decide what belongs to us in the first place, nor the power to make whatever use we want of our bodies and personal space. The freedom from interference with my body protects me from unwanted invasions of my physical space, but it does not give me the liberty to place my body wherever I want, including other people's properties or other people's bodies. Likewise, I cannot designate a stranger's apartment—especially if it is the place where *that* person lives—as my personal space just by fiat. Conceiving the right to stay as a control right tells us that once we have established our domicile somewhere, we have a fundamental right not to be displaced against our will; it does not imply that we can go wherever we want and establish our domicile there.

This has important implications for the case of immigrants. Unlike the arguments based on an opportunity notion of freedom, which advocate both the right to leave and the right to stay as instrumental to make opportunities available to people (Oberman 2015), the argument for the right to stay based on freedom as control establishes an asymmetry between emigration and immigration. Having a right to stay implies that we cannot be forced to relinquish the place we inhabit; it does not imply that we have the right to move wherever we want. If such a universal right to immigration exists, it must rest on a different basis. However, it is worth noting that the argument for the right to stay based on control, like the arguments based on social ties and on located life plans, establishes a right not to be removed from where one lives that also extends to immigrants once they have set their residence in the host country, including those who were not authorized to do so. Deportation is a serious infringement of people's control rights, which can only be excused—like the limitation of other fundamental civil rights—in exceptional circumstances. This does not imply that states have no right to prevent immigrants from accessing their territory, or to sanction unauthorized immigration; it just implies that, even assuming that states have such rights, deportation is not an admissible way to enforce them. With respect to immigration, the main difference between the justifications of the right to stay based on control and those based on social ties or located life plans is that the former also apply to those immigrants who have not established valuable ties or cannot count on valuable opportunities in the host society. This is in fact an expansive implication of the right to stay as a control right, as compared to those alternative understandings of the same right. Notice, however, that this is also what we should expect if we want to vindicate the right to stay as a universal civil right, rather than a right that is attached to citizenship, or to social ties as a proxy for full membership within a society. The right to stay, so conceived, protects people wherever they are, and also protects those who might fail to be recognized as members of the host society because of their marginal position or lack of valuable opportunities.

On the other hand, construing the right to stay as a control right prevents other exceedingly expansive consequences which would follow instead from conceiving it as based on social ties or located life plans. Claiming a right to stay as a fundamental human right, rather than simply as an interest worthy of protection, serves to prevent forced displacement on mere utility-maximizing grounds.[16] However, conceiving the right to stay as a control right, rather than as a right based on the irreplaceable ties and plans that people have in the site where they reside, allows for negotiating conditions of voluntary movements in those cases in which serious reasons of public utility are at stake. In fact, the right to stay, if conceived as a control right, does not rest on a sedentary bias; what counts, is not that people actually stay where they are, but that if they decide to move, they do so voluntarily. These considerations support a generous interpretation of the *Guiding Principles of Internal Displacement*, by which displacement for reasons of public utility can only take place if the affected people are offered a relocation plan that improves their condition (rather than mere compensation) and they give their free and informed consent.[17]

---

[16] Needless to say, like any other fundamental civil right, the right to stay can be limited, upon judicial decision, when reasons of public safety or other compelling circumstances require it. This does not make the right to stay and the other civil rights any less fundamental and undeafisible in ordinary circumstances.

[17] For an analysis of this requirement, see Penz, Drydyk and Bose 2011, especially ch. 8.

These considerations might prompt a different, and indeed opposite, line of objection. It might be felt, in fact, that conceiving the right to stay as a control right produces too modest implications: by separating the value and meaning of such a right from the ties and attachments people have to their society of origin and its social and communal relations, the control-based approach cannot fully account for all the wrongs and harms done in cases of massive displacements, such as the loss of cultural heritages, shared social life, or self-determination of territorially localized communities. However, this consequence of the control-based approach should be seen as a virtue, rather than a fault. In fact, nothing is to be gained by mingling the right to stay as a basic, civil freedom with other rights and interests of individuals and communities that can be harmed by displacement. For example, displaced people may suffer separation from their close family members, which counts as the infringement of a fundamental human right to family life (Savino 2016), and may also suffer economic damages by the dispossession of their property and loss of work. These wrongs need to be addressed and compensated by specific measures, rather than conflated under the generic notion that people have a right to stay. This is even more evident in the case of the displacement of entire communities. Displacing communities, especially when they are culturally oppressed or politically marginalized, can cause a wrong that needs to be accounted for in its own terms, rather than subsumed under the individual right of its members not to be displaced. At the local level, this is paradigmatically exemplified by gentrification. In many cases gentrification occurs through a forceful displacement of individual people that violates their right to stay; however, the wrong of gentrification cannot be reduced to the violation of the right to stay of those so displaced and needs instead to be accounted for as a form of structural injustice that perpetuates the spatial and cultural marginalization of disadvantaged social groups.[18] Again, there is no advantage in trying to account for these forms of socio-economic injustice by shoving them under the umbrella of individuals' right to stay. Accounting for the right to stay in terms of social ties and attachments or located life plans tends to do so by conflating the individual interest in staying with the communal goods and social

---

[18] See for example Wyly and Hammel 2004; Rerat 2018.

environment that can be enjoyed in the place of residence. A central point of the foregoing discussion was that in many cases this makes it impossible to account for the loss incurred by individuals; in addition, we can now see that it can lead to misrecognizing the wrongs and injustice suffered by communities and disadvantaged social groups.

Conclusion

In this chapter, I have tried to uncover and analyse a conundrum that emerges when we seek to make sense of an individual right to stay as a fundamental right of every human being: many of the harsher and most obvious cases in which the right to stay is violated are also those in which staying, for the people involved, has very little instrumental value. This conundrum is not just a conceptual problem, but uncovers a fundamental unfairness in the arguments that make the right to stay depend on the value of the relations and opportunities that people have where they reside. In fact, this makes the value and importance of the right to stay directly proportional to people's status, wealth, and good fortune in the society and place where they live. Conversely, it suggests that the most destitute and vulnerable have nothing to lose when they are chased from their place of residence. In response to this challenge, I have argued that the right to stay should be conceived as a fundamental civil right that protects people's control over their own bodies and personal space. This points to a fundamental loss people incur when they are forced to move, which is independent of the value they place in the site and society in which they reside.

Conceiving the right to stay as a control right not only accounts for the right to stay as a separate, fundamental right that cannot be reduced to other wrongs that people suffer before or after they are displaced, but it avoids the risk of over-romanticizing the relation that many people who are forced to move—and especially the most disadvantaged and socially unprivileged among them—have to their community or site of origin, or the society in which they have landed as immigrants. Those people may have good reasons to leave with no regret the place where they were born or have long lived, and still claim that in being forced to leave they suffered a major wrong and a violation of a fundamental right they have as human beings.[19]

References

Adeola, Romola (2016). "The Right Not to Be Arbitrarily Displaced under the United Nations Guiding Principles on Internal Displacement," *African Human Rights Law Journal* 16: 83–98.

Abebe, Allehone M. (2017). *The Emerging Law of Forced Displacement in Africa* (Abingdon, Oxon: Routledge).

Altman, Alex (2018). "A Syrian Refugee Story," *TIME* Magazine. Available at: http://time.com/a-syrian-refugee-story/ (accessed 10 February 2018).

Angell, Kim (2017). "A Forward-Looking Justification of Territorial Rights," *Political Studies* 65: 231–47.

Archard, David (2007). "The Wrong of Rape," *The Philosophical Quarterly* 57: 374–93.

Bacon, David (2013). *The Right to Stay Home* (Boston: Beacon Press).

Bakewell, Oliver (2008). "Keeping Them in Their Place: The Ambivalent Relationship between Development and Migration in Africa," *Third World Quarterly* 29: 1341–58.

Barutciski, Michael (1998). "Tensions between the Refugee Concept and the IDP Debate," *Forced Migration Review* 3: 11–14.

Barutciski, Michael (2002). "A Critical View on UNHCR's Mandate Dilemmas," *International Journal of Refugee Law* 14: 379–81.

Buckinxy, Barbara and Filindraz, Alexandra (2015). "The Case against Removal: Jus Noci and Harm in Deportation Practice," *Migration Studies* 3: 393–416.

Carens, Joseph (2010). *Immigrants and the Right to Stay* (Cambridge, MA: MIT Press).

---

[19] Previous versions of this chapter were presented at the University of Milano, University of Pavia, and University of Amsterdam. I wish to thank the organizers and the public of these events for the very helpful comments I received. I also greatly benefited from discussions and written comments by Gabriele Badano, Alasia Nuti, Laura Santi Amantini, Adam Swift, Aart Van Gils, and the editors of this volume. I am especially indebted to Ian Carter for very detailed written feedback and invaluable, lengthy discussions.

Cohen, Roberta (2002). "The Guiding Principles: How do they Support IDP Response Strategies?" in *Response Strategies of the Internally Displaced: Changing the Humanitarian Lens*, edited by Norwegian Refugee Council (Oslo: Norwegian Refugee Council).

Deng, Francis M. (1999). "Guiding Principles on Internal Displacement," *International Migration Review* 33: 484–93.

Du Plessis (2005). "The Growing Problem of Forced Evictions and the Crucial Importance of Community-Based, Locally Appropriate Alternatives," *Environment &Urbanization* 17: 123–34.

Entwisle, Hannah (2005). "Tracing Cascades: The Normative Development of the U.N. Guiding Principles on Internal Displacement," *Georgetown Immigration Law Journal* 19: 369–90.

Goffman, Erwig (1961). *Asylums* (New York: Anchor Books).

Hartman, Stephen W. (2010). "NAFTA, the Controversy," *The International Trade Journal* 25: 5–34.

Hathaway, James C. (1995). "New Directions to Avoid Hard Problems: The Distortion of the Palliative Role of Refugee Protection," *Journal of Refugee Studies* 8: 288–94.

Hathaway, James C. (2007a). "How Refugee Laws Still Matter," *Melbourne Journal of International Law* 8: 89–103.

Hathaway, James C. (2007b). "Forced Migration Studies: Could We Agree Just to 'Date'?," *Journal of Refugee Studies* 20: 349–69.

Heyes, Cressida J. (2016). "Dead to the World: Rape, Unconsciousness, and Social Media," *Signs* 41: 361–83.

Holland, Gale (2014). "On L.A.'s Skid Row, Homeless Woman Stands Her Ground to Stay Put," *LA Times*, 29 April 2014, available at: http://touch.latimes.com/#section/-1/article/p2p-80041700/ (accessed 10 April 2018).

Huber, Jakob and Wolkenstein, Fabio (forthcoming). "Gentrification and Occupancy Rights," *Politics, Philosophy & Economics*.

Kahn, Jonathan (2003). "Privacy as a Legal Principle of Identity Maintenance," *Seton Hall Law Review* 33: 371–410.

Katselli Proukaki, Elena (2018). "The Right Not to Be Displaced by Armed Conflict under International Law," in *Armed Conflict and Forcible Displacement*, edited by Elena Katselli Proukaki (Abingdon, Oxon: Routledge): 1–45.

Kibreab, Gaim (1999). "Revisiting the Debate on People, Place, Identity and Displacement," *Journal of Refugee Studies* 12: 404–5.

Laqueur, Walter (2001). *Generation Exodus* (Hanover: Brandeis University Press).

Lefkowitz, David (2015). "Autonomy, Residence, and Return," *Critical Review of International Social and Political Philosophy* 18: 529–46.

Loizos, Peter (2009). "The Loss of Home," in *Struggles for Home: Violence, Hope and the Movement of People*, edited by Stef Jansen and Staffan Löfving (New York: Berghahn Books): 66–84.

Malkki, Liisa (1992). "National Geographic: The Rooting of Peoples and the Territorialization of National Identity among Scholars and Refugees," *Cultural Anthropology* 7: 24–44.

Malkii, Liisa (1995). *Purity and Exile: Violence, Memory and National Cosmology among the Hutu Refugees in Tanzania* (Chicago: University of Chicago Press).

Margalit, Avishai (1996). *The Decent Society* (Cambridge, MA: Harvard University Press).

Medecins sans frontières (2017). *Forced to Flee Central America's Northern Triangle*, available at: https://www.doctorswithoutborders.org/sites/default/files/2018–06/msf_forced-to-flee-central-americas-northern-triangle.pdf

Meyers, Diana Tietjens (2014). "Rethinking Coercion for a World of Poverty and Transnational Migration," in *Poverty, Agency and Human Rights*, edited by Diana Tietjens Meyers (Oxford: Oxford University Press): 68–93.

Miller, David (2012). "Territorial Rights: Concept and Justification," *Political Studies* 60: 252–68.

Moore, Adam (2008). "Defining Privacy," *Journal of Social Philosophy* 39: 411–28.

Moore, Barrington Jr. (2017) [1984]. *Privacy* (Abingdon, Oxon: Routledge).

Moore, Margaret (2015). *A Political Theory of Territory* (Oxford: Oxford University Press).

Morel, Michèle, Stavropoulou, Maria, and Durieux, Jean-François (2012). "The History and Status of the Right Not to Be Displaced," *Forced Migration Review* 41: 5–7.

Nine, Cara (2016). "Water Crisis Adaptation: Defending a Strong Right against Displacement from the Home," *Res Publica* 22: 37–52.

Nine, Cara (2018). "The Wrong of Displacement: The Home as Extended Mind," *The Journal of Political Philosophy* 26: 240–57.

Oberman, Kieran (2011). "Immigration, Global Poverty and the Right to Stay," *Political Studies* 59: 253–68.

Oberman, Kieran (2015). "Poverty and Immigration Policy," *American Political Science Review* 109: 239–51.

Ochoa Espejo, Paulina (2016). "Taking Place Seriously: Territorial Presence and the Rights of Immigrants," *The Journal of Political Philosophy* 24: 67–87.

Ottonelli, Valeria and Torresi, Tiziana (2013). "When Is Migration Voluntary?," *International Migration Review* 47: 783–813.

Patosalmi, Mervi (2009). "Bodily Integrity and Conceptions of Subjectivity," *Hypatia* 24: 125–41.

Penz, Peter, Drydyk, Jay, and Bose, Pablo S. (2011). *Displacement by Development* (Cambridge: Cambridge University Press).

Pitarokoili, Vasileia M. (2014). "The Internally Displaced Persons and the Need of a Normative Framework," *International Journal of Human Rights and Constitutional Studies* 2: 384–98.

Reiman, Jeffrey (1976). "Privacy, Intimacy, and Personhood," *Philosophy & Public Affairs* 6: 26–44.

Rerat, Patrick (2018). "Spatial Capital and Planetary Gentrification: Residential Location, Mobility and Social Inequalities," in *Hanbook of Gentrification Studies*, edited by Loretta Lees and Martin Phillips (Northampton: Edward Elgar): 103–17.

Ryder, Richard D. (1978). "Postscript: Towards Humane Methods of Identification," in *Animal Marking*, edited by B: Stonehouse (Palgrave: London): 229–34.

Savino, Mario (2016). "The Right to Stay as a Fundamental Freedom?" *Transnational Legal Theory* 7: 70–94.

Simons, Marco (2002). "The Emergence of a Norm against Arbitrary Forced Relocation," *Columbia Human Rights Law Review* 34: 95–156.

Springer, Cheryl (1997). "Female Adolescents, the Experience of Violence, and the Meaning of the Body," *Clinical Social Work Journal* 25: 281–96.

Stilz, Anna (2011). "Nations, States, and Territory," *Ethics* 121: 572–601.

Stilz, Anna (2013). "Occupancy Rights and the Wrong of Removal," *Philosophy & Public Affairs* 41: 324–56.

Taracena, Maria Ines (2018). "La Caravana de la Resistencia," *NACLA Report on the Americas* 50: 386–91.

Waldron, Jeremy (2004). "Settlement, Return, and the Supersession Thesis," *Theoretical Inquiries in Law* 5: 237–68.

Winkler, Tanja (2009). "Prolonging the Global Age of Gentrification," *Planning Theory* 8: 362–81.

Wyly, Elvin K. and Hammel, Daniel J. (2004). "Gentrification, Segregation, and Discrimination in the American Urban System," *Environment and Planning* 36: 1215–41.

Zetter, Roger (1999). "Reconceptualizing the Myth of Return: Continuity and Transition amongst the Greek-Cypriot Refugees of 1974," *Journal of Refugee Studies* 12: 1–22.

Zetter, Roger (2015). *Protection in Crisis: Forced Migration and Protection in a Global Era* (Washington, DC: Migration Policy Institute).

5

Global Equality and Open Borders

Nils Holtug

1. Introduction

In contemporary liberal democracies, it is difficult to find a policy issue as divisive as immigration. Elections are fought and sometimes won on immigration issues and electorates are deeply torn over how to control immigration and to manage diversity. Travel bans, non-arrival measures, and policies to render immigration less attractive are among the measures used to limit the influx of, in particular, refugees and low-skilled migrant labor. Furthermore, xenophobia and nationalism are on the rise in a number of countries, not least in response to immigration. Nor is there any sign that these are political issues that are going to go away, as people in poor countries experience economic progress and hence increased prospects for mobility, the number of forcibly displaced persons worldwide is at a record high of 65.6 million (UNHCR 2018) and estimates of how many people will be displaced by 2050 by climate change alone range from twenty-five million to one billion (with 200 million being the most cited estimate; IOM 2009; Byvaran and Rajan 2010). Simultaneously, policies of attracting foreign (in particular skilled) labor are actively being pursued to solve demographic challenges, fill shortages on labor markets, and boost national economies.

In the present article, my concern is with a particular aspect of immigration policy, namely the extent to which borders should be open, or at least more open than they presently are in most liberal democracies. More specifically, my concern is with the implications of egalitarian justice for the question of open borders. In order to address this issue, I need to answer two distinct questions, namely (1) what is the scope of egalitarian justice, and (2) what does the appropriately-scoped

Nils Holtug, *Global Equality and Open Borders* In: *Oxford Studies in Political Philosophy Volume 6.* Edited by: David Sobel, Peter Vallentyne, and Steven Wall, Oxford University Press (2020). © Nils Holtug. DOI: 10.1093/oso/9780198852636.003.0005 egalitarian principle imply for the issue of (more) open borders? Thus, the question of scope plays an important role for how we should think about restrictions on immigration. Indeed, we find some egalitarians arguing for restrictive immigration policies and other egalitarians arguing for open borders, where at least part of their disagreement is due to the fact that the latter take equality to have global scope and the former take it to have domestic scope only.

According to one line of argument, liberal democracies should have restrictive immigration policies because this is necessary to protect their welfare states. This is sometimes referred to as the 'progressive's dilemma', the idea being that liberal democracies can have a liberal immigration policy or a generous welfare state but not both (Goodhart 2004). In fact, there are two distinct arguments for restrictive immigration policies in play here. According to the first, extensive welfare states tend to attract low-skilled migrants who stand to benefit from, for example, high level social services and free health-care, but who are a net economic burden to the state. This is what Milton Friedman had in mind when he famously stated that it is obvious that you cannot have free immigration and a welfare state (Legrain 2006: 144). According to the second, immigration causes ethnic diversity, where ethnic diversity drives down social cohesion, including trust and solidarity, and so the basis for support for the welfare state (Miller 2004; Goodhart 2013). This version relies on what has been called the 'heterogeneity/redistribution trade-off hypothesis' (Banting and Kymlicka 2006: 3).

However, independently of whether such empirical assumptions about the impact of immigration on the welfare state are true, global or cosmopolitan egalitarians have argued that these arguments for restrictive immigration policies make the mistake of assuming that equality has domestic scope only. After all, these arguments assess immigration simply in terms of the impact on the welfare state of the receiving country. But if, on the other hand, equality has global scope, we would need to assess immigration in terms of its impact on inequality in the world as a whole. And here, there are reasons to think that not least the forms of migration that worry egalitarians who invoke the progressive's dilemma, namely South-North migration, will be beneficial for global equality, both because poor, low-skilled migrants are able to achieve a higher standard of living and because they tend to send back remittances at considerable levels to their families who remain in their country of origin. I make this argument in greater detail below.

I should emphasize that I am concerned only with the implications of equality for open borders. I do not argue that it is the only relevant concern to consider. I do, however, briefly consider the overall weight of considerations of equality for immigration policy in the final section of the chapter, where I consider other concerns such as national self-determination and freedom of movement. I should also emphasize that I will not be arguing for equality as a principle of distributive justice, rather, I simply assume egalitarianism and critically examine its scope.

In the following, I first argue that equality has global scope and then consider what this implies, more specifically, for the question of (more) open borders. But before I develop my argument, there is a certain methodological point I want to make, namely that we need to separate issues of basic justice and issues of regulation. Thus, following Cohen (2008; cf. Holtug forthcoming a: ch. 1), I believe that, at the most basic level, principles of justice and their justifications are purely normative. This means, among other things, that issues of feasibility do not apply at this level. A certain social arrangement may be what justice requires even though, as it turns out, it is unfeasible to (fully) implement it. This is the level at which I argue that equality has global scope. When I turn to the question of open borders, my discussion becomes, in part, empirical, because I need to say something about how open borders would impact global equality. Among other things, this involves considering feasibility constraints on promoting global equality through migration policies. The policies I discuss here pertain to the regulative level of justice, that is, what policies to implement. More specifically, we should adopt the policies that best fulfil the aims set out in our basic level principles. Thus, there will sometimes be a gap between basic level principles and principles of regulation, and immigration policy may be a paradigm case of this, where cosmopolitan ideals meet feasibility constraints in terms of, for example, popular opposition to immigration.

The question, then, is what kind of immigration policy will best (or to the greatest extent) promote global equality in the present circumstances, where the present circumstances include facts about, for example, institutions, distributions and motivations (and so it is a question in what

Rawls called non-ideal theory). Of course, the reference to existing institutions, distributions, and motivations is not meant to rule out that these should be changed—indeed, this chapter is concerned with how global distributions should be altered—but to emphasize that migration policies of regulation should aim to move us forward from our present predicament.

The article is structured as follows. In Section 2, I clarify the form(s) of egalitarianism I am concerned with and provide an argument for global scope. In Sections 3 and 4 I discuss, respectively, nationalist and statist restrictions on scope and argue that both are flawed. In Section 5, I suggest that (more) open borders would lead to a higher level of global equality. In Section 6, I consider various possible limitations to equality-promoting migration policies. In Section 7, I consider policy alternatives and conclude that while migration policy (or more open borders) may not be the most important tool in the toolbox, it nevertheless has a role to play as regards promoting global justice. Finally, in Section 8, I consider the significance of egalitarian vis-à-vis other normative concerns pertaining to immigration.

2. On the Scope of Egalitarian Justice

Before I consider the question of scope, I need to be more specific about the form of egalitarianism I have in mind. My concern is with responsibility-catering egalitarianism, which comprises more specific doctrines such as equality of opportunity and luck egalitarianism. According to equality of opportunity, it is unjust if individuals do not have equal opportunities for acquiring a range of goods, including offices and positions, income, education, and health-care; and, more specifically, if they do not have the same prospects for doing so regardless of their lot in the social lottery (cf. Rawls 1971: 72–3). Here, the 'social lottery' refers to the fact that everyone is born into a specific social class and, more generally, social setting, and that the particular setting into which one is born has an impact on one's prospects for obtaining the goods in question.

According to luck egalitarianism, it is unjust if, through no responsibility of their own, some individuals have lower levels of advantages than others. Here, I shall not assume any particular theory of responsibility or of advantages, primarily because I do not need to do so for the purposes of the chapter. Thus, whatever the particular currency of egalitarian justice, it is simply a separate question whether an egalitarian principle that incorporates it should have domestic or global scope. Furthermore, whether we take the currency to be, for example, resources (Dworkin 2000), opportunity for welfare (Arneson 1989), access to advantage (Cohen 1989), or capabilities (Sen 1980), inequality looms large on a global scale, as exemplified by that fact that income inequality is significantly higher at the global level than even in very unequal societies such as the United States. While the Gini-coefficient, which measures the level of redistribution necessary to achieve perfect equality, was 41 in the US in 2007 (World Bank 2018), it was 71 for the world as a whole in 2008 (Lakner and Milanovic 2015: 226).

As regards responsibility, I do not need to adopt a particular theory thereof either, because any plausible theory will imply that the globally worse off are not to any significant extent responsible for so being themselves. Even if, like Rawls (1999), we were to hold that lack of development is largely due to the quality of government in developing nations (which is in any case a questionable claim), it is far from clear that this would translate into personal responsibility for low distributive shares, not least in light of people's limited influence on policies in these countries (many of which are not democratic by any reasonable standard). In an interesting study, Branko Milanovic (2015: 458) finds that more than half of the variability in income in the world is explained by two factors alone, namely GDP per capita and income inequality in country of residence. And, as he suggests, we cannot reasonably believe that an individual is responsible for the average GDP and level of inequality in the country in which she lives. Furthermore, income and wealth are of course impacted by a number of further factors for which people are not themselves responsible, some of which pertain to the social lottery.

For present purposes, the differences between equality of opportunity and luck egalitarianism are not too important. Global inequalities are huge regardless of whether we conceive of them in terms of opportunities for jobs, income, health, etc., or in terms of more general currencies such as opportunities for resources, welfare, etc. Furthermore, my concern is to a considerable extent with inequalities that are captured by the social lottery, and so for example the difference in opportunities between growing up in a well-educated, high-income family of engineers in Germany and growing up in an uneducated, low-income family of peasants in Ethiopia. But, of course, South-North inequality comprises not only social inequality but also natural inequality due to, for example, droughts.

There are two further assumptions I need to make about egalitarianism before I move on. First, I assume a 'whole lives' view according to which equality should obtain between entire lives rather than between temporal segments of lives.[1] This also means that equality applies between generations. Second, I assume that equality should be combined with a concern for efficiency. If egalitarians did not combine concerns in this manner, they would have no reason to prefer equality at high levels of advantages to equality at low levels.

Here is an argument for global scope that derives from the egalitarian principles outlined above. Consider first luck egalitarianism. According to luck egalitarianism, what makes a particular distribution unjust (insofar as it is unjust for egalitarian reasons) is that (1) it is unequal (as regards the relevant currency); and (2) those who are worse off than others are not themselves responsible for being so. The point is that (1) and (2) apply just as much to global distributions as to domestic ones. So, if the joint satisfaction of (1) and (2) is what *makes* distributions unjust, equality has global scope (cf. Moellendorf 2002; Caney 2005: 107; Holtug 2011: 150–1). Furthermore, a parallel argument is available in the case of equality of opportunity. According to equality of opportunity, what makes a particular distribution unjust is that (1*) there is an unequal distribution of jobs, and/or income, and/or education, and/or health-care; and (2*) this inequality reflects that individuals did not have the same prospects for acquiring these goods regardless of their lot in the social lottery. Again, (1*) and (2*) apply just as much to global distributions as to domestic ones, and so equality has global scope.

While this is, I believe, a forceful argument for the global scope of equality, it is of course not a knock-down argument. Consider that the egalitarian principles under consideration may be construed as conditional forms of egalitarianism, where the injustice of a particular

---

[1] Ultimately, I believe we should adopt a more complex view of justice and time (Holtug 2010a: ch. 10), but for present purposes the difference between this view and whole lives does not matter much.

inequality is conditional on the appropriate non-responsibility of those who are worse off. If the injustice of inequality is conditional in this manner, it may be asked, why could it not also be conditional on other factors, such as certain relations between the individuals who are unequally well off, for example, that they are members of the same society? Indeed, it cannot be ruled out in advance that such further conditions apply. Rather, further conditions should be assessed on the basis of two considerations, namely: (a) how plausible are they in their own right; and (b) how plausible are they in conjunction with the condition pertaining to responsibility? Here, (a) concerns the extent to which the proposed relation of societal membership (say, citizenship or nationality) is significant for whether an inequality should be considered unjust; and (b) pertains to the interaction of membership and responsibility as regards the injustice of inequality. Thus, as regards the latter, if appropriate lack of responsibility for distributive shares tends to transform an inequality into an unjust inequality, why would it matter for whether this tendency materializes whether the individuals in question belong to the same society? This, at least, seems to require some kind of explanation.

So far, I have been concerned with whether equality has global scope in the sense that inequalities between individuals (that are not in appropriate ways linked to responsible agency) are unjust independently of whether these individuals belong to the same society. However, there is a related, but separate question of what the obligations are of a particular state as regards inequalities between individuals and whether this depends upon the relation in which they stand to the state. That is, it may be suggested that even if an inequality between, say, a Frenchman and a Tanzanian is unjust, this inequality is of no concern from the point of view of the French state (although perhaps the French state has other, non-egalitarian obligations towards Tanzanians that may, e.g., be based on humanitarianism). To further illustrate this point, some would argue that while it is equally bad if a Tanzanian and a Frenchman starves, the French state has a special responsibility for the Frenchman and so a special obligation to prevent his starving. Such special obligations rely on a species of *agent-relative reasons*, which are moral reasons an agent (or state) has to promote a particular goal that are reasons for *her* (or it), but not necessarily reasons for others. Thus, the reason to prevent the starving of a Frenchman would be a reason for the French state, but not necessarily a reason (or a reason of the same strength) for other states, such as the US or Tanzania.

Therefore, in what follows, I need to consider not only the justice of distributions, but also whether states are equally obligated towards all unjustly unequal distributions or whether such obligations are partial and track societal membership. Note, however, that insofar as global inequality is unjust, presumably there is a *pro tanto* reason for states to rectify it—a reason that would have to be defeated by other reasons (e.g., agent-relative ones) in order to establish that states have egalitarian obligations towards their own members but not towards the global community.[2]

One such reason, it may be thought, pertains to the demandingness of global egalitarianism (cf. Tan 2012: 166–70). As we have seen, there obtains a grossly unequal global distribution of advantages and, at least for rich, Western democracies, presumably it would be rather costly to aim for global equality. And indeed, in moral theory, the idea of an agent-relative option to give greater weight to one's own interests than to those of others is sometimes invoked in response to the demandingness of morality. However, agent-relative options cannot justify restrictions on the scope of equality. After all, it may be just as costly for a Swede, or the Swedish state, to raise a poor, homeless Swedish citizen to a given level of advantages as to raise a poor Sudanese person to the same level. Thus, invoking agent-relative options may serve to reduce the demandingness of morality, but it does not serve to distinguish between fellow citizens and non-citizens in this regard. So, while agent-relative options may tend to downplay egalitarian obligations, they are of little relevance for the question of scope.

3. Restrictions on Scope: Nationalism

In this section and the next, I consider some objections to the suggestion that equality has global scope. Indeed, these are arguments for why equality has domestic scope only. According to the first argument, nations are sources of restrictions on scope. Here, it is a specific aspect

---

[2] See, e.g., Kagan (1989: 15–19, 47–64) on the *pro tanto* reason to promote the good.

of nationalism I engage with, namely the claim that we have stronger obligations towards co-nationals than towards non-nationals. This implies, according to the argument under consideration, that egalitarian obligations apply only among co-nationals.

Nationalists argue that the relation of co-nationality generates special obligations (Tamir 1993; Miller 1995, 2007). And, as they sometimes argue, this is not a strange or unfamiliar doctrine, but similar to how most people think about certain other relations, such as the parent-child relationship. Parents have stronger obligations towards their own children than towards other people's children, simply in virtue of the nature of the particular relationship in which they stand to their own children. Likewise, according to nationalists, special obligations emerge from the relation of co-nationality. In either case, agent-relative reasons to cater for those to whom one stands in the relevant relationship arise.

Of course, not just any kind of relationship can generate special obligations. Miller (2007: 35–6) proposes three requirements that attachments must satisfy in order to generate such duties: (1) the relationship must be intrinsically valuable; (2) the duties must be integral to the relationship such that it could not exist in the same form unless the duties were generally acknowledged; and (3) the relationship must not be inherently unjust. Miller believes that nations, or at least certain nations, satisfy (1)–(3) and so that special obligations obtain between co-nationals. Strictly speaking, it does not follow that the (less extensive) obligations that may obtain between non-nationals are not nevertheless strong enough to give rise to a concern for global equality, but I shall not consider this possibility any further here. Miller (2007: 167) believes that, at the global level, our obligations are sufficientist, and so that we should aim to provide a certain minimum level of advantages for all.

National partiality, it is sometimes argued, finds support in our actual pattern of commitments, where we in various ways tend to favor co-nationals. Thus, we tend to root for our national football team, care in particular about the thriving of our own nation-state, and are more willing to redistribute within it than to members of other states. However, I'm inclined to think that, on further reflection, our commitments and intuitions are more complicated than this. Miller (2007: 29) considers a case in which a child goes missing, and the extent to which we have an obligation to try to find her, depending on whether it is our own child, a child from our village, or a co-national of ours. He argues that while it is equally bad that any child goes missing, in each of these cases, we have a special obligation to try to find her based on the relation in which we stand to her.

However, whatever intuitive plausibility partiality may have when based on family or even village membership, where also the latter may (at least if the village is small enough) be based on personal relations, it seems to me to lose in the case of the nation. Suppose I find not one but two children who have gone missing and have to make the choice of whom to bring home to her parents (for some reason, I cannot bring both). Should their nationality play a role for whom I should help, such that I should first inquire about this before I make my decision? This, it seems to me, is an extreme view. It does not strike me as problematic, for example, to inquire if any of them is injured, because that would clearly be relevant, but to inquire about their nationality as a basis for choice seems to me almost *obscene*.

What, then, is the specific content of the relation between co-nationals that is supposed to justify special obligations? It involves sharing a national identity with which one identifies such that it is partly constitutive of one's own identity. The content of that identity may of course vary, and here, conservative and liberal nationalists will disagree on what the appropriate content of such an identity is. But at a somewhat general level, it will contain elements of the national culture, a shared political culture, recognizing special obligations to compatriots, a commitment to the continued existence of the nation, and an aspiration to political self-determination at the level of the nation-state (Miller 2007: 124–6). Nevertheless, it cannot be required for co-nationality that all members share the very same cultural characteristics and commitments; discrepancies must be permitted to allow that (at least some) states are nation-states and so that nationalist partiality applies in them. We may wonder why this impersonal and looser relation would generate something as morally fundamental as special obligations.

Furthermore, not all community members will share the national identity, even on this looser construal. Not only because some members have another cultural background, but also because infants and (other) young children and some people with severe cognitive disabilities will for obvious reasons not share the national culture and nor will they have commitments to their co-nationals. Thus, nationalism seems to imply that some of the most vulnerable people, whom we ordinarily think welfare states should care especially for, do not fall within the scope of egalitarian justice.

In response to the objection that the relations in which co-nationality consists do not seem suited to ground special obligations, Miller (2011: 167–8) has argued that the beneficial consequences of sustaining a national community, not least as regards democracy and social justice, are sufficient to ground national partiality. Here, the point is that the national community, and the special duties on which it relies, are necessary to maintain democratic institutions and social justice. However, note that Miller here shifts from discussing the intrinsic significance of co-nationality to an instrumental argument for the importance of a national community. And this argument puts the cart before the horse. Thus, we need to know what the scope of (egalitarian) justice is before we can morally assess the impact of sustaining a national community, which according to Miller includes compatriot partiality. So, even if Miller were correct in assuming that, empirically, such partiality is necessary for national democracy and redistribution, we would need to know what standard to assess this impact on the basis of, which requires that we have already settled the scope question. Suppose, then, that we believe that equality has global scope, but also that for democracy and redistribution to thrive at the level of states, states need to exhibit some level of national partiality. In that case, we may have an instrumental argument for allowing some level of national partiality, insofar as this would best promote our global aims as regards institutions and distribution, but what this would amount to would be a policy of regulation, not a restriction on scope at the level of basic justice. I shall return to the question of feasibility for global egalitarianism in Section 6, where I consider regulative principles of immigration.

Of course, as we have seen, Miller holds not only that nations have instrumental value (in facilitating democracy and social justice), but also that they have intrinsic value (which is a requirement for their being sources of special obligations). However, even if we were to grant Miller the claim about intrinsic value (which I am not inclined to do), we would need a separate argument for why this value gives rise to special obligations, which rely on agent-relative reasons (cf. Hurka 1997;

McMahan 1997). More specifically, we may hold that, in response to the intrinsic value of nations, we have reason to care especially about our own nation and to give priority to our co-nationals. But we may also hold that we have reason to care about all nations, irrespective of our own particular national membership, where this involves caring about relations between co-nationals, irrespective of whether they are co-nationals of our own. The latter would involve the claim that the intrinsic value of nations gives rise to agent-neutral (impartial) rather than agent-relative (partial) reasons. And it would not justify the form of national partiality that is supposed to ground a restriction on the scope of egalitarianism.[3]

Finally, let us consider how, more specifically, national partiality is supposed to impact the scope of equality. One possibility is to claim that global inequality is unjust, but that nation-states only have egalitarian obligations towards members of their own nation. This would mirror Miller's account of how it is equally bad if any child goes missing, but that one has stronger obligations for some children than for others. However, *if* global inequality is unjust, why would nation-states not have *some* reason to try to eradicate it? Suppose, *ex hypothesi*, that a state could reduce global inequality at no cost to its members, and with no undesirable side-effects? Assuming that global inequality is indeed unjust, would it then not have at least some reason to do so? Of course, this is compatible with stronger obligations towards its own members, and stronger reasons to reduce domestic inequality (but even such partiality would, of course, be based on premises I have argued above we should reject).

Then consider the possibility that global inequality is not unjust, more specifically, that lack of membership of the same nation somehow annuls the injustice of inequality. Suppose we know of two people that one is worse off than the other through no responsibility of her own. Suppose, for example, that the difference in their advantage levels can be explained entirely in terms of one of them being born in a privileged, upper class family and the other being born by poor, uneducated

---

[3] Miller (2007: ch. 3; 2016: 46–7) has raised two further objections to global egalitarianism, according to which (a) there is no culturally neutral way to define a global currency of egalitarian justice; and (b) global egalitarianism tends to undermine national self-determination. I critically discuss these arguments in Holtug (2011), and Miller responds in Miller (2011).

parents in a neighborhood with very few opportunities, educational or otherwise. They have both worked hard, and equally so, to get where they are, but because of differences in social background, one of them is rewarded much more generously for her efforts than the other. According to the suggestion under consideration, we would not be able to tell if the inequality is unjust unless we know whether they have the same nationality. This seems counterintuitive. If the less privileged person's lack of responsibility for being worse off would under other conditions transform this inequality into an unjust inequality, why does the fact that they are non-nationals prevent this from happening?

Here, the point is not just that, as I have argued above, nationality seems to lack relevance for the question of scope, but also more specifically how the absence of co-nationality would block the transformative force of non-responsibility as regards the injustice of inequality? Intuitively, non-responsibility seems to bestow injustice on the inequality quite independently of the presence or absence of other factors. In this respect, it seems similar to undeserved pain. Intuitively, pain is (intrinsically) bad if it is undeserved (and, presumably, there will be at least a *pro tanto* reason to prevent it), quite irrespective of the presence or absence of other factors. Its badness is settled by its being undeserved, and we do not need to begin to consider other factors to see whether they might somehow block the transformative force of undeservedness. In conclusion, neither the claim that global inequality is not unjust nor the claim that (while unjust) global inequality does not generate reasons for states to rectify it seems capable of justifying restrictions on scope.

4. Restrictions on Scope: Statism

Statism or institutionalism is another possible source of restrictions on the scope of equality. Where nationalism restricts equality on the basis of membership of the nation, statism restricts it on the basis of membership of a political (or institutional) community. The general structure of the statist argument for domestic scope is this: (1) in order for egalitarian concerns to pertain to the distribution of advantages between individuals, certain institutional arrangements need to exist and these individuals need to be appropriately related in terms of them; and (2) while these arrangements and relations (often) obtain domestically, they do not obtain at the global level. Such institutional arrangements may be (and have been) specified in different ways, resulting in different justifications for domestic scope. To some extent, these different justifications mirror Rawls' (1971: 7) suggestion that social justice applies only to the basic structure of society and the different things he had to say about what characterizes the basic structure and why it is the primary site of justice.

Rawls (1971: 7) describes the basic structure as 'the way in which major social institutions distribute fundamental rights and duties and determine the distribution of advantages from social cooperation'. This structure includes the political constitution (such as legal rights and duties), legally recognized forms of property, taxation, and the ways in which markets are organized. According to Rawls (1971: 7), 'the basic structure is the primary subject of justice because its effects are so profound and present from the start', where such effects pertain not least to inequalities that are 'pervasive' and 'affect men's initial chances in life'.

Indeed, if we are concerned with equality, it seems reasonable to focus on the main factors that shape it. Furthermore, on the assumption that there is no global basic structure, it may be argued that egalitarian justice does not obtain at this level, because the institutions it is concerned with regulating are absent. And so egalitarian justice has domestic scope only (assuming that a basic structure *does* exist at the state level).

However, first, this argument conflates two distinct questions, namely what the scope of egalitarian justice is; and what institutions we have reason to be concerned about insofar as we are concerned with egalitarian justice. The argument points to the instrumental role of the basic structure for implementing egalitarian distributions, but it does not tell us what scope our egalitarian concern should have when we assess the significance of that role. Second, as Thomas Pogge (1989: sect. 3; 2002) has forcefully argued, existing institutions have a profound impact on the global distribution of advantages and, on this basis, there is reason to posit the existence of a global basic structure.

As we have seen, Rawls also stresses the significance of the basic structure for social cooperation and the distribution of rights and resources it gives rise to. Here, according to Rawls, social cooperation consists not only in social coordination and interaction, but 'includes the idea of fair terms of cooperation' (Rawls 2001: 6), which again refers to reciprocity or mutual advantage. On this basis, it may be suggested that egalitarian concerns arise only where there is social cooperation and that while such cooperation obtains within states, at the global level, there are no institutions that, to any substantial degree, ascribe to people rights and duties, regulate legal forms of property and tax, and more generally distribute the benefits of social cooperation to the mutual advantage of participants.

However, first, this 'cooperation' account also conflates the question of the scope of justice and the question of what reasons we have to be concerned about the basic structure. It ascribes to the basic structure the purpose of regulating the distribution of the fruits of cooperation, but we still need to determine the scope of our egalitarian concern when assessing the distributions that arise from it. Second, the claim that, in order for social justice to apply to a system of social interaction, that interaction must already in a certain respect be *fair*—it must be to the mutual advantage of the participants—seems dubious (Abizadeh 2007: 332). Why would the fact that a given system of social interaction is not to the mutual advantage of the parties, or is even exploitative, be a reason to hold that we should not be concerned about the inequality to which it gives rise?

There is, however, a final statist argument for domestic scope I want to consider. It pertains to a particular aspect of the basic structure, namely the legal system and the coercive structures it instantiates. Michael Blake (2001) suggests that states need to be able to justify the ways in which their legal institutions coerce citizens because coercion is in a *prima facie* conflict with autonomy. However, at the same time, state coercion makes it possible for individuals to live autonomous lives in virtue of the protections it offers. In order for the state to be justified in this overall legal system of coercion, it must be capable of justifying it to each citizen (or person coerced by the system) by giving them reasons they could not reasonably reject (Blake 2001: 283). This includes justifying it to the individuals who do most poorly under the system, that is, the worst off. And in order for the worst off not to have a ground for reasonable rejection, it must be the case that the worst off are as well off as possible, which means that the difference principle must be satisfied.

Thus, according to Blake, the concern for egalitarian justice derives from the need to justify state coercion to citizens. Furthermore, there are no global legal institutions that engage in this sort of coercion of individual agents and, therefore, there is no basis for saying that global institutions have egalitarian obligations (Blake 2001: 280). Finally, state institutions do not coerce non-citizens (or non-residents) so they do not have egalitarian obligations towards them (Blake 2001: 287). Therefore, egalitarianism has domestic scope only.

I believe there are a number of problems with this argument. First, and most generally, an appeal to state coercion does not seem to me to be the best way to explain the unfairness of inequality. I briefly return to this point at the end of the section (see also Caney 2015). Second, even if we were to assume that the need to justify state coercion is what generates a concern with equality, the argument for why this would rule out egalitarian concern for non-citizens is questionable. As others have also pointed out, this is particularly obvious in the case of immigration policies (Abizadeh 2007: 345–57; Carens 2013: 257–8). States engage in a variety of activities to keep immigrants out, including controlling borders, building walls, non-arrival measures, and push-backs on open sea, and it can hardly be denied that these are forms of coercion. Blake (2001: 280) does consider border control in a footnote, but in a rather puzzling manner suggests that we should distinguish between prospective and current membership, and that it is only the latter that generates egalitarian concern. If a system of coercion requires a justification to those coerced, and this requires providing a reason they cannot reasonably reject, which again requires satisfying the difference principle, it remains a mystery why states are not obligated in terms of this principle towards would-be immigrants they coercively deny entry.

More recently, however, Blake (2013: 105–6; cf. 2008) has responded in somewhat greater detail to the objection that coercive border control generates egalitarian obligations to outsiders:

the state here has an easy reply to the individual who wishes to immigrate—namely, you have access to all those goods you are entitled to in your own society; we have no obligation to provide them to you, given that they are adequately distributed as things stand.

However, denying a would-be immigrant access on this basis is to pre-suppose what needs to be shown, namely that she is not entitled to any-thing over and above what she has in her country of origin. In particular, assuming she is coercively denied access, a justification needs to be provided to her to which she could not reasonably reject.

Assume, for the sake of argument, that both the sending and the receiv-ing society secure the autonomy of their citizens and a distribution that is consistent with the difference principle. Nevertheless, by further assump-tion, immigration would significantly improve a migrant's standard of liv-ing, because the receiving society is much wealthier. What we need to settle is whether she is entitled to the difference between her standard of living in these two Rawlsian societies, and so it cannot simply be taken for granted that she is not. Furthermore, if a citizen of the receiving society could reasonably reject the level the would-be immigrant receives in her country of origin, why cannot the would-be immigrant reject this level when she is being coercively prevented from entering and obtaining a higher level? By imposing coercive border control, the receiving state includes the would-be immigrant in the set of people to whom it owes a justification they cannot reasonably reject, and since what people in this set cannot reasonably reject is settled on the basis of the available resources in *this* society, this society's resources also becomes a standard for evaluat-ing what the would-be immigrant is entitled to.[4]

I should perhaps emphasize that I do not believe it is only border control that exemplifies coercion of foreigners and so, on a coercion-based statist account such as Blake's, implies egalitarian obligations to out-siders. It is just that border control is a particularly obvious example. Blake (2013: 97–8) does suggest that international coercion, with few exceptions, is directed at states rather than individual foreigners and so does not generate claims for egalitarian shares. However, while I cannot do so here, I would argue that many forms of international coercion, including war, trade sanctions, and international courts also amount to the coercion of individual foreigners in the relevant sense.

I have now considered three distinct statist (or institutional) theories of why equality has domestic scope only and argued that none of them

---

[4] Thomas Nagel (2005) has proposed an alternative coercion-based justification of domestic scope but it is, I believe, no less problematic than Blake's. See, for example, Abizadeh (2007).

construes institutional relations in a manner that justifies this claim about scope. Now I want to very briefly point to a couple of further problems statism shares with the nationalist justification of domestic scope. First, there is the question of whether these institutional relations are supposed to give rise to agent-relative or agent-neutral reasons. Consider, for example, the coercion account. According to this account, when a state coerces its citizens but does not ensure among them an egalitarian distribution of advantages, it cannot justify its coercive structures to them. We might think this gives rise to an agent-relative reason, that is, a reason for the state to ensure equality, but not a reason for other states to contribute thereto. However, we might instead think that it gives rise to an agent-neutral reason, which would also be a reason for other states (such that, e.g., they have a *pro tanto* reason to transfer resources to this state insofar as it is incapable of providing the required distribution itself). This latter view would not be cosmopolitan, because it would not require equality between individuals independently of the coercive states they belong to, but nor would it be a traditional domestic view, because it would imply that states have reasons to contribute to equality in other states.

Finally, consider the question of how institutional relations are supposed to impact the scope of equality. One possibility is to claim that global inequality is unjust, but that states only have egalitarian obligations towards their own citizens. Again, if global inequality *is* unjust, would this not it itself provide a *pro tanto* reason to try to eradicate it? Then suppose instead the statist claims that global inequality is not unjust. Suppose also that two people have made a large and equal effort to get to where they are but that because of her privileged social background, one ends up much better off than the other. According to statism, we would not be able to tell whether the inequality that prevails between them is unjust unless we know whether they are co-citizens (and so, e.g., are subjected to the same coercive structure). This is counterintuitive, or so it seems to me.

This completes my discussion of the scope of equality. I have argued that equality has global scope, both by providing an independent argument for the global scope of egalitarianism and by raising a number of objections to nationalist and statist justifications for domestic scope only.

5. Migration for Global Equality

What does global egalitarianism imply for the question of open borders? A case for open borders is often made on the basis of the roughly global luck egalitarian argument that since no one chooses where he or she is born, the inequalities in life-chances that flow from such circumstances are unfair and so are the coercive barriers that prevent people from migrating to places where they might improve their standard of living (Carens: 1992, 2013: part 2; Cole 2000, 2011). As Carens (1987: 252) puts it: 'citizenship in Western liberal democracies is the modern equivalent of feudal privilege—an inherited status that greatly enhances one's life chances. Like feudal birthright privileges, restrictive citizenship is hard to justify when one thinks about it closely'.

This argument, of course, relies on the assumption that migration, and in particular South-North migration, tends to promote global equality. And indeed, economists sometimes argue that open borders are the quickest way to equalize the global distribution of income (Hamilton and Whalley 1984: 73–4; Begg, Fisher, and Dornbusch 1997: 644). In fact, there are two main ways in which open borders will tend to promote global equality. First, poor migrants can improve their standard of living by migrating to wealthy liberal democracies. Thus, wages in developed countries typically exceed those of developing countries by four to twelve times and large disparities remain even when comparing wages for similar jobs requiring similar skills across countries (Freeman 2006: 14–17).

Second, immigrants often help their families in their country of origin through remittances and thereby further stimulate its economy (World Bank 2006). Indeed, recorded remittances to developing nations in 2007 were four and a half times the size of total global development aid (UNDP 2009: 78). In 2011, personal remittances contributed 21 per cent of the GDP in Haiti, 23 per cent in Liberia, 22 per cent in Nepal, 22 per cent in Somoa, and 47 per cent in Tajikistan (World Bank 2013). Furthermore, there is evidence that remittances contribute to poverty reduction in recipient households, increase investment in human capital (education and health), reduce child labor, and increase entrepreneurship (Özden and Schiff 2006: 14).

According to some estimates, the effects of increasing South-North migration by an annual 3 per cent might produce net benefits that exceed the combined effect of meeting national targets for development aid, cancelling all Third World debt and abolishing all barriers to Third World trade (World Bank 2006; Putnam 2007: 141). For reasons such as these, we find the UNDP (2009) proposing more open borders as a means for promoting development and global equality.

As noted above, egalitarians are concerned not only with equality but also efficiency, and so let us briefly look more generally at the impact of migration on economic growth. Such calculations are difficult and somewhat imprecise (Geddes 2003). Nevertheless, it is generally acknowledged that international migration tends to increase global growth (Hamilton and Whalley 1984; Moses and Letnes 2004; Pécoud and Guchtenaire 2005; Legrain 2006; Ugur 2007). According to a study by Hamilton and Whalley (1984), lifting immigration controls could more than double the world GNP, and later studies have suggested even larger effects (Moses and Letnes 2004). This is because free migration tends to redeploy workers to where they are more productive, resulting in large increases in the global economy (Legrain 2006: ch. 3). According to Moses and Letnes (2004: 1610), even small increases in international migration could produce highly significant economic gains, exceeding those generated by traditional development policies. The World Bank (2006: 34) similarly finds that if rich countries increased their workforce by 3 per cent by taking in migrants from developing nations, the net gains would amount to 356 billion USD, where natives in high-income countries gain 139 billion USD, people who remain in the countries of origin 143 billion USD, and the migrants themselves 162 billion USD. Thus, the case for (more) open borders seems to be supported not only by considerations of equality, but also of efficiency.[5]

---

[5] It is sometimes argued that in particular low-skilled immigration tends to increase unemployment and drive down wages for worse off natives, which poses a problem for social justice. However, first, the available evidence seems to suggest that effects on the unemployment and wages of natives tend to be small or non-existent (Nannestad 2007: 526; Ugur 2007: 21–3; Foged and Peri 2015). Second, we need to remember that, at the basic level, the relevant concern is global rather than domestic equality, and worse off members of liberal welfare states may still be quite well off by global standards, and so even if their shares are reduced this need not increase global inequality.

Importantly, concerns for equality and efficiency are supposed to work in tandem in this argument. Thus, if a formerly impoverished migrant gains a higher standard of living this may not increase global equality, namely if the migrant ends up sufficiently well above the global average of advantages. Nevertheless, holding everything else constant, since this is a Pareto improvement, efficiency-sensitive egalitarianism implies that it is a change for the better.[6]

6. Limitations on Equality-Promoting Migration Policies

In this section, I want to briefly address three arguments for why migration policy may be less well suited to promote global equality than has been suggested so far. First, there is the worry that international migration leads to brain drain from developing nations (Özden and Schiff 2006: 11; Eyal and Hurst 2008). And indeed, brain drain is a significant problem in a number of such nations. Nevertheless, importantly, brain drain impacts developing nations differently. Indeed, a recent study finds a positive effect of the prospect of skilled migration on human capital formation in a cross-section of 127 developing countries (Beine, Docquier and Rapoport 2008; cf. Stark 2004). This effect is primarily due to the fact that the prospect of migration increases the incentive to educate oneself, resulting in a surplus of skilled workers who end up remaining. However, for Central America, the Pacific region, and Sub-Saharan Africa brain drain is a significant problem (Beine, Docquier and Rapoport 2008: 644).

Nevertheless, note that brain drain may be impacted through policy. In sending countries, higher education could be provided on the basis of contracts where students commit themselves to work in the country for a certain number of years after having earned their degree. And as regards receiving countries, policies could be implemented that limit the number of green cards awarded to high-skilled migrants from developing nations and/or compensate these nations insofar as high-skilled migrants are admitted. This would limit the extent to which poor

---

[6] It may, of course, be questioned whether global growth is a desirable aim, not least in light of global warming. Unfortunately, I cannot go into this discussion here.

developing countries are subsidizing, for example, health-care services in rich Western democracies.

Another worry about (more) open borders pertains to the sustainability of welfare states. Thus, there are differences between welfare states as regards the fiscal impact of immigration. A number of studies suggest that the impact of immigration on fiscal balances in developed countries is small, and sometimes even positive (Legrain 2006: ch. 7; World Bank 2006: 39–41; Ugur 2007; d'Albis, Boubtane and Coulibaly 2018). However, fiscal impacts are likely to depend upon both the composition of the immigrant group and the type of welfare state that admits them. In particular, extensive welfare states face challenges in relation to low-skilled migration. A case in point is the fiscal loss imposed by non-Western immigration into the Nordic countries (Storsletten 2003: 500; Nannestad 2007: 527–8; Brockmann et al 2017: 156–7; Danish Ministry of Finance 2017: 9).

Thus, for at least some welfare states, there is a trade-off to be made in terms of immigration and other ways of promoting global equality, and this trade-off is not unlikely to be faced by more countries the further we move towards open borders. That is, immigration above a certain level may be costly, and so costs and benefits need to be compared to alternative ways of promoting global equality. Furthermore, open borders may weaken the ability of rich, Western democracies to promote global equality in the long run. I shall return to the comparison of alternative ways of promoting global equality in the next section. However, for now, it is worth keeping in mind that even relatively small steps towards liberalization of immigration policies may be expected to lead to (disproportionally) large gains in efficiency and global equality (Hamilton and Whalley 1984: 75; World Bank 2006: ch. 2).

A further possible limitation on equality-promoting migration policies pertains to the willingness of domestic populations to accept (more) immigration. Thus, according to an influential argument, solidarity is bounded and reaches out primarily to members of one's own in-group. For example, as we have seen, Miller (1995: chs. 5–6; 2004; Miller and Ali 2014) argues that solidarity at substantial levels requires a national community and does not extend beyond it.[7] Indeed,

---

[7] For this reason, Miller (2004) likewise argues that immigration drives down the social cohesion required for social justice. I critically discuss this argument in Holtug (2010b).

according to a European study (Noël and Thérien 2002: 641), there is stronger support for domestic than for international redistribution (although support for international redistribution is also high). As regards immigration, slightly more than 50 per cent of Europeans hold either that no poor migrants from outside the EU, or only a few, should be admitted (Heath and Richards 2016). This may seem to indicate that there are limits to solidarity at the global level. In addition, a number of studies in social psychology confirm that people are biased towards their in-group (Balliet, Wu, and de Dreu 2014).[8]

Note, incidentally, that these concerns pertain to the feasibility of promoting global equality through migration policy and so do not challenge the claim that, at the basic level, justice may require (more) open borders. They pertain to the regulative level of justice, or more specifically, the migration policies we have reason to try to implement. And even if there are limits to popular support for immigration, this does not pose a reason to resist equality-promoting policies that are in fact feasible.

Furthermore, patterns of identification and the solidarities that may flow from them do not seem immune from policy. Of course, this is also an underlying assumption when states engage in nation-building, although regrettably, the particular identities promoted often tend towards excluding rather than including immigrants. Nevertheless, studies in social psychology suggest that identities in social groups can be made more inclusive and indeed that negative bias may be reduced by re-categorizing the identities of different groups into a single, overarching identity (Dovidio, Gaertner, Validzic, and Matoka 1997). Likewise, Esses, Dovidio, Semenya, and Jackson (2005: 330–2) find that when research subjects are primed with an international identity, which emphasizes their being part of a single worldwide community, individuals who are high in social dominance orientation (where such individuals tend to hold particularly unfavorable attitudes to immigration) become significantly more favorable towards immigration. While, then, there may well be limits to the solidarity required for implementing

---

[8] This literature, however, does not directly support the nationalist claim that high levels of solidarity require a national community (Holtug 2017: 1090–2). Nor do studies of the effects of national identification seem to confirm this (Breidahl, Holtug, and Kongshøj 2018; Holtug forthcoming b).

more open borders, there is also reason to believe that levels of solidarity cannot simply be taken for granted but are sensitive to identity-building and institutional policies.

7. Policy Alternatives and their Efficiency

While I have argued that migration can potentially provide a considerable positive impact on global equality, I have also considered some possible limitations to equality-promoting migration policies. Sometimes brain drain poses a problem, but it seems possible to address this problem through policies. There is also a question of the sustainability of welfare states and their ability to aid developing nations in the longer run if a policy of open borders is adopted. However, as I have argued, even small steps towards more open borders may lead to large increases in efficiency and global equality. Finally, I have considered limitations to solidarity based on in- and out-group dynamics, and argued that while there are such limitations, we should not simply take existing levels for granted, because it is likely that they can be impacted through policies.

Thus, none of the considered limitations to equality-promoting migration policies suggests that more open borders cannot indeed promote global equality. However, as with any policy, we should consider policy alternatives. And, indeed, it has been suggested that there are more efficient ways of promoting global equality than by promoting migration, and in particular that aiding people in their countries of origin will have a number of advantages, including the following (Pogge 1997): (1) the costs of benefiting the worse off will generally be lower in developing nations because a given sum of money will have greater purchasing power there; (2) spending the money in developing nations will tend to stimulate local markets; and (3) the poorest people in the world are much less likely to migrate, and so opening borders will in general not promote *their* interests (cf. UNDP 2009: 25).

While there is much more to be said about the relative efficiency of different equality-promoting policies, I believe that, in part because of efficiency concerns, (more) open borders are not in general the answer to global inequality. Furthermore, there are other reasons to prefer to improve people's conditions in their country of origin, where these reasons pertain to their already being embedded in particular social and cultural communities there. But even if, for this reason, we conclude that other policies should take precedence in the promotion of global equality, this should not be taken to imply that migration has no role to play in the promotion of global justice. One reason for this is that it is simply unrealistic to imagine that liberal democracies will begin to implement optimal policies to promote global equality from one day to the next, and so arguably the best strategy for those who want to promote global equality will be to aim for piecemeal improvements in many different policy domains, including global economic institutions, development aid, *and* immigration policies. Another reason is that, presumably, many rich countries are capable of higher rates of immigration before they reach a level where further immigration becomes a net cost, and below this level there is no issue of weighing immigration against other equality-promoting policies in terms of which is most cost-effective. Finally, there are a number of people it is very difficult to help in their country of origin, at least in the short term, including, most notably, many refugees.

These, of course, are highly pragmatic considerations about what policies to try to implement here and now, and so pertain to regulative rather than basic level justice. At more basic levels, justice may well require something close to open borders, although as a regulative policy for the present, this would be counterproductive, for example, because it would most likely lead to a backlash and cripple long-term efforts towards global equality (cf. Carens 2013: 296).

8. On the Significance of Equality for Migration Policy

Before I end, I want to briefly consider the significance of egalitarian concerns for the overall assessment of (more) open borders and more specifically, whether these concerns are defeated or outweighed by other concerns. Opponents of open borders have appealed to national self-determination (Miller 2007: ch. 8; 2016: ch. 4) and, as an aspect of self-determination, freedom of association (Wellman 2011) to justify their opposition. However, these arguments seem to me problematic. Even if states have a right to self-determination, for example on the basis of freedom of association, there is an independent question of how they should use that right, that is, what decisions they should collectively make. The right to self-determination does nothing to settle that question; it is a question that should be settled on the basis of reasons for specific policies, and states can be criticized if, for example, they make decisions about immigration that do not conform to those reasons. Furthermore, while proponents of the self-determination argument tend to assume priority to compatriots when they emphasize that restrictions on immigration may facilitate a number of benefits from self-determination for members of the receiving society (Miller 2016: 71), I have argued that there is no basis for such priority.

While there are thus political principles that have been taken to defeat or outweigh the egalitarian argument for (more) open borders, it might also be suggested that the egalitarian case for open borders is too contingent and unduly restrictive. Thus, it may be suggested that in order for a state to respect people's freedom of movement (Carens 1992, 2013; Cole 2000, 2011; Oberman 2016), it should only deny them entry in exceptional circumstances (say, if they pose a clear threat to national security).

However, our response to this conflict of concerns will depend upon the relative weight we assign to different values, how we justify them, and the structure we believe they have. First, there is a question of the relative weight we assign to equality and freedom of movement. Second, and related to this, our justifications and the structure we assign to these values may impact our priorities. Suppose our concern for freedom of movement is basically motivated by a concern for human interests (as argued by, e.g., Oberman 2016). In that case, what do we do if open borders are in tension with the aim of maximally promoting human interests, or an efficiency-sensitive egalitarian distribution of interest-fulfilment? If freedom of movement is construed as an agent-relative constraint on limiting people's mobility, then restrictions on immigration cannot be justified merely by reference to the availability of more efficient ways of promoting interests or equality on a global scale. If, on the other hand, our concern with freedom of movement is more consequentialist in nature, we may be willing to accept restrictions to the extent these allow for more efficient interest- or equality-promoting policies.

Similar considerations apply if, instead, we justify freedom of movement in terms of autonomy. According to an influential account, autonomy requires (1) the ability to make plans and to comprehend the means necessary to realize them; (2) an adequate range of valuable options to choose from; and (3) freedom from coercion and manipulation from others (Raz 1986: 372–3; and for the claim that a right to immigration should be based, at least in part, on access to an adequate range of options, see Miller 2007: 207). It is easy to see how closed borders may conflict with both (2) and (3) here. And again, if freedom of movement is construed as an agent-relative constraint, then pointing out that there are more efficient ways of furthering global equality will not suffice to override this constraint. But if we are basically concerned with promoting people's ability to live autonomous lives, we may be more willing to accept restrictions on migration in cases where, for example, this would provide access to an adequate range of options for a greater number of people.

For reasons of space, I cannot here argue in any degree of detail for a particular way of resolving the potential conflict between equality and freedom of movement as regards immigration policy. But, for what it is worth, I believe that in cases where we can do more to reduce global poverty and inequality by imposing restrictions on immigration, say because we can then spend the surplus directly in poor nations and on modifying unfair international institutions, doing so does not amount to an unjustifiable restriction on freedom of movement.[9] In such cases, to put it crudely, helping the many in the global South is more important than helping the smaller number of would-be immigrants to the global North (which is not to say that *any* kind of restrictive border control is justified, of course). However, note first that this trade-off applies only in situations in which global equality and freedom of movement are in fact in conflict, and as I have argued, this will far from always be the case. Second, note that none of this challenges my main conclusion, namely that migration has an important role to play in the promotion of global justice.

---

[9] Perhaps the tension between equality and freedom can be reduced by increasing the proportion of a state's budget that is spent on the globally poor, which I wholeheartedly endorse, but even with a higher budget presumably there will sometimes be a conflict between these two aims.

References

Abizadeh, A. (2007), 'Cooperation, Pervasive Impact, and Coercion: On the Scope (not Site) of Distributive Justice', *Philosophy and Public Affairs*, 35/4: 318–58.

Arneson, R.J. (1989), 'Equality and Equal Opportunity for Welfare', *Philosophical Studies*, 56/1: 77–93.

Balliet, D., Wu, J., and de Dreu, C.K.W. (2014), 'Ingroup Favouritism in Cooperation: A Meta-analysis', *Psychological Bulletin*, 140/6: 1556–81.

Banting, K., and Kymlicka, W. (2006), 'Introduction. Multiculturalism and the Welfare State: Setting the Context', in K. Banting and W. Kymlicka (eds.), *Multiculturalism and the Welfare State* (Oxford: Oxford University Press), 1–45.

Begg, D., Fischer, S., and Dornbusch, R. (1997), *Economics*, 5th edition (London: McGraw-Hill).

Beine, M., Docquier, F., and Rapoport, H. (2008), 'Brain Drain and Human Capital Formation in Developing Countries: Winners and Losers', *The Economic Journal*, 118/4: 631–52.

Blake, M. (2001), 'Distributive Justice, State Coercion, and Autonomy', *Philosophy and Public Affairs*, 30/3: 257–96.

Blake, M. (2008), 'Immigration and Political Equality', *San Diego Law Review*, 45/3: 963–79.

Blake, M. (2013), *Justice and Foreign Policy* (Oxford: Oxford University Press).

Breidahl, K.N., Holtug, N., and Kongshøj, S. (2018), 'Do Shared Values Promote Social Cohesion? If So, Which? Evidence from Denmark', *European Political Science Review*, 10/1: 97–118.

Brockmann, G., Djuve. A.B., Eriksen, T., Holmøy, E., Horst, C., Nordahl, T., Riekeles, H., Skaksen, J.R., Taraku, S., Toje, A., and Østensjø, I. (2017), *Integrasjon og tillit. Langsiktige konsekvenser av høy innvandring, Norges Offentlige Udredning*, 17: 2.

Byvaran, S., and Rajan, S.C. (2010), 'The Ethical Implications of Sea-level Rise Due to Climate Change', *Ethics and International Affairs*, 24/3: 239–60.

Caney, S. (2005), *Justice Beyond Borders: A Global Political Theory* (Oxford: Oxford University Press).

Caney, S. (2015), 'Coercion, Justification, and Inequality: Defending Global Egalitarianism', *Ethics and International Affairs*, 29/3: 277–88.

Carens, J. (1987), 'Aliens and Citizens: The Case for Open Borders', *Review of Politics*, 49/2: 251–73.

Carens, J. (1992), 'Migration and Morality. A Liberal Egalitarian Perspective', in B. Barry and R.E. Goodin (eds.), *Free Movement: Ethical Issues in the Transnational Migration of People and of Money* (New York: Harvester Wheatsheaf), 25–47.

Carens, J. (2013), *The Ethics of Immigration* (Oxford: Oxford University Press).

Cohen, G.A. (1989), 'On the Currency of Egalitarian Justice', *Ethics*, 99/4: 906–44.

Cohen, G.A. (2008), *Rescuing Justice and Equality* (Princeton: Princeton University Press).

Cole, P. (2000), *Philosophies of Exclusion: Liberal Political Theory and Immigration* (Edinburgh: Edinburgh University Press).

Cole, P. (2011), 'Open Borders: An Ethical Defense', in C.H. Wellman and P. Cole (eds.), *Debating the Ethics of Immigration: Is There a Right to Exclude?* (Oxford: Oxford University Press), 159–313.

d'Albis, H., Boubtane, E., and Coulibaly, D. (2018), 'Macroeconomic Evidence Suggest that Asylum Seekers Are Not a "Burden" for Western European Countries', *Science Advances*, 4/6.

Danish Ministry of Finance (2017), *Økonomisk analyse: Indvandrenes nettobidrag til de offentlige finanser i 2015* (Copenhagen: Danish Ministry of Finance).

Dovidio, J.F., Gaertner, S.L., Validzic, A., and Matoka, A. (1997), 'Extending the Benefits of Recategorization: Evaluations, Self-disclosure, and Helping', *Journal of Experimental Social Psychology*, 33/4: 401–20.

Dworkin, R. (2000), *Sovereign Virtue* (Cambridge, MA: Harvard University Press).

Esses, V.M., Dovidio, J.F., Semenya, A.H., and Jackson, L.M. (2005), 'Attitudes Toward Immigrants and Immigration: The Role of National and International Identity', in D. Abrams, M.A. Hogg and J.M. Marques (eds.), *The Social Psychology of Inclusion and Exclusion* (New York: Psychology Press), 317–37.

Eyal, N., and Hurst, S. (2008), 'Physician Brain Drain: Can Nothing Be Done?', *Public Health Ethics*, 1/2: 180–92.

Foged, M., and Peri, G. (2015), 'Immigrants Effect on Native Workers: New Analysis of Longitudinal Data', *American Economic Journal: Applied Economics*, 8/2: 1–34.

Freeman, R.B. (2006), 'People Flows in Globalization', NBER Working Paper Series (Cambridge, MA: National Bureau of Economic Research).

Geddes, A. (2003), 'Migration and the Welfare State in Europe', in S. Spencer (ed.), *The Politics of Migration. Managing Opportunity, Conflict and Change* (Malden, MA: Blackwell Publishing), 150–62.

Goodhart, D. (2004), 'Too Diverse?', *Prospect Magazine*, February.

Goodhart, D. (2013), *The British Dream: Successes and Failures of Post-war Immigration* (London: Atlantic Books).

Hamilton, B., and Whalley, J. (1984), 'Efficiency and Distributional Implications of Global Restrictions on Labour Mobility: Calculations and Policy Implications', *Journal of Development Economics*, 14/1: 61–75.

Heath, A., and Richards, L. (2016), 'Attitudes towards Immigration and Their Antecedents: Topline Results from Round 7 of the European Social Survey', ESS Topline Results Series, Issue 7.

Holtug, N. (2010a), *Persons, Interests, and Justice* (Oxford: Oxford University Press).

Holtug, N. (2010b), 'Immigration and the Politics of Social Cohesion', *Ethnicities*, 10/4: 435–51.

Holtug, N. (2011), 'The Cosmopolitan Strikes Back: A Critical Discussion of Miller on Nationality and Global Equality', *Ethics and Global Politics*, 4/3: 147–63.

Holtug, N. (2017), 'Identity, Causality and Social Cohesion', *Journal of Ethnic and Migration Studies*, 43/7: 1084–100.

Holtug, N. (forthcoming a), *The Politics of Social Cohesion: Immigration, Community and Justice* (Oxford: Oxford University Press).

Holtug, N. (forthcoming b), 'Does Nationhood Promote Egalitarian Justice? Challenging the National Identity Argument', in G. Gustavsson and D. Miller (eds.), *Liberal Nationalism and Its Critics: Normative and Empirical Questions* (Oxford: Oxford University Press).

Hurka, T. (1997), 'The Justification of National Partiality', in R. McKim and J. McMahan (eds.), *The Morality of Nationalism* (New York: Oxford University Press), 139–57.

IOM (2009), *Migration, Environment and Climate Change: Assessing the Evidence* (Geneva: International Organization of Migration).

Kagan, S. (1989), *The Limits of Morality* (Oxford: Oxford University Press).

Lakner, C., and Milanovic, B. (2015), 'Global Income Distribution: From the Fall of the Berlin Wall to the Great Recession', *World Bank Economic Review*, 30/2: 203–32.

Legrain, P. (2006), *Immigrants. Your Country Needs Them* (Princeton: Princeton University Press).

McMahan, J. (1997), 'The Limits of National Partiality', in R. McKim and J. McMahan (eds.), *The Morality of Nationalism* (New York: Oxford University Press), 107–38.

Milanovic, B. (2015), 'Global Inequality of Opportunity: How Much of Our Income is Determined by Where We Live?', *Review of Economics and Statistics*, 97/2: 452–60.

Miller, D. (1995), *On Nationality* (Oxford: Clarendon Press).

Miller, D. (2004), 'Social Justice in Multicultural Societies', in P. van Parijs (ed.), *Cultural Diversity versus Economic Solidarity* (Brussels: De Boeck University Press).

Miller, D. (2007), *National Responsibility and Global Justice* (Oxford: Polity Press).

Miller, D. (2011), 'On Nationality and Global Equality: Reply to Holtug', *Ethics and Global Politics*, 4/3: 165–71.

Miller, D. (2016), *Strangers in Our Midst: The Political Philosophy of Immigration* (Cambridge, MA: Harvard University Press).

Miller, D., and Ali, S. (2014), 'Testing the National Identity Argument', *European Political Science Review*, 6/2: 237–59.

Moellendorf, D. (2002), *Cosmopolitan Justice* (Boulder, CO: Westview Press).

Moses, J.W., and Letnes, B. (2004), 'The Economic Costs to International Labor Restrictions: Revising the Empirical Discussion', *World Development*, 32/10, 1609–26.

Nagel, T. (2005), 'The Problem of Global Justice', *Philosophy and Public Affairs*, 33/2: 113–47.

Nannestad, P. (2007), 'Immigration and Welfare States: A Survey of 15 Years of Research', *European Journal of Political Economy*, 23/2: 512–32.

Noël, A., and Thérien, J-P. (2002), 'Public Opinion and Global Justice', *Comparative Political Studies*, 35/6: 631–56.

Oberman, K. (2016), 'Immigration as a Human Right', in S. Fine and L. Ypi (eds.), *Migration in Political Theory* (Oxford: Oxford University Press), 32–56.

Özden, C., and Schiff, M. (eds.) (2006), *International Migration, Remittances and the Brain Drain* (Basingstoke: Palgrave Macmillan and World Bank).

Pécoud, A., and de Guchteneire, P. (2005), 'Migration without Borders: An Investigation into the Free Movement of People', Global Migration Perspectives 27, Global Commission on International Migration.

Pogge, T. (1989), *Realizing Rawls* (New York: Cornell University Press).

Pogge, T. (1997), 'Migration and Poverty', in V. Bader (ed.), *Citizenship and Exclusion* (Basingstoke: Macmillan), 12–27.

Pogge, T. (2002), *World Poverty and Human Rights* (Cambridge: Polity).

Putnam, R.D. (2007), '*E Pluribus Unum*: Diversity and Community in the Twenty-first Century', *Scandinavian Political Studies*, 30/2: 137–74.

Rawls, J. (1971), *A Theory of Justice* (Oxford: Oxford University Press).

Rawls, J. (1999), *The Law of Peoples* (Cambridge, MA: Harvard University Press).

Rawls, J. (2001), *Justice as Fairness: A Restatement*, ed. E.I. Kelly (Cambridge, MA: Harvard University Press).

Raz, J. (1986), *The Morality of Freedom* (Oxford: Clarendon Press).

Sen, A. (1980), 'Equality of What?', in S. McMurrin (ed.), *Tanner Lectures on Human Values* (Cambridge: Cambridge University Press), 197–220.

Stark, O. (2004), 'Rethinking the Brain Drain', *World Development*, 32/1: 15–22.

Storsletten K. (2003), 'Fiscal Implications of Immigration: A Net Present Value Calculation', *Scandinavian Journal of Economics*, 105/3: 487–506.

Tamir, Y. (1993), *Liberal Nationalism* (Princeton: Princeton University Press).

Tan, K-C. (2012), *Justice, Institutions, and Luck* (Oxford: Oxford University Press).

Ugur, M. (2007), 'Migration without Borders: the Ethics, Economics and Governance of Free Movement', MPRA Paper No. 26007.

UNDP (2009), *Overcoming Barriers: Human Mobility and Development* (Basingstoke: Palgrave Macmillan).

UNHCR (2018), *Figures at a Glance*. http://www.unhcr.org/figures-at-a-glance.html

Wellman, C.H. (2011), 'Freedom of Association and the Right to Exclude', in C.H. Wellman and P. Cole (eds.), *Debating the Ethics of Immigration: Is There a Right to Exclude?* (Oxford: Oxford University Press), 13–155.

World Bank (2006), *Global Economic Prospects: Economic Implications of Remittances and Migration* (Washington, DC: World Bank).

World Bank (2013), Databank. http://data.worldbank.org/indicator/BX.TRF.PWKR.DT.GD.ZS

World Bank (2018), Gini Index. https://data.worldbank.org/indicator/SI.POV.GINI?locations=US

6

National Partiality, Immigration, and the Problem of Double-Jeopardy

Johann Frick

From this moment on, it's going to be America First. Every decision on trade, on taxes, on immigration, on foreign affairs, will be made to benefit American workers and American families. (…) We will seek friendship and goodwill with the nations of the world—but we do so with the understanding that it is the right of all nations to put their own interests first.

Donald Trump, Inaugural Address, January 20, 2017

1. Introduction

A foundational conviction of contemporary liberal thought is that all persons possess equal basic worth.[1] Modern moral philosophy in general takes it as axiomatic that, in the words of Thomas Nagel,

> no one is more important than anyone else. (…) [E]veryone counts the same. For a given quantity of whatever it is that's good or bad—suffering or happiness or fulfilment or frustration—its intrinsic impersonal value doesn't depend on whose it is. (Nagel 1991, 14)

In light of this professed belief that, impersonally considered, everyone's interests and well-being matter equally, it is striking that at the same

---

[1] See, among many others, Dworkin (1977, 180–3).

Johann Frick, *National Partiality, Immigration, and the Problem of Double-Jeopardy* In: *Oxford Studies in Political Philosophy Volume 6*. Edited by: David Sobel, Peter Vallentyne, and Steven Wall, Oxford University Press (2020). © Johann Frick.
DOI: 10.1093/oso/9780198852636.003.0006

time most people view their lives as governed by a host of *particularistic attachments*—to family, friends, co-religionists, etc.—all of which, according to common-sense morality, entail the permission, in many cases the duty, to care *especially* for the interests and well-being of these people.

One domain in which such partiality is particularly prominent is the sphere of collective political action. Modern states, as the primary organs of our collective self-governance, frequently pursue policies that strongly favor the interests of compatriots over those of foreigners. Though the degree of priority that states may assign their citizens is, of course, a matter of dispute, the more fundamental thought that states are permitted and often morally required to give some measure of priority to the interests of citizens over non-citizens, is rarely contested.[2] Let us call this the **Priority for Compatriots Claim**, or **PCC** for short. Being someone's "compatriot", in my sense, designates a legal condition of shared citizenship, not adherence to a shared culture or ethnicity (though these are, of course, characteristics that compatriots often have in common).

The apparent tension between the impartiality of our general moral and political convictions and the particularistic obligations suggested by common-sense moral principles like the PCC calls for a philosophical explanation. By far the most common strategy for justifying the PCC in the literature is to appeal to *associative duties*. Partiality towards our compatriots is justified and even required, it is argued, because we stand with them in special *associative relations*, which give rise to special obligations to promote their interests.[3] By contrast, we do not stand in these relations with foreigners.[4]

---

[2] Even avowedly cosmopolitan thinkers such as Thomas Pogge, while arguing that the scope of national priority is circumscribed by duties of global justice, hold that some degree of partiality towards our fellow citizens is justified. See Pogge (1998).

[3] We shall survey some suggestions from the literature in Section 4.

[4] Of course, this is not the only way in which one might argue in support of the PCC. In "What is So Special about Our Fellow Countrymen?", Robert Goodin (1988) argues that duties of partiality towards our compatriots are not the result of associative obligations. Rather, they "derive the whole of their moral force from their connections to general duties (p. 679). According to Goodin, "[s]pecial obligations [in general] are (…) merely devices whereby the moral community's general duties get assigned to particular agents (p. 678). These general duties, Goodin maintains, include a duty to ensure that everyone's interests are protected and promoted. For various empirical reasons, including the avoidance of co-ordination problems and the fact that sentiments of closeness may make fellow citizens more disposed to help each other than others (p. 682), Goodin thinks that this general moral obligation will be most

This chapter issues a challenge to such arguments. I will seek to convince you that arguments from associative obligation in support of the PCC are crucially incomplete in the absence of a justification for the restrictions that most contemporary states place on immigration. Only if we can supply an *independent* justification for existing restrictions on immigration can we then appeal to the associative relations that exist among fellow citizens to justify the PCC (or at least certain strong versions of that claim).[5]

This connection is not often drawn. Indeed, to the extent that political philosophers have made links between the PCC and the topic of immigration, they typically view the connection as running in the *reverse* direction: we are justified in restricting immigration, it is suggested, *on grounds* of legitimate partiality towards our compatriots—for example, to protect domestic workers from the competition of would-be immigrants.[6] Michael Sandel gives an admirably forthright statement of this position:

> Why should we protect our most vulnerable workers if it means denying job opportunities to people from Mexico who are even less well-off? From the standpoint of the least advantaged, a case could be

effectively fulfilled by *assigning* special responsibilities to prioritize the interests of their citizens to individual states and their officials.

Though theoretically elegant, Goodin's account seems unpromising as a defense of the PCC in the political here and now. Given the vast disparities of resources between states, Goodin's suggestion that assigning each state a duty to give priority to the interests of its own citizens is the best way of promoting everyone's interests is surely questionable. In the words of David Miller (1988, 652), why should we expect the best results to be achieved by putting "the well-off in charge of the well-off and the badly-off in charge of the badly-off"? Goodin responds that this "is not a critique of [his] model but, instead, a critique of existing international boundaries from within [his] model" (p. 685). This concession, however, robs Goodin's proposal of much of its practical relevance. What we want to know is whether states can justifiably show a measure of partiality towards their own citizens in the *given* international set-up, or something closely resembling it, not in some distant possible world in which international boundaries have been radically redrawn to equalize states' resources.

---

[5] See the following section for an elucidation of the kind of *strong* priority for compatriots thesis that, I will argue, would be invalidated by the absence of a successful justification for restrictions on immigration.

[6] This claim, of course, is also a staple of current *political* debates about immigration, in the United States and elsewhere. The epigraph from Donald Trump's Inaugural Address, with its declaration that "every decision on (...) immigration (...) will be made to benefit American workers and American families", is remarkable only in the bluntness with which it expresses the view that special duties towards compatriots are a legitimate ground for limiting immigration.

made for open immigration. And yet, even people with egalitarian sympathies hesitate to endorse it. Is there a moral basis for this reluctance? Yes, but only if you accept that we have a special obligation for the welfare of our fellow citizens by virtue of the common life and history that we share. (Sandel 2009, 232)

In a similar vein, Stephen Macedo writes:

[W]e ought to take seriously the proposition that recent patterns of immigration to the United States have been bad for distributive justice. Members of political communities have special obligations of distributive justice to one another. There is a prima facie case in light of these considerations for the United States to move toward a more restrictive immigration policy, perhaps especially with respect to those low-skilled immigrants who compete with the poorest Americans for jobs. John Rawls, meet Lou Dobbs. (Macedo 2011, 320)

I will argue that, given the present state of play in political philosophy, such arguments put the cart before the horse.[7] If I am right, then—on pain of circularity—restrictions on immigration cannot *in the first instance* be justified by requirements of national partiality that derive from associative relationships among compatriots. This is because, in order to work, such associative arguments must *presuppose* that existing policies restricting immigration are morally permissible. However, it remains hotly contested among political philosophers whether states (in particular *affluent* states) are morally justified in restricting immigration, and if so, to what extent and by what criteria.[8] In the absence of a resolution to this debate, any defense of the PCC from associative duties remains at best provisional.

---

[7] Another, quite explicit, attempt to derive principled restrictions on immigration from the PCC is David Miller's argument in *National Responsibilities and Global Justice*. See Miller (2007, 223).

[8] For a powerful statement of the case for largely open borders, see Joseph Carens (1987). For an updated and expanded discussion of these issues, see Carens (2013).

2. The Effects of Acquiring an Associative Duty

Let us begin by reviewing the notion of an "associative duty". Over and above the *general duties* that we owe to everyone in virtue of their simple humanity, it is often claimed that participation in significant social groups or personal relationships may, in addition, give rise to *associative duties*, which act to strengthen our existing (positive) duties vis-à-vis members of these groups or take the form of new (positive) duties not included in the set of our general duties.[9] Thus, our (positive) associative duties go beyond our general (positive) duties, in the sense that they are either more extensive in content or more stringent, or both. There are certain kinds of *prima facie* duties that I have towards my friend that I don't have towards strangers, for instance to act as their confidant. (This is an example of my duties to associates being more extensive than my general duties.) And although I can be expected to bear some personal cost in order to provide assistance to strangers, I am required to bear *greater* costs to provide comparable assistance to my friend. (This is an example of my duties to associates being more stringent.) Thus, one effect of acquiring an associative duty towards person A is that there are now things I have a duty to do for A that I didn't previously have a general duty to do.[10]

But acquiring an associative duty towards A may also affect how I can permissibly treat *non-associates*. Besides those persons to whom the special duties are owed—what Samuel Scheffler (2001a) has called the "In Group"—there are typically other persons who fall outside the scope of our particularistic concern. Call these the "Out Group". Sometimes, these persons do so by their own choosing, but in other instances they are *excluded* from joining those special associative relationships,

---

[9] For some influential discussions of the notion of associative duty, see Waldron (1993), Brink (2001), Scheffler (2001a) and (2001b), and Kolodny (2010).

[10] All my claims about associative duties in the following are claims about *positive* associative duties. Whether associative ties can also strengthen my existing *negative* duties vis-à-vis associates or give rise to new kinds of negative duties towards associates is much more controversial. As Robert Goodin observes, in some cases, the *opposite* appears to be the case: we have certain negative duties towards non-associates that we do not have towards associates. For instance, we can deprive our compatriots of liberty by conscripting them into the army, while we are not permitted to do this to foreigners (Goodin 1988, 667–71).

membership of which would allow them, too, to lay claim to our special concern.

According to common-sense morality, positive duties to one's associates in the In Group sometimes *take precedence* over one's positive general duties vis-à-vis people in the Out Group, in cases where the two conflict.[11] As a result, having an associative duty to members of the In Group can license doing *less* for people in the Out Group than one would otherwise have been required to do by general duty. For instance, special duties towards my children may make it permissible for me to do less to fight world poverty than I would have been morally required to do, had I remained childless.

Seeing this allows us to distinguish two versions of the PCC. According to the

> **Strong PCC:** States are permitted and often morally required to give some measure of priority to the interests of citizens over non-citizens, even when doing so would mean overriding *prima facie* general duties vis-à-vis non-citizens.

By contrast, according to the

> **Weak PCC:** States are permitted and often morally required to give some measure of priority to the interests of citizens over non-citizens, but only when doing so does not lead us to override *prima facie* general duties vis-à-vis non-citizens.[12]

Correspondingly, we can distinguish two ways in which non-citizens might be affected by the existence of associative duties to our compatriots. If the Weak PCC is true, the existence of associative duties would

---

[11] In the following, I am only concerned with cases where positive duties to associates may override one's *positive prima facie* duties vis-à-vis non-associates. I will not address the question whether the existence of special duties to associates could ever make it permissible to override *negative* general duties to non-associates. I will henceforth take this qualification as read.

[12] Notice that if the Weak but not the Strong PCC is correct, associative relations with our compatriots do not give us new moral *permissions* (they do give us new *duties*). Rather, whatever duties or permissions we have to be partial towards our compatriots under the Weak PCC must be compatible with meeting all our *prima facie* general duties vis-à-vis non-citizens. By contrast, if the Strong PCC is true, associative relations with compatriots *do* generate new moral permissions, since *prima facie* general duties vis-à-vis non-citizens can sometimes be permissibly overridden by associative duties to compatriots.

lead non-citizens to be 'disadvantaged' compared to citizens, but only in a *relative* sense: the existence of associative duties makes it the case that our duties to citizens go beyond our duties vis-à-vis non-citizens. But this is not because we owe non-citizens absolutely less than we would have in the absence of associative duties to our compatriots—we just owe absolutely more to our compatriots. By contrast, if the Strong PCC is true, non-citizens would be 'disadvantaged' in an *absolute* sense. Since associative duties to our compatriots can sometimes override *prima facie* general duties to non-citizens, we may be permitted to do absolutely less for non-citizens than would have been the case, had associative duties to our compatriots not been a factor.

I believe that most people who are attracted to the PCC would embrace the Strong PCC. Consider the following case:

> *Two Natural Disasters*: A larger and a smaller natural disaster occur at the same time. The smaller natural disaster takes place at home and affects compatriots. The larger disaster takes place abroad and affects foreigners. Our state could either direct our resources to help at home or abroad (at the same low cost), but it cannot do both. Our state could save more lives by helping abroad.

Now, in the absence of special associative obligations, I take it that our state ought to have helped where it can save more lives. To see this, imagine a variation on this case in which *both* disasters happen in foreign countries. Intuitively, our state ought to help in that country where our help will save more lives, all else equal.[13] That is our *prima facie* general duty. But I believe that most people who endorse the PCC would hold that, since in *Two Natural Disasters* the lives threatened by the smaller disaster are actually those of our compatriots with whom we have various associative ties, our state may, all things considered, have a duty to help at home, where it will save fewer lives.[14] This is consistent with the Strong but not the Weak PCC.

---

[13] This, at least, is the majority view in the literature on the so-called "numbers problem" in normative ethics. For a dissenting view, see Taurek (1977). For a convincing rejoinder, see Parfit (1978).

[14] Thus, David Miller maintains that whereas our *negative* duty not to violate the human rights of foreigners is no weaker than our negative duty not to violate the human rights of compatriots, "the picture changes quite radically [when we turn to] the duty to provide resources

In this chapter, I will focus on the Strong PCC. Thus, when I say in what follows that the presence of associative duties is thought to make it permissible to "give priority" to the interests of compatriots over non-compatriots, I will have in mind situations, like *Two Natural Disasters*, where the presence of an associative duty to compatriots is thought to make it permissible to treat non-compatriots in a way that overrides a *prima facie* general duty.

3. Two Worries about the Appeal to Associative Duties

Let me distinguish two sources of resistance to associative arguments in support of the PCC.

In his paper "Families, Nations, and Strangers", Samuel Scheffler discusses an objection which, if successful, would support a general skepticism about associative duties. For Scheffler, associative duties arise out of relationships that one has reason to value non-instrumentally. On Scheffler's account, one cannot value a relationship non-instrumentally without seeing it as a source of special responsibilities. To see a relationship with another person as a source of special responsibilities means to be disposed to see that person's needs, interests, and desires as, in themselves, providing presumptively decisive reasons for action which would not have existed in absence of the relationship.[15]

But what functions as an *explanation* of associative duties at the same time gives rise to a potent worry about the notion of associative duty itself: Can there really be associative duties, this so-called "Distributive Objection" asks, given their often highly *inegalitarian* implications? Associative duties, coming on top of the intrinsic rewards that standing in valuable relationships with other members of the In Group often brings, seem to *compound* one kind of inequality with another. As Scheffler writes:

of various kinds (...). In this case most people would accept a fairly strong version of priority for compatriots: if because of potential shortages we have to choose between securing the subsistence rights of compatriots and the equivalent rights of others, we should favour our compatriots....[H]ere perhaps we should apply a weighing model, and think of partiality towards compatriots as a matter of giving their rights-claims greater (though not absolute) weight when deciding how to use scarce resources" (Miller 2005, 75).

---

[15] See Scheffler (2001a and 2001b).

> If (…) A and B have associative duties to each other, then, in addition
> to enjoying the rewards of Group membership, which C lacks, A and B
> also get the benefit of having stronger claims on each other's services
> than C has. Why should this be? Why should the fact that A and B are
> in a position to enjoy the first sort of advantage give rise to a moral
> requirement that they should also get the second, and that C, who has
> already lost out with respect to the former, should now lose out with
> respect to the latter?   (Scheffler 2001a, 57)

In what follows, I will not attempt to assess the merits of Scheffler's
Distributive Objection to associative duties.[16] Instead, I want to press a
distinct but related worry. Even supposing that Scheffler's skeptical
worry about associative duties can be overcome, is it licit to appeal to
associative duties to justify giving lesser priority to members of the Out
Group, given that we may have deliberately *excluded* these people from
becoming members of the In Group?

Let me motivate this abstract concern with a concrete illustration:
Suppose it was claimed—perhaps not very plausibly—that membership
of a certain educational institution, such as Princeton University, gave
rise to associative duties of partiality vis-à-vis other members or alumni
of this institution.

Now, it seems to me that even if this type of associative relation were
in principle apt to give rise to associative duties, partiality would in fact
be justified only if the *boundaries* of the In Group were themselves
drawn in a justifiable manner. If, for instance, membership of Princeton
University were unjustifiably restricted on the basis of race or gender
or religion (as, of course, it was for much of its history), this would
invalidate claims to permissible partiality from the get-go.

This, I take it, is part of the explanation why we find "old-boy networks"
morally odious: It isn't just that the members show partiality or favoritism
to other members on the basis of a kind of associative tie—having gone
to the same school or university—that, even in the best case, is *probably*
not apt to give rise to permissible partiality. Setting aside this first worry,
there is a second and independent source of concern: Partiality towards
fellow "old boys" is often practiced in conditions where eligibility for

---

[16] For a cogent critique of the distributive objection, see Lazar (2009).

membership of these very schools or universities was unjustly restricted in the first place, for example on the basis of race or gender or religion. But, the thought goes, if we *impermissibly* exclude a person from attending our university, then we cannot licitly appeal to the fact that she does not stand in this special associative relation with us to justify giving less weight to her interests than to those of our associates—at least not in a way that absolutely disadvantages her.[17]

I propose, then, the following minimal necessary condition that associative relationships must meet, if they are to give rise to justifiable partiality. I call it the

> **Boundary Principle:** If we are deliberately and avoidably preventing another person from becoming one of our associates (either by directly refusing to stand in the relevant associative relation with her, or by otherwise making it impossible for her to enter into the relevant associative relation with us), then we cannot appeal to the fact that she *isn't* one of our associates in order to justify giving her interests less priority (in a way that absolutely disadvantages her), unless we act *permissibly* in preventing her from becoming one of our associates.

Let us familiarize ourselves with this principle by thinking through its implications for a variety of cases.

There are two types of cases in which the Boundary Principle is trivially satisfied. The first easy case is one in which the relevant associative duties, if they exist, arise out of relational ties which are *in principle unextendable* to other people. Take, for instance, the *genetic* relation between progenitor and offspring, or the involuntary *historical* relation of having been through a shared experience of involuntary suffering, such as being interned together in a labor camp under a dictatorship. Ethnic and racial ties also belong into this category. *If* relations of these kinds are apt to give rise to associative duties—which of course will only be plausible for *some* relations in this category—there is no *separate* problem of justifying the make-up of the relevant In Group, and the fact that it does not include certain people. The Boundary Principle is trivially

---

[17] I do not mean to rule out that members of even an unjustly delimited educational institution might have various associative duties to one another whose performance does not absolutely disadvantage outsiders, for instance duties to support one another's academic work.

satisfied, since its antecedent is false. We are not *deliberately and avoidably preventing* another person from becoming one of our associates, in the relevant sense. Rather, the relevant associative relation is in principle unextendable to them.

In the second easy case, justifying the boundaries of the In Group poses no difficulty either, because membership of the In Group is open to anyone who desires it. This is true, for instance, in the case of some religions, such as Islam or Christianity. Anyone can become a Muslim by pronouncing the *Shahada* or join the community of Christians by being baptized. Since membership in the In Group is open to anyone who wants it, the Boundary Principle is again trivially satisfied.

By contrast, the types of associative relations that exist between citizens, and which are thought by some to give rise to legitimate partiality, belong to a harder class of cases. Duties of partiality towards compatriots, if they exist, do not supervene on a natural relation, but are the result of these persons occupying the legal status of citizen. Citizenship is *conferred*—typically at birth, but in some cases later in life, as in the case of naturalized immigrants. Unlike in the first easy case, the scope of the relevant In Group is fixed, not by natural or historic ties that are in principle unextendable to members of the Out Group, but by the policies of the state in question. Unlike religious communities, however, states typically exercise their ability to confer membership in the In Group with extreme discretion. At present, citizenship, or even residency, especially in the affluent societies, is denied to most foreigners who would want it.[18]

These two factors combine to make it the case that for the kinds of associative ties that exist between compatriots, the Boundary Principle gives rise to a *non-trivial* justificatory demand.

Before I say more about the associative relations between compatriots, let me pause to address a question that may be forming in your mind: There is a structural similarity between the associative relations among compatriots and the intimate associative relations among friends or

---

[18] Consider the figures for the annual U.S. Diversity Visa Lottery ("Green Card Lottery"), which allocates permanent resident visas to persons from countries with low rates of immigration to the United States—primarily developing countries: For the fiscal year 2018, this lottery received 14,692,258 qualified entries for 50,000 visas, or almost 294 applications per slot. https://travel.state.gov/content/travel/en/legal/visa-law0/visa-bulletin/2017/visa-bulletin-for-july-2017.html

spouses. In all these cases, membership of the In Group is not open to everyone who may want it, and, in addition, it is, *de facto*, left to members of the In Group to determine who is eligible for membership. Thus, it is up to me to decide who I want to be friends with or marry, and moreover, this is a power I exercise with great discretion: I am married to only one woman, and am close friends with no more than a few dozen people. And yet, we think of friendship and spousal relations as paradigmatic instances where partiality towards one's associates *is* justified. Do these cases, then, raise a challenge to the Boundary Principle?

I do not think they do. It is not that, when I appeal to the fact that I am friends with Peter but not with Paul in order to justify giving priority to the interests of Peter over Paul, I *escape* a requirement, under the Boundary Principle, to show that withholding my friendship from Paul but not from Peter is permissible. Rather, it is that such a justification is readily to hand: it is generally accepted that we have a broad *personal prerogative* to determine the make-up of our elective intimate associations, which I exercise when I decide to be friends with Peter but not with Paul. And, as a general matter, a demand to show that one's φ-ing is permissible is conclusively met by citing a valid moral prerogative to φ.[19]

---

[19] The claim that (1) S has a moral *prerogative* to φ is distinct both from the claim that (2) S has a *moral right* to φ and the claim that (3) S is *not making a moral mistake* in φ-ing. (1) and (2) are not equivalent, since having a moral right to φ does not entail that one's φ-ing is morally permissible. Rather, if S has a moral right to φ, this entails that it is typically impermissible for *third parties* to prevent S from φ-ing. We can have rights to do what is wrong. See Waldron (1981). (1) and (3) are not equivalent, since it being morally permissible for S to φ does not entail that this is the option that S has *most* moral reason to choose, or that S's *motivating* reasons for φ-ing aren't morally bad ones. Doing φ could involve what Elizabeth Harman calls a "morally permissible moral mistake". See Harman (2016).

These distinctions matter, because they help us make sense of the common intuition that even friendships among bigots can be a source of permissible partiality. Suppose that I readily form friendships or intimate relationships with members of my own ethnic or religious group, but, due to bias, I avoid intimate bonds with members of other groups. Plausibly, although I am not morally *required* to be friends or lovers with anyone in particular, nor to give everyone a "fair chance" of being my friend or lover, I am nonetheless morally criticizable for the bigoted way in which I choose my intimate associates. It is a moral mistake to discount someone as a potential friend or lover because of their ethnicity or religion. Yet, as long as such morally questionable behavior still falls under a broad personal *prerogative* to determine the make-up of my intimate associations (and isn't just protected by a right to do *wrong*), I am not behaving *impermissibly* by being friends with the people I am friends with, and not with others. Hence, even under these circumstances, there would be no objection from the Boundary Principle to giving priority to my intimates over non-associates. I thank Doug Portmore and an anonymous referee for helpful discussion of these issues.

Of course, philosophers will want to ask further questions, for instance about what *explains* the fact that we have such a personal prerogative to determine the make-up of our elective intimate associations. I don't here have the space to go very deep into this question, but a satisfying answer might appeal, *inter alia*, (a) to the costs of maintaining friendships and intimate partnerships; and (b) to conditions on the value of friendships and intimate partnerships.

Relationships take *work*. They require lots of time, and emotional and mental energy. Moreover, at least when it comes to the most intimate ones, their value is diluted when one has more tokens of the type. My relationship with my friend Peter, or my wife Ekédi, would not be quite so valuable if I had very numerous friends or multiple intimate partners. (I don't want to make this claim in too sweeping a fashion; other people, and perhaps people in other social forms, might be able to avoid this dilution.) Friendships and intimate partnerships are also less valuable when at least one party's heart isn't in it, so to speak. Put together, these facts might help explain the prerogative to choose the friendships and intimate partnerships that one wants.[20] Of course, not every instance in which I *exercise* this personal prerogative and permissibly decline to enter into an intimate association with another person need be one where taking on another relationship would be too much work or where the value of my other relationships would be diluted. In general, to claim that some set of considerations C explains why I have a prerogative to perform actions of type X is not to claim that every instance in which I exercise my prerogative and permissibly perform a token of type X is one in which considerations C apply.[21]

What is more important for my argument than these cursory attempts to *explain* the personal prerogative in question is the fact that few

---

[20] I am indebted to Adam Kern for helpful discussions of these points.

[21] Compare: according to interest theories of rights, the function of a right is to further the right-holder's interests. (The *locus classicus* is Raz (1986)). Thus, a promisee has a claim-right in the performance of the promised action because, in general, promisees have an interest in the performance of the promise which is a sufficient reason for holding the promisor to be under a duty to perform the promised action. But this is not to say that every instance in which a promisee asserts her right to the performance of the promise is one where the promised action furthers the right-holder's interests. I can have a right that you keep your promise to return my borrowed bicycle *tonight* rather than tomorrow, even though I won't need the bicycle until next week and, in fact, it is less convenient for me to receive the bicycle tonight rather than tomorrow.

philosophers deny that we do indeed *possess* such a prerogative, whatever its exact explanation may be.[22] Hence, relationships between friends
and spouses are not counter-examples to the Boundary Principle, but
rather cases where it is not *trivially* but nonetheless *uncontroversially*
satisfied.

Let us return now to the main line of the argument.

4. The Argument from the Boundary Principle and the Problem of Double-Jeopardy

If the Boundary Principle is correct, it follows that in order to justify the
PCC by giving an associative argument, we must not only identify a feature of the relationship between compatriots that might ground an associative duty. In addition, we must also explain why outsiders are
permissibly excluded from entering those relationships which give rise
to associative obligations between compatriots. The argument for this
could be stated as follows:

Argument from the Boundary Principle

(1) If we are deliberately and avoidably preventing another person
    from becoming one of our associates (either by directly refusing
    to stand in the relevant associative relation with her, or by other-
    wise making it impossible for her to enter into the relevant asso-
    ciative relation with us), then we cannot appeal to the fact that
    she *isn't* one of our associates in order to justify giving her inter-
    ests less priority (in a way that absolutely disadvantages her),
    unless we act *permissibly* in preventing her from becoming one of
    our associates.

---

[22] For an interesting dissenting view, see Brownlee (2015). Brownlee contends that at least
in certain cases, where a person's 'fundamental associative needs' cannot be met by others, we
have a duty to associate with her, for example by being friends. Hence, our permission not to
associate with others is at most conditional. While I do not have the space to discuss Brownlee's
argument, suffice it to say that if Brownlee is correct, this would in no way undermine the case
for the Boundary Principle; rather, it would give it more bite, in the case of intimate relationships. Far from showing that we *escape* a justificatory demand when it comes to partiality
towards our intimates, Brownlee's view suggests that this demand may be less easy to satisfy
than most philosophers assume. I thank Kimberley Brownlee and Laura Valentini for a helpful
discussion of this issue.

(2) We are deliberately and avoidably preventing many would-be immigrants from settling in our country and becoming our fellow citizens.

(3) By preventing would-be immigrants from settling in our country and becoming our fellow citizens, we make it impossible for them to enter into the relevant associative relations with us.

Therefore, we cannot appeal to the fact that would-be immigrants do not stand in the relevant associative relations with us to justify giving their interests less priority *unless* it is permissible for us to prevent them from settling in our country and becoming our fellow citizens.

However, as we shall now see, most attempted justifications of the PCC from associative duties in the literature do not meet this justificatory demand, and hence cannot provide a complete justification of the PCC.

Let us consider two representative examples from the literature. They stand in for many other discussions with a similar structure.

A common strategy for justifying the PCC starts from the assumption that states are, essentially, cooperative social enterprises for mutual advantage. Our membership in these joint cooperative ventures, in the words of Charles Taylor, is a means "to obtain benefits through common action that [we] could not secure individually" (Taylor 1989, 16). The most prominent modern proponent of this conception of the state is, of course, John Rawls (1971). In this chapter, however, I shall focus on an article by Richard Dagger (1985).

In "Rights, Boundaries, and the Bonds of Community", Dagger develops an account of our special obligations towards compatriots as grounded in the principle of fair play. Participating as equals in such cooperative enterprises for mutual advantage, which typically include welfare provisions, such as health insurance and unemployment benefits, gives us reciprocal duties to accept the burdens that maintaining these social institutions and caring for needy compatriots places on us. If we refused to take the burdens of cooperation with the benefits, we would be treating our co-nationals "merely as means not as ends", and would thereby violate their right to autonomy. Given that like relations of cooperation do not exist between us and non-nationals, Dagger argues, we are justified in assigning considerably lower priority to their interests.

This strategy for justifying the PCC faces some well-known objections. Thus, as Robert Goodin (1988) and Andrew Mason (1997) point out, if the PCC is grounded in a duty of fair play, this fails to explain why special duties of partiality are not equally owed to resident aliens who contribute to the cooperative social enterprise of their host-nations. On the other hand, we should give little if any special weight to promoting the well-being of co-nationals permanently living abroad, or to those fellow citizens who have not been able to significantly contribute to the social product of our country, for instance due to a severe congenital handicap.

The Argument from the Boundary Principle raises a different worry about Dagger's argument: Modern states severely limit the scope of economic migration, and thereby *prevent* many would-be contributors to the collective enterprises of our affluent societies from ever entering into relations of reciprocal cooperation with us that would give rise to special duties of partiality on our part. Not only are potential immigrants excluded from the benefits that participation in these schemes would *itself* confer on them.[23] In addition, the fact that we so exclude them is indirectly regarded as justifying us in assigning significantly lesser weight to their interest in the formulation of state policy. But, in the absence of a valid moral justification for our restrictive immigration policies, this would be implausible.[24]

A similar problem besets Andrew Mason's civic republican case for national partiality in "Special Obligations to Compatriots". Mason's argument draws inspiration from Joseph Raz's (1989) account of why friendship justifies special obligations. Raz makes three main claims: (1)

---

[23] Stephen Macedo cites work by the economist Mark Rosenzweig, which estimates that Mexican high school graduates can, by leaving Mexico and finding a job in the United States, increase their income sevenfold; Mexican college graduates can increase their income ninefold (Macedo 2011, 317). For less developed countries than Mexico, this figure must be higher still.

Moreover, the consequences of exclusion are not only felt by those who are excluded. It is estimated that worldwide about 200 million migrants help to support about 800 million family members in their home countries through regular remittances from their wages. The amount of money involved is more than the total amount of bi- and multi-lateral foreign aid. Hence, excluding one person from entry into the labor market of a developed country excludes several from the benefits of participation in the labor market. For more data, see World Bank Group, *Migration and Development Brief 27* (April 2017). My thanks to Chuck Beitz for discussion of these issues.

[24] For a broadly similar critique of Dagger's argument, albeit one that does not explicitly articulate the Boundary Principle, see Abizadeh (2016).

friendship is an intrinsically valuable relationship, that is, it is properly valued for its own sake; (2) part of what it is for two people to be friends is for each to be under certain obligations to the other, and these obligations are justified by the moral good of friendship; (3) these special obligations are internally related to the good of friendship, that is, they are part of that good.

Mason suggests that the most promising argument in support of special obligations among compatriots takes an analogous form:

> Citizenship has intrinsic value because in virtue of being a citizen a person is a member of a collective body in which they enjoy equal status with its other members and are thereby provided with recognition. This collective body exercises significant control over its members' conditions of existence (a degree of control which none of its members individually possesses). It offers them the opportunity to contribute to the cultural environment in which its laws and policies are determined, and opportunities to participate directly and indirectly in the formation of these laws and policies. Part of what it is to be a citizen is to incur special obligations: these obligations give content to what it is to be committed or loyal to fellow citizens and are justified by the good of the wider relationship to which they contribute. In particular, citizens have an obligation to each other to participate fully in public life and an obligation to give priority to the needs of fellow citizens. A good citizen is, in part, someone who complies with these various obligations and responsibilities, and in doing so realizes the good of citizenship.   (Mason 1997, 442)

Like Dagger's argument from fair play, Mason's civic republican argument for partiality fails to account for the Boundary Principle. According to Mason, the normative basis for giving priority to the interests of our compatriots is simply that we stand with them in a valuable relationship—that of shared citizenship—which constitutively entails certain special obligations towards them. Vis-à-vis foreigners, we lack this relationship. But, of course, it is true of many foreigners that the only reason why they don't stand with us in this valuable relationship is precisely that we are deliberately *preventing* them from doing so, by stopping them from immigrating to our country and becoming our fellow citizens. Surely, some independent argument is needed to justify *this* fact in order for Mason's argument to get off the ground.

The general problem that Dagger's and Mason's arguments have in common is one that infects many other associative arguments for the PCC.[25] It is this: All these arguments take the boundaries of citizenship as *given*, and then seek to derive an account of the PCC from certain features of the relationship among fellow citizens. What this overlooks, as we have seen, is the fact that most modern states severely limit the scope of migration, and thereby *prevent* many would-be immigrants from ever entering into the relevant associative relations that would give rise to associative duties on our part. Not only are would-be immigrants excluded from the benefits that settling in our country would itself confer on them. In addition, the fact that we so exclude them, and thus prevent them from standing in the relevant associative relations with us, is regarded as justifying us in giving significantly less weight to their interests.

However, in the absence of a moral *justification* for placing restrictions on migration, this inference is implausible. To see this, suppose there was no adequate justification for the ways in which we limit migration. In attempting to justify the priority we give to the interests of compatriots, we would, in effect, be saying to would-be immigrants: "Given that we are *impermissibly excluding* you from entering into certain valuable relationships with us, we are justified in giving less weight to your interests, in a way that absolutely disadvantages you, *because* you do not stand in these relationships with us." This, I believe, is a justification that they could reasonably reject. By adding partiality to impermissible exclusion, we would simply be compounding one injustice by another. Call this the *Double-Jeopardy Problem* for the PCC.

The Double-Jeopardy Problem should be distinguished from a superficially similar argument presented by Javier Hidalgo (2013) in "Associative Duties and Immigration". Like Scheffler, Hidalgo believes that associative duties arise only from relationships that are intrinsically valuable. In addition, however, Hidalgo maintains that only relationships that do not reliably cause injustice to outsiders can be intrinsically

---

[25] See, for instance, Nathanson (1989), Simmons (1996), Miller (2005), and Seglow (2010).

valuable. By contrast, if a special relationship systematically involves injustice to outsiders, then we have no reason to value this relationship, and hence it necessarily fails to ground any associative duties. Hidalgo then suggests that the relationship between compatriots may be just such a relationship, given the way in which restrictions on immigration limit membership in the In Group of compatriots: "Immigration restrictions may in general be impermissible. The explanation is that immigration restrictions impinge on important liberties and our reasons to refrain from interfering with these liberties defeat the reasons in favor of these restrictions"(Hidalgo 2013, 719).

One obvious difference between Hidalgo's argument and my own is that since Hidalgo affirms that existing restrictions on immigration are unjust, in virtue of impinging on the liberties of would-be immigrants, his conclusion is an *unconditional* one: the relations between compatriots cannot give rise to justified partiality. By contrast, the conclusion of the Argument from the Boundary Principle has a *conditional* form: *if* existing restrictions on immigration are impermissible, then the associative relations among compatriots could not support the Strong PCC.

Beyond this, Hidalgo's argument strikes me as too procrustean, for two reasons. First, it relies on the axiological premise that a relationship which involves systematic injustice to outsiders (e.g. by involving morally indefensible restrictions on membership) must for that reason be devoid of intrinsic value. This seems too strong. For instance, even at a time when women and religious and ethnic minorities were unjustifiably excluded from Princeton University, I believe that the relationships within the community of scholars and students at Princeton possessed some intrinsic value. It was something they had non-instrumental reason to value as such (though, all else equal, they would of course have had stronger reasons to value a relationship not marred by this kind of injustice). The same may be true, on an account like Mason's, of the relationships of equal citizenship among citizens in a democratic polity, even if we assume that membership in their political community is unjustly closed off to outsiders.

Second, Hidalgo's account suggests that *all* associative duties among citizens are lost, if their relationship involves systematic injustice to outsiders, for example by operating a morally indefensible immigration policy. This, again, seems false. There is no reason to assume that associative duties which do not absolutely disadvantage outsiders need lose their force, just because the boundaries of their political community are unjustly drawn. With regard to such associative duties, there is no problem of *double*-jeopardy. Although some would-be members of our community are impermissibly excluded, it is not the case that, as a result, we do less for them than we are required to by general duty.

The Argument from the Boundary Principle avoids both these shortcomings. The argument does not rely on the axiological claim that, if a state unjustly excludes would-be immigrants from citizenship, the relations between citizens necessarily lose all intrinsic value. Rather, the Boundary Principle makes a purely *deontic* claim: it is a necessary condition on us having justified partiality towards our compatriots, in a way that absolutely disadvantages foreigners, that foreigners not be unjustly excluded from citizenship. If this necessary condition is not satisfied, then *even if* the associative relations between compatriots possess intrinsic value, they do not give rise to legitimate partiality in the strong sense.

Second, my argument is compatible with the claim that citizens may have some associative duties to one another even if the boundaries of their political community are not justly drawn. The Boundary Principle makes a more limited claim: if some foreigners are being unjustly excluded from citizenship, then we may not be partial towards our citizens in a way that *absolutely* disadvantages these foreigners, by overriding a *prima facie* general duty. But this is consistent with us having other associative duties towards our compatriots that we lack vis-à-vis foreigners. A failure to satisfy the Boundary Principles rules out *strong*, but not *weak*, priority for compatriots.

What types of policies weak priority for compatriots might license in practice will depend both on the correct substantive theory of states' general duties to non-citizens and the correct substantive theory of states' associative duties to citizens. In general we can say: the more extensive and stringent a states' general duties towards non-citizens, the less room this will leave for associative duties towards citizens under the Weak PCC, since fulfilling these duties is more likely to *conflict* with fulfilling our demanding general duties. Suppose, for instance, that the correct account of our general duties was a Singerian account, on which we have extensive and stringent general duties of beneficence towards non-compatriots.[26] If the Weak PCC is true, then such a demanding view of our general duties would leave little room for associative duties towards compatriots, since acting on our associative duties would often mean doing less for non-compatriots than we owe them as a matter of general duty. Likewise, if we had extensive and stringent duties of *cosmopolitan justice* vis-à-vis foreigners.[27]

By contrast, if our general duties towards non-compatriots are relatively undemanding (for instance: very basic duties of humanitarian assistance, but no more), then it will often be possible for states to fully meet their general duties towards foreigners and, in addition, to comply with quite robust associative duties towards compatriots. [28]

5. Two Kinds of Double-Jeopardy Argument

I have labeled my worry about associative arguments for the PCC the problem of "Double-Jeopardy". This is not so much a reference to the legal doctrine prohibiting double trial and double conviction as a nod to a famous argument in bioethics with a structure similar to my own: John Harris's (1987) "Double-Jeopardy Objection" to the use of so-called QALY (or "Quality-Adjusted Life-Year") maximization in bioethics and health economics in Harris (1987). Since I believe Harris's argument to be subject to forceful objections, it will be instructive to compare and contrast our two Double-Jeopardy arguments, to see how they differ.

QALY maximization (or some variant thereof) is a widely-employed method for the allocation of scarce health resources. The basic idea behind QALY maximization is that, in deciding who should receive a scarce health resource (such as an organ transplant or an expensive

---

[26] See Singer (1972) and Singer (2009).   [27] See, for instance, Beitz (1979).
[28] An example of this type of view may be Thomas Nagel's (2005) position in "The Problem of Global Justice". In that paper, Nagel defends an anti-cosmopolitan "political conception" of justice, according to which robust demands of distributive justice arise only among citizens of the same state, and have their source in features of their political association—in particular, the fact that the state organizes coercive authority over its citizens (in a way that claims their active cooperation). By contrast, according to Nagel, our *general* positive duties to foreigners are limited to "humanitarian" duties to assist foreigners threatened with starvation or death. However, lest his view violate the Boundary Principle, Nagel would have to maintain that, if the boundaries of our state are unjustly drawn then, if our political duties of justice vis-à-vis compatriots were ever to conflict with our general duties towards foreigners, the latter would have to take precedence.

medical procedure) or which of two medical programs we should finance, it is not enough to attend only to how many lives will be saved through either option, or even to how many *life-years* will be preserved. Both these measures ignore an important factor: *quality* of life. The QALY is a measure of the effectiveness of health interventions that takes into account both *length* of life and *quality* of life. A year of completely healthy life is assigned the numerical value 1. A year of life at *less* than full health is assigned a value between 1 and 0. The size of the discount factor depends on the severity of the health problem (e.g. a year as a paraplegic might be assigned a score of 0.5). QALY *maximization* is the consequentialist notion that, for a given input of money or resources, we ought to select that medical intervention which maximizes the number of quality-adjusted life-years that are lived.

Harris points out that QALY maximization renders intuitively troubling verdicts in cases like the following:

> *Choice of Life-Extension*: Hannah and Sally are two 55-year-old patients who have both contracted a deadly virus. Either patient will die within days unless she receives a dose of some scarce drug. Unfortunately, we have only one dose of the drug. Whoever receives the drug will be expected to live another twenty years. There is only one difference between the patients: Hannah has a congenital spinal problem which forces her to use a wheel-chair. Assume that an additional year of life for Hannah would have a QALY score of 0.8. By contrast, other than having contracted the virus, Sally is completely healthy. An additional year of life would for Sally would have a QALY score of 1.

The problem with QALY maximization, Harris points out, is that in cases involving life-extending treatment, the use of QALYs produces a systematic 'bias' against the disabled and sick. Fewer QALYs will be produced by extending their lives than by extending the lives of the otherwise fully healthy, all else equal. (In the present case, Hannah will receive only 16 QALYs to Sally's 20). So QALY maximization recommends against giving them the life-extending treatment.

But this, Harris argues, is unfair. It imposes on the sick and disabled a form of "double-jeopardy":

QALYs dictate that because an individual is unfortunate, because she has once become a victim of disaster, we are required to visit upon her a second and perhaps graver misfortune. The first disaster leaves her with a poor quality of life and QALYs then require that in virtue of this she be ruled out as a candidate for life-saving treatment (…). Her first disaster leaves her with a poor quality of life and when she presents herself for help, along come QALYs and finish her off!   (Harris 1987, 120)

Harris's objection and my own Double-Jeopardy Problem have the following structure in common: Both concern cases where some agent *A* seeks to appeal to a fact *p*, the obtaining of which is *independently* a set-back to the interests of some subject *S*, in order to justify treating *S* in a way that *further* disadvantages *S* in an absolute sense. In Harris's case, the relevant fact *p* is that the patient in question enjoys a lower quality of life due to her congenital disability; in the context of associative arguments for the PCC, it is the fact that a would-be immigrant does not stand in the same, independently valuable, relationships with us as do our compatriots.

These surface similarities notwithstanding, there is an important difference between the two cases: The fact *p* that the QALY maximizing agent appeals to is true *independently* of this agent. That Sally suffers from a congenital disability which gives her a lower quality of life is in no way owed to the behavior of the deliberating agent. By contrast, in the context of national partiality, the relevant fact *p* (that *S*, a would-be immigrant, does not stand in the relevant associative relations with us) is a fact that the relevant agent—our state—*makes* true through its choice of immigration policy. I believe that this empirical difference makes for an important moral disanalogy between the two cases.

Harris's Double-Jeopardy Objection to QALY maximization seems to implicitly appeal to what Frances Kamm has called the

Non-Linkage Principle: "The fact that some undeserved bad thing has happened to you [ought] not make it more likely that another bad thing will happen"   (Kamm 2004, 240).[29]

---

[29] For further discussion, see also Kamm (2013).

However, despite its *prima facie* attractiveness, this principle does not in fact appear to be valid, as Kamm herself points out. Suppose we must choose whether to give a life-saving heart transplant to a quadriplegic or a non-disabled person. The non-disabled person is expected to live for another twenty years, whereas the quadriplegic, because she is unable to exercise, is unlikely to survive for more than eighteen months with the transplanted heart.[30] Surely, *pace* the Non-Linkage Principle, it is *not* wrong to appeal to the fact that some undeserved bad thing (quadriplegia) has happened to a person as a ground for imposing on them a further disadvantage (not receiving the heart transplant), given how the fact that the patient is quadriplegic will affect her ability to benefit from the heart transplant. But, if this is true, it appears to undermine the central normative principle underpinning Harris's Double-Jeopardy Objection to QALY maximization.[31]

My own Double-Jeopardy Worry does not rely on the flawed Non-Linkage Principle. According to my argument, if the exclusion of would-be immigrants is morally permissible, then we *could* appeal to the fact that foreigners do not stand in the relevant associate relations with us to justify giving their interests lesser priority. This would be true *even though* the fact of their exclusion would constitute an *undeserved* disadvantage. (That we are permitted to exclude them, after all, does not mean that they *deserve* to be excluded.)

My argument relies not on the simple "anti-compounding" idea of the Non-Linkage Principle, but instead on the Boundary Principle from Section 3. What this principle picks up on is not just the fact that foreigners do not stand in the relevant associative relations with us, but moreover that this fact is *of our own making*, indeed the deliberate result of our state's immigration policies. That we ourselves *cause* this fact to obtain, I argued, places us under a justificatory demand, which we fail to satisfy if our state's immigration policies are morally impermissible.

Consider the following analogy from distributive desert: A father has a policy of giving his children pocket-money for little extra tasks they perform around the house. However, although all his three children are

---

[30] The case is Kamm's.
[31] This is not to say that QALY maximization isn't subject to other, more successful objections. These are explored with great subtlety by Frances Kamm in the two articles cited above.

eager, the available tasks are always assigned to the same favorite child, who as a result has lots of pocket-money while his siblings have none. When challenged about the resulting inequalities among his children, it would be preposterous for the father to reply that the other two children "just aren't doing anything to deserve pocket-money". This, after all, is a fact which the father himself deliberately and avoidably *causes to obtain* (by only giving opportunities to earn pocket money to his favorite child) and which he therefore can be called on to justify. But, of course, the father has no good justification for his behavior—his blatant favoritism is morally wrong.

I maintain that the fundamental normative idea underlying both this example and the Boundary Principle is captured the following principle:

> **Cohen's Principle:** If an agent is making it the case that some fact p obtains by deliberately and avoidably doing φ, then she cannot appeal to p to justify performing some other action ψ, unless she is morally *permitted* to do φ.[32]

Elsewhere, I argue that Cohen's Principle is a corollary of a plausible account of interpersonal justification, according to which A succeeds in justifying to B her action(s) X in circumstances c just in case B cannot make a successful normative "counter-proposal" concerning how A should act in c.[33] By a successful normative counter-proposal, I mean a proposed course of action for A in c, whereby (i) A does not do X, but instead performs some other action(s) Y and (ii) doing Y is a more plausible answer to the question "How ought A to act in c?" than doing X.

In the class of cases to which Cohen's Principle applies, A's actions in c consist in doing φ (thereby making it the case that p obtains) and doing ψ. A can successfully justify her actions to B just in case B cannot make a successful normative counter-proposal concerning A's actions in c. But if A is not morally permitted to do φ in c, then we know that B must be able to offer a successful normative counter-proposal. For, given that doing φ is impermissible in c, there must be a more plausible answer to

---

[32] The principle is named in honor of G.A. Cohen, who was the first to explore principles of this general kind. See Cohen (1991) and Cohen (2008), ch. 1.

[33] See Frick (2016), especially sections 5 and 6.

the question "How ought *A* to act in *c*?" than a course of action that involves *A* doing φ (and ψ).[34] Hence, if doing φ is impermissible, the fact that *A* does φ (and thereby makes *p* true) can play no role in justifying *A*'s doing ψ; for we already know that any course of action that involves *A* doing φ is subject to a successful normative counter-proposal. This gives us Cohen's Principle.

The Boundary Principle, in turn, is a straightforward corollary of Cohen's Principle: In the Boundary Principle, the fact *p* is the fact that non-citizens do not stand with us in the relevant associative relationships. The act φ which makes *p* obtain is the state's deliberate and avoidable act of excluding would-be immigrants from coming to our country and becoming our compatriots. And the act ψ, which according to associative arguments for national partiality is justified by *p*, is the act of giving priority to the interests of our compatriots, even in a way that disadvantages non-citizens in an absolute sense.[35]

---

[34] I am assuming that there are no moral dilemmas, that is, situations where all courses of action available to *A* are morally impermissible. For an argument in support of this assumption, see my "Dilemmas, Luck, and the Two Faces of Morality" (ms).

[35] Note that the antecedent of Cohen's Principle (as well as that of the Boundary Principle, which it underpins) is stated in the present progressive tense. As Kimberley Brownlee's contribution to this volume makes clear, there are cases where having acted wrongly *in the past* can give an agent moral permissions in the present which she otherwise would have lacked. See Brownlee (2020). Cohen's Principle does not exclude this possibility. What it rules out is that an agent, seeking to justify some action of hers, can appeal to a fact *p* which is made to obtain by her deliberate and avoidable wrongdoing *in the present*. Likewise, the Boundary Principle is violated if the state gives less priority to the interests of would-be immigrants on the basis of some fact *p* that obtains only because of our state's *current* immigration policies, and in addition these policies are morally wrong. For Dagger and Mason the relevant facts which are thought to justify priority for compatriots are, respectively, the fact that foreigners do not participate in the cooperative enterprise for mutual advantage that is our society, or the fact that they do stand with us in the intrinsically valuable relationship of shared citizenship. For many would-be immigrants, I submit, these facts are indeed true only because of policies of immigration-restriction that our state *currently* engages in. If our immigration policies changed, many would-be immigrants would seek citizenship virtually overnight, and would become contributors to the collective enterprise of our society. So if our present immigration policies are morally indefensible, then Dagger's and Mason's arguments for partiality violate the Boundary Principle. (The same, I believe is true of the other accounts listed in note 25.)

By contrast, some writers, notably Tom Hurka (1997), claim that the relevant fact which licenses partiality towards our compatriots is the obtaining of *historical* associative ties, such as having a *history* of doing good together. However, that such *historical* relations obtain among us, but not vis-à-vis foreigners, is a function, not of our state's *present* immigration policies, but of its immigration policies in the past. Even if those policies *unjustly* excluded some would-be immigrants at the time, there is nothing we can do *now* to make it the case that a history of shared good-doing exists between us and these individuals. (The relation is "in principle unextendable", as I put it in Section 3.) Hence, arguments from *historical* associative ties, such as Hurka's, do not fall within the scope of the Argument from the Boundary Principle.

Despite their surface similarities, my Double-Jeopardy Problem thus differs in its deeper moral underpinnings from Harris's Double-Jeopardy Objection to QALY maximization. At the most fundamental level, my Argument from the Boundary Principle is grounded in Cohen's Principle, a plausible moral principle which itself is a corollary of an attractive account of interpersonal justification, not in the flawed Non-Linkage Principle that underlies Harris's argument. My argument therefore does not suffer from the problems that beset Harris's argument.

6. Responding to the Problem of Double-Jeopardy: Justifying Limits on Immigration

If the Argument from the Boundary Principle is sound, then much of the published literature on the PCC is flawed. It is flawed insofar as it presupposes that we can provide a *free-standing* defense of the PCC, based only on the associative relations in which we stand to our fellow citizens. This, I have argued, is not the case. Lest we confront the Double-Jeopardy Problem, we must *first* be able to give a principled moral justification for the restrictions that virtually all contemporary states place on immigration. Moreover, on pain of circularity, this justification cannot *itself* appeal to the idea of permissible partiality to compatriots.

This is not to maintain that the PCC can play no role in justifying limitations on immigration. Suppose it could be shown, on *independent* grounds, that the state has a right to exclude would-be immigrants from becoming members of our political community. We could *then*, in a second step, appeal to the associative relations that exist among the members of our *justly delimited* political community to vindicate the PCC. And the PCC, in turn, could then give us *further* reasons to limit immigration, for example reasons of the kind sketched by Sandel and Macedo in the passages quoted at the outset of this chapter. By contrast, in the absence of a free-standing defense of the right to exclude, appealing to the PCC to justify restrictions on immigration would be to put the cart before the horse.

What would such a free-standing defense of existing immigration restrictions involve? First and foremost, it would have to successfully rebut the powerful case mounted in recent years by cosmopolitan and libertarian political philosophers to the effect that justice requires largely open borders.[36] Even successfully clearing that hurdle, however, would not ensure that the Problem of Double-Jeopardy is avoided. Showing that some restrictions on immigration are permissible in principle does not entail that the *extent* of such restrictions in practice, or the particular *criteria* for exclusion, are also permissible.[37] So a fuller response to the Problem of Double-Jeopardy would in addition have to investigate, in a more fine-grained fashion, the various actual policies of immigration restriction practiced by contemporary states.

Of course, political philosophers have risen to this challenge, and recent years have seen a wealth of sophisticated and credible defenses of some form of 'right to exclude'.[38] Assessing which side has the better of this debate is beyond the scope of the present chapter. However, given the quality of interventions on *both* sides, the question whether existing practices of immigration, or something resembling them, can be morally justified certainly strikes me as one on which reasonable people can disagree for the time being. Unlike the claim that we have a personal prerogative to determine the make-up of our *intimate* associations, which is rarely challenged, we are still quite far from a reasonable consensus on the question of immigration.

7. Conclusion

The upshot of my discussion is not that a defense of national partiality in terms of associative obligations cannot succeed. I do not deny that *if* we can give an independent justification for the way in which existing limits on immigration restrict eligibility for membership in the In

---

[36] See Joseph Carens (1987) and (2013). See also Huemer (2010), Caplan and Naik (2015), Oberman (2016), and Hidalgo (2017). For an argument from democratic theory against a state's right to unilaterally exclude outsiders, see Abizadeh (2008).

[37] Indeed, even supposing that a state was permitted to exclude *all* would-be immigrants— that is, to have a policy of entirely closed borders—this would not imply that all grounds for *less comprehensive* practices of exclusion would *ipso facto* be permissible. There could be *conditional* obligations restricting the grounds on which a state may permissibly choose among would-be immigrants, *if* it decides to allow any immigration, for example, not to discriminate on the basis of race or ethnicity or religion, or, more controversially, on the basis of education or professional qualifications. Thus even the permissibility of entirely closed borders would not entail the permissibility of full discretionary control over immigration.

[38] Some of the most important contributions to this literature include Walzer (1983), Wellman (2008), Pevnick (2011), Blake (2013), Miller (2016), and Stilz (forthcoming).

Group, we might *then* appeal to associative accounts like Dagger's or Mason's to ground the Strong PCC. What I have argued is that a successful defense of national partiality in these terms is more closely tied to issues concerning the ethics of immigration than most political philosophers have hitherto acknowledged. An associationist defense of the Strong PCC cannot be free-standing. Rather, it depends for its success on questions concerning the state's right to exclude that must, for the time being, be considered unresolved.[39]

Works Cited

Abizadeh, Arash. (2008) "Democratic Theory and Border Coercion: No Right to Unilaterally Control Your Own Borders", *Political Theory* Vol. 36, No. 1, pp. 37–65.

Abizadeh, Arash. (2016) "The Special Obligations Challenge to More Open Borders" in Sarah Fine and Lea Ypi (eds.) *Migration in Political Theory: The Ethics of Movement and Membership* (Oxford: Oxford University Press).

Beitz, Charles. (1979) *Political Theory and International Relations* (Princeton: Princeton University Press).

Blake, Michael. (2013) "Immigration, Jurisdiction, and Exclusion", *Philosophy & Public Affairs* Vol. 41, No. 2, pp. 103–30.

Brink, David. (2001) "Impartiality and Associative Duties", *Utilitas* Vol. 13, No. 2, pp. 152–72.

Brownlee, Kimberley. (2015) "Freedom of Association: It's Not What You Think", *Oxford Journal of Legal Studies* Vol. 35, No. 2, pp. 267–82.

Brownlee, Kimberley. (2020) "Getting Rights out of Wrongs" in David Sobel, Peter Vallentyne, and Steven Wall (eds.) *Oxford Studies in Political Philosophy*, Volume 6 (Oxford: Oxford University Press).

[39] For helpful comments and feedback, I thank Sara Amighetti, Arthur Applbaum, Ralf Bader, Eric Beerbohm, Chuck Beitz, Selim Berker, Mitch Berman, Luc Bovens, Kimberley Brownlee, Tom Dougherty, David Estlund, Maddalena Ferranna, Aart van Gils, Elizabeth Harman, Grace Helton, Louis-Philippe Hodgson, Desmond Jagmohan, Mark Johnston, Frances Kamm, Adam Kern, Melissa Lane, Harvey Lederman, Christian List, Steve Macedo, Michal Masny, Ekédi Mpondo-Dika, Oded Na'aman, Eric Nelson, Laura Ong, Valeria Ottonelli, Japa Pallikkathayil, Alan Patten, Doug Portmore, Theron Pummer, Lucia Rafanelli, Joseph Raz, Mathias Risse, James Rosenberg, Tim Scanlon, Amy Sepinwall, David Sobel, Lucas Stanczyk, Zofia Stemplowska, Annie Stilz, Patrick Tomlin, Laura Valentini, Peter Vallentyne, Alec Walen, and Steve Wall, as well as audiences at Princeton University, Harvard University, Columbia University, and the Oxford Studies in Political Philosophy Conference in Pavia. I also thank two anonymous referees for Oxford Studies in Political Philosophy.

Caplan, Bryan and Vipul Naik. (2015) "A Radical Case for Open Borders" in Benjamin Powell (ed.) *The Economics of Immigration* (New York: Oxford University Press).

Carens, Joseph. (1987) "Aliens and Citizens: The Case for Open Borders", *Review of Politics* Vol. 49, No. 2, pp. 251–73.

Carens, Joseph. (2013) *The Ethics of Immigration* (New York: Oxford University Press).

Cohen, G.A. (1991) "Incentives, Inequality, and Community", Tanner Lectures in Human Values, delivered at Stanford University.

Cohen, G.A. (2008) *Rescuing Justice and Equality* (Cambridge, MA: Harvard University Press).

Dagger, Richard. (1985) "Rights, Boundaries, and the Bonds of Community: A Qualified Defense of Moral Parochialism", *The American Political Science Review* Vol. 79, No. 2, pp. 436–47.

Dworkin, Ronald. (1977) *Taking Rights Seriously* (London: Duckworth).

Frick, Johann. (2016) "What We Owe to Hypocrites: Contractualism and the Speaker-Relativity of Justification", *Philosophy & Public Affairs* Vol. 44, No. 4, pp. 223–65.

Frick, Johann. (ms) "Dilemmas, Luck, and the Two Faces of Morality".

Goodin, Robert. (1988) "What is So Special about Our Fellow Countrymen?", *Ethics* Vol. 98, No. 4, pp. 663–86.

Harman, Elizabeth. (2016) "Morally Permissible Moral Mistakes", *Ethics* Vol. 126, No. 2, pp. 366–93.

Harris, John. (1987) "QALYfying the value of life", *Journal of Medical Ethics* Vol. 13, No. 3, pp. 117–23.

Hidalgo, Javier. (2013) "Associative Duties and Immigration", *Journal of Moral Philosophy* Vol. 10, No. 6, pp. 697–722.

Hidalgo, Javier. (2017) "The Libertarian Case for Open Borders" in Jason Brennan, David Schmidtz, and Bas van der Vossen (eds.) *The Routledge Handbook of Libertarianism* (London: Routledge).

Huemer, Michael. (2010) "Is There a Right to Immigrate?", *Social Theory and Practice* Vol. 36, No. 3, pp. 429–61.

Hurka, Thomas. (1997) "The Justification of National Partiality" in McKim and McMahan (eds.) *The Morality of Nationalism* (Oxford: Oxford University Press).

Kamm, Frances. (2004) "Deciding Whom to Help, Health-Adjusted Life Years and Disabilities" in S. Anand, F. Peter, and A. Sen (eds.) *Public Health, Ethics, and Equity* (Oxford: Oxford University Press).

Kamm, Frances. (2013) "Aggregation, Allocating Scarce Resources, and the Disabled", *Bioethical Prescriptions: To Create, End, Choose, and Improve Lives* (Oxford: Oxford University Press).

Kolodny, Niko. (2010) "Which Relationships Justify Partiality? The Case of Parents and Children", *Philosophy & Public Affairs* Vol. 38, No. 1, pp. 37–75.

Lazar, Seth. (2009) "Do Associative Duties Really Not Matter?", *The Journal of Political Philosophy* Vol. 17, No. 1, pp. 90–101.

Macedo, Stephen. (2011) "When and Why Should Liberal Democracies Restrict Immigration" in Rogers M. Smith (ed.) *Citizenship, Borders, and Human Needs* (Philadelphia: University of Pennsylvania Press).

Mason, Andrew. (1997) "Special Obligations to Compatriots", *Ethics* Vol. 107, No. 3, pp. 427–47.

Miller, David. (1988) "The Ethical Significance of Nationality", *Ethics* Vol. 98, No. 4, pp. 647–62.

Miller, David. (2005) "Reasonable Partiality Towards Compatriots", *Ethical Theory and Moral Practice* Vol. 8, No. 1–2, pp. 63–81.

Miller, David. (2007) *National Responsibilities and Global Justice* (Oxford: Oxford University Press).

David Miller. (2016) *Strangers in our Midst* (Cambridge, MA: Harvard University Press).

Nagel, Thomas. (1991) *The View from Nowhere* (New York: Oxford University Press).

Nagel, Thomas. (2005) "The Problem of Global Justice", *Philosophy and Public Affairs* Vol. 33, No. 2, pp. 113–47.

Nathanson, Stephen. (1989) "In Defense of 'Moderate Patriotism'", *Ethics* Vol. 99, No. 3, pp. 535–52.

Oberman, Kieran. (2016) "Immigration as a Human Right" in Sarah Fine and Lea Ypi (eds.) *Migration in Political Theory: The Ethics of Movement and Membership* (New York: Oxford University Press).

Parfit, Derek. (1978) "Innumerate Ethics", *Philosophy & Public Affairs* Vol. 7, No. 4, pp. 285–301.

Pevnick, Ryan. (2011) *Immigration and the Constraints of Justice* (Cambridge: Cambridge University Press).

Pogge, Thomas. (1998) "The Bounds of Nationalism" in J. Couture, K. Nielsen, and M. Seymour (eds.) *Rethinking Nationalism* (Calgary: University of Calgary Press).

Raz, Joseph. (1986) *The Morality of Freedom* (Oxford: Oxford University Press).

Raz, Joseph. (1989) "Liberating Duties", *Law and Philosophy* Vol. 8, No. 1, pp. 3–21.

Sandel, Michael. (2009) *Justice: What's the Right Thing to Do?* (New York: Farrar, Straus and Giroux).

Scheffler, Samuel. (2001a) "Families, Nations, and Strangers", *Boundaries and Allegiances* (New York Oxford University Press).

Scheffler, Samuel. (2001b) "Relationships and Responsibilities", *Boundaries and Allegiances* (New York: Oxford University Press).

Seglow, Jonathan. (2010) "Associative Duties and Global Justice", *Journal of Moral Philosophy* Vol. 7, No. 1, pp. 54–73.

Singer, Peter. (1972) "Famine, Affluence, and Morality", *Philosophy and Public Affairs* Vol. 1, No. 3, pp. 229–43.

Singer, Peter. (2009) *The Life You Can Save: Acting Now to End World Poverty* (New York: Random House).

Simmons, John. (1996) "Associative Political Obligations", *Ethics* Vol. 106, No. 2, pp. 247–73.

Rawls, John. (1971) *A Theory of Justice* (Cambridge, MA: Harvard University Press).

Stilz, Anna. (forthcoming) *Territorial Sovereignty: A Philosophical Exploration* (Oxford: Oxford University Press).

Taurek, John. (1977) "Should the Numbers Count?", *Philosophy and Public Affairs* Vol. 6, No. 4, pp. 293–316.

Taylor, Charles. (1989) "Cross-Purposes: The Liberal Communitarian Debate" in Nancy Rosenblum (ed.) *Liberalism and the Moral Life* (London: Harvard University Press).

Waldron, Jeremy. (1981) "A Right to Do Wrong", *Ethics* Vol. 92, No. 1, pp. 21–39.

Waldron, Jeremy. (1993) "Special Ties and Natural Duties", *Philosophy and Public Affairs* Vol. 22, No. 1, pp. 3–30.

Walzer, Michael. (1983) "Membership", *Spheres of Justice* (New York: Basic Books).

Wellman, C.H. (2008) "Immigration and Freedom of Association", *Ethics* Vol. 119, No.1, pp. 109–41.

PART III
OTHER MATTERS

7

What Normative Facts Should Political Theory Be About?

Philosophy of Science Meets Political Liberalism

Christian List and Laura Valentini

1. Introduction

We are familiar with the idea that different theories in the sciences deal with different classes of facts: they have, in that sense, different ontologies. For example, fundamental physics deals with facts about particles, fields, and forces; biology deals with facts about cells, organisms, and ecosystems; and the social sciences deal with facts about people and various social phenomena. The ontologies of these different sciences are related— social-scientific and biological facts depend on physical ones, for instance—but they are not the same. The ontologies of "higher-level" theories are more coarse-grained than those of "lower-level" theories. Biology and the social sciences, to take our examples, abstract away from micro-physical details. They are not committed to any particular such details. Instead, they deal with facts about certain higher-level entities and properties. Similarly, we may ask whether different *normative* theories, specifically moral and political ones, are concerned with different classes of facts. In particular, do moral and political theories deal with the same normative facts, or with different ones? Do they have different ontologies?

Of course, normative theories do not deal with empirical or positive facts, like the sciences, but with normative ones: facts about what is permissible, impermissible, right, wrong, desirable, undesirable, and so on. We understand normative facts, broadly, to include both "deontic" facts

Christian List and Laura Valentini, *What Normative Facts Should Political Theory Be About? Philosophy of Science Meets Political Liberalism* In: *Oxford Studies in Political Philosophy Volume 6*. Edited by: David Sobel, Peter Vallentyne, and Steven Wall, Oxford University Press (2020). © Christian List and Laura Valentini. DOI: 10.1093/oso/9780198852636.003.0007 (facts about what is obligatory or permissible) and "evaluative" facts (facts about what is good, bad, desirable, etc.). Reference to such facts need not be metaphysically suspicious. On most interpretations—setting aside some strong anti-realist ones—normative theories are intended to capture certain normative facts. This leaves open whether those facts are independently given, natural or non-natural, humanly constructed, and if so how, universal or relative to some standpoint, and so on.

So, do moral and political theories deal with the same normative facts, or different ones? Here are two common answers (cf. Larmore 2013):

- *The domain view*: Political and moral theories are concerned with the same normative facts. They just address different questions in light of them: moral theories focus on individual conduct, political theories on institutional design, and social organization. In other words, political theories explore what morality implies for political questions: for instance, what forms of social organization would be recommended by utilitarianism, prioritarianism, Kantianism, and so on. This view about the nature of moral and political theory was arguably held by Robert Nozick (e.g., 1974) and G. A. Cohen (e.g., 2008).
- *The core-value view*: Political and moral theories are concerned with different normative facts in light of their different core values. Moral theories focus on facts about what is right, just, and good. Political theories focus on facts about legitimacy, order, and stability. Political realists, in Bernard Williams's tradition (e.g., 2005), arguably hold this view (cf. Rossi and Sleat 2014).

Our aim is to defend a third, principled way of distinguishing between the ontologies of moral and political theories:

- *The levels view*: Political and moral theories are concerned with different normative facts, which belong to different ontological levels. The normative facts of political theory belong to a higher—more coarse-grained—ontological level than those of moral theory. Normative political facts are "multiply realizable" by moral facts, so that competing facts at the moral level can underpin the same facts at the political one. Consequently, some normative questions on which we tend to assume the existence of facts at the moral level are indeterminate at the political level. Normative political ontology is thinner than moral ontology.

Our development of this view builds on a hitherto overlooked analogy with the sciences. We argue that, despite interpretational differences, the relationship between the moral level and the political one is structurally similar to the relationship between a lower level and a higher level in the empirical sciences.

Although our analysis draws on this philosophy-of-science background and is a little outside the box, the picture we propose fits well with liberal political theory. The suggestion that political theories are associated with a thin ontology of normative facts echoes John Rawls's idea, expressed in *Political Liberalism* (1996), that at the political level we should abstract away from any comprehensive moral doctrines. However, there is much disagreement among political theorists on how to understand this idea. We make no claims about whether our proposal is faithful to Rawls's own view; our aim is not exegesis. But we suggest that it offers a plausible (re)interpretation of the ontology of political liberalism and of the demarcation between comprehensive and political morality. A key implication of our proposal is that full-blown moral realism—the thesis that all normative questions have determinate "true"/"false" answers—is not defensible *at the political level*. Only a thinner set of normative questions—"political" ones—have determinate answers at that level.

In Section 2, we outline a framework for thinking about levels. In Sections 3 and 4, we bring this framework to bear on the relationship between the ontologies of moral and political theory, and we contrast our distinction between facts at different levels (an ontic distinction) with the more familiar distinction between admissible and inadmissible evidence (an epistemic distinction). In Sections 5 to 7, we describe the virtues of the levels view from a liberal perspective and discuss some implications for the practice of political theory.

We should emphasize that, in drawing a distinction between the ontologies of moral and political theory, we are proposing a particular meta-theoretical account of how political theory should be done. Not everyone will agree with this account, and we do not mean to suggest that others could not reasonably prefer different conceptions of political theory. However, our account should be congenial to those who share the particular liberal view about the point and purpose of political theory we discuss in Section 5.

2. The Framework of Levels

We begin with some background on how the positive sciences depict the world and the sense in which different sciences operate at different levels of description. For the moment, we set aside anything related to moral and political theory, to which we will return subsequently. The framework sketched in this section draws on List (2018).

2.1 Scientific Explanation and Levels of Description

Even though it is widely accepted that, from a scientific perspective, the world is ultimately governed by physical laws, it is also widely accepted that fundamental physics by itself is insufficient for explaining and making sense of the world. While fundamental physics can explain some basic features of the world, such as the behaviour of elementary particles, forces, and fields, it cannot adequately explain many other, higher-level phenomena. Special sciences such as biology, psychology, and the social sciences are needed to make sense of them. We would get overwhelmed with an unnecessary volume of detail and a computational overload if we tried to explain biological, psychological, or social phenomena in micro-physical terms: we wouldn't see the forest for the trees (see, e.g., Putnam 1967, Fodor 1974, Owens 1989, and List and Spiekermann 2013). Even chemical explanations must set aside certain micro-physical details. To explain chemical, biological, psychological, and social phenomena, we must employ higher-level descriptions, which abstract away from fundamental physical underpinnings and invoke a different, higher-level repertoire of concepts and categories. Micro-physical concepts such as *quarks*, *bosons*, and *leptons* are absent in biology and the social sciences; instead, we speak about *cells*, *organisms*, and *institutions*.

Higher-level descriptions are more coarse-grained than lower-level descriptions: a variety of different lower-level configurations can each realize or instantiate the same higher-level phenomenon. This is a by-product of the process of abstraction. For example, different combinations of micro-states of the individual water molecules in a water tank can each realize the same macro-state of liquid water at a particular temperature. A temperature of 80 degrees Celsius can be realized by an astronomical number of different micro-configurations of molecules. We say that the higher-level phenomenon—here, water at 80 degrees Celsius—is "multiply realizable" at the lower level (Putnam 1967, Fodor 1974).

If we want to explain how a steam engine works, for example, the macro-states of the water are much more relevant than the micro-states. It matters that water turns into steam when heated and that the pressure is such-and-such, but we need not describe the micro-states of the billions of water molecules involved (see, e.g., Jackson and Pettit 1990). A specification of those micro-states is not only unnecessary for an adequate explanation of the steam engine, but even distracting. Similarly, if we want to explain the population dynamics in an ecosystem, the appropriate level of description is the biological one, not the level of the underlying elementary particles. Good scientific methodology mandates that we explain the phenomena in question in the simplest possible way. Often, higher-level explanations are simpler than lower-level ones, as illustrated by the examples of the steam engine and population dynamics.

In fact, higher-level explanations are often not just simpler than lower-level ones, but they also pick up regularities that cannot be found at the lower level. It is a striking fact about the world that it displays regularities at more than one level. There are not only micro-physical regularities, but also regularities at various macroscopic levels—such as biological, psychological, and social ones—which are robust to changes in their lower-level realizations (see, e.g., Dennett 1991 and List and Menzies 2009). For instance, the way in which the price of a good depends on the supply and demand is independent of the detailed physical nature of the good, the structure of the economy, and the currency in question. The laws of supply and demand apply irrespective of whether the economy is a traditional agricultural economy, and money takes the form of gold or whether it is an advanced industrial economy in which money is electronic and virtual. Those same economic laws apply even in informal prison economies where cigarettes play the role of cash (Radford 1945).

2.2 From Levels of Description to Ontological Levels

The point we have made so far is a basic one about scientific explanation: we employ different levels of description for different explanatory purposes, where higher-level descriptions involve different concepts and categories than lower-level ones and are more coarse-grained, deliberately abstracting away from lower-level details. At first sight, one might think that this is merely an epistemological point: our cognitive limitations as human beings, such as our limited knowledge and limited computational capacities, lead us to focus on macroscopic data and to ignore microscopic foundations when we explain certain phenomena.

However, one may coherently and plausibly interpret the different levels of description in science as markers of different ontological levels (List 2018). The idea can be summarized as follows. Because different levels of description provide different conceptual schemes for thinking and speaking about the world, they carve up the world in different ways; they pick out different "real patterns" (Dennett 1991). Each level of description thus allows us to refer to a specific class of facts. We call these the "facts at that level". At a biological level, for instance, we refer to facts about organisms and ecosystems, but not to facts about the underlying quantum-mechanical processes. The latter can be described only using the resources of fundamental physics, and so they belong to a lower level. At a macro-economic level, we refer to facts about macro-economic properties, such as inflation, unemployment, and growth, but not to facts about the detailed psychological processes in the minds of individual market participants. The latter can be described only using the resources of micro-economics or psychology, and so they belong to a lower level.

It might be objected that although we talk about macro-level facts—for example, biological, medical, chemical, and social ones—these are just ways of speaking and do not entail any ontological commitments. The only "real reality" is to be found at the most fundamental, micro-physical level. This, the objection suggests, is what we should conclude if we subscribe to Occam's Razor principle—the principle that tells us not to multiply ontological commitments unnecessarily.

One can give at least three responses to this objection. First, Occam's Razor principle only says that we should not make ontological commitments when these are explanatorily unnecessary. But as we noted earlier, positing facts at the higher level is explanatorily useful, often even indispensable. Most macroscopic phenomena cannot be explained without referring to higher-level facts. So, Occam's Razor principle does not speak against higher-level ontological commitments. Second, the burden of proof falls on the objector. The existence of higher-level facts is part of our ordinary understanding of reality. We talk about chemical compounds, plants, organisms, books, money, companies, economies, and states, and we think of them as real phenomena, about which we can establish facts. Denying the existence of these facts flies in the face of scientific practice as well as common sense. That we talk about them using the vocabulary of certain special sciences, rather than that of fundamental physics, makes them no less real. The objector would have to explain how we can make sense of the macroscopic world without recognizing such higher-level facts. Third, the jury is still out on whether there is a fundamental level at all. Perhaps the world can be understood in ever-more fine-grained ways, and we will never hit rock bottom (Schaffer 2003). In case there is no fundamental level, every level can be viewed as being a higher level, relative to some other, lower levels.

2.3 Possible Worlds at Different Levels

It is helpful to think of about the relationship between different levels in terms of the idea of possible worlds. Each level of description gives us a particular way of specifying what the world is like. The term "possible world" normally stands for a full specification of the way the world might be: the totality of facts. As Wittgenstein (1922) famously put it, "the world is everything that is the case". Now, once we recognize that facts can be associated with different levels, we must conclude that possible worlds can also be specified at different levels. A "possible world at a particular level" is a full specification of the facts at that level. Adjusting Wittgenstein's dictum, we get the following level-relativized variant: "the world at a particular level is everything that is the case at that level" (List 2018). So, a physical-level world is a full specification of the physical-level facts; a chemical-level world is a full specification of the chemical-level facts; a biological-level world is a full specification of the biological facts; and so on. Physical descriptions speak about the world at the physical level; chemical descriptions speak about the world at the chemical level; and so on. In short, instead of speaking about "worlds simpliciter", the various sciences, in effect, speak about "worlds at a particular level".

Higher-level worlds are more coarse-grained than lower-level worlds, in that they specify a thinner set of facts. Each higher-level world corresponds to an entire equivalence class of lower-level worlds: its possible lower-level realizers. For instance, each chemical-level world corresponds to the equivalence class of all physical-level worlds that could realize it and that are, therefore, equivalent with respect to chemical properties. Similarly, each world at the macro-economic level corresponds to the equivalence class of all the micro-economic worlds that may realize it and that are therefore macro-economically equivalent. The relationship between lower-level worlds and higher-level worlds is one of "supervenience with multiple realizability": there exists a many-to-one correspondence between lower-level worlds and higher-level worlds.[1]

We can think of a possible world at a particular level as determining the truth-values ("true", "false") of all sentences or statements at that level; so, a lower-level world determines the truth-values of all lower-level sentences or statements, while a higher-level world determines the truth-values of all higher-level sentences or statements. Since higher-level worlds are more coarse-grained than lower-level worlds, the truth-values of many lower-level sentences or statements are left open by higher-level worlds. At the higher level, there is no fact of the matter about those lower-level sentences or statements: they are indeterminate at that level. For example, a possible world at the level of statistical mechanics determines the truth-values of sentences about the temperature

---

[1] If Ω and Ω' are the sets of all possible worlds at the lower and higher levels, respectively, then each world in Ω' corresponds to the equivalence class of worlds in Ω that could realize it. This is precisely developed in List (2018).

and other aggregate states of a liquid, but not of sentences about the micro-configurations of the underlying molecules. A world at the level of macro-economics determines the truth-values of sentences about inflation and unemployment, but not of sentences about the activities of each individual market participant. Another way of expressing this point is to say that higher-level worlds are more abstract than lower-level worlds: they omit certain facts that are filled in only by their lower-level realizers. With this philosophy-of-science background in place, we return to the topic of moral and political theory.

3. The Levels View about Political and Moral Ontology

The present framework allows us to clarify the relationship between the ontologies of moral and political theory.[2] Political theory, we suggest, can be associated with a different level of description and a different body of normative facts than moral theory. Specifically, moral theory operates at a more fine-grained level than political theory. This means, in particular, that political theories have a thinner normative ontology and thinner truth-conditions than moral theories, while moral theories have a richer normative ontology and richer truth-conditions.

This insight is arguably implicit in Rawls's *Political Liberalism* (1996), and so we will develop it by reference to Rawls. As noted, however, our aim is not exegetical, and if what we offer is a revisionary re-interpretation of Rawls, then we have no problem with that. Recall the following claims from *Political Liberalism*:

- *The negative claim*: At the political level, we should not take a stand on the core concerns of comprehensive moral and religious doctrines—for instance, what a person is, what makes something valuable, what fundamentally explains the rightness or wrongness of an action.
- *The positive claim*: Normative political questions, especially about how to organize the basic structure of society, should be answered by reference to freestanding political principles, namely principles

---

[2] For an earlier, but different application of levelled thinking to political theory, see Carter (2015), who uses grounding hierarchies to investigate value-freeness and value-neutrality in political concepts.

that do not presuppose the truth of any particular comprehensive moral doctrine.

- *The "overlapping consensus" claim*: The answers to normative political questions—including the freestanding political principles—should be compatible with a variety of comprehensive moral doctrines and supported by an overlapping consensus among them.

These claims can be explicated through the framework of levels. We will employ the idea of "possible worlds at different levels", but we will understand "worlds" for present purposes not as specifications of positive facts, but as specifications of normative facts. In particular, we will define a "possible normative world" as a specification of the totality of normative facts, as posited by some normative theory. Under this definition, different normative theories disagree about which normative world is actual: which encodes the "true" or "correct" set of normative facts. By positing different rightness or wrongness facts, for example, Kantian and utilitarian theories give us different accounts of what the normative facts are, thereby depicting different possible normative worlds as actual. The "levels view" asserts the following claims:

- Possible normative worlds can be specified at different levels of grain. The set of possible normative worlds at the political level is more coarse-grained than the one at the comprehensive moral level. A normative political theory specifies a thinner set of normative facts than a comprehensive moral doctrine.
- Normative political questions should be answered at the political level, not the moral one. By implication, there are questions addressed by comprehensive moral doctrines on which there is no political fact of the matter, hence no "normative political truth". Those questions are indeterminate at the political level.
- Any "normative political truth" may be compatible with a variety of "moral truths". Political-level truths can, in this sense, be multiply realized at the comprehensive moral level. By implication, competing comprehensive moral doctrines, which take incompatible moral-level worlds to be actual, can agree on the same normative world at the political level. The competing moral-level worlds can then be viewed as different possible "realizers" of the same

normative political-level world. (This multiple-realizability claim must not be confused with the more trivial claim that the same normative political principles may be satisfied by a variety of different behaviours, policies, or institutions, which is obviously the case.[3])

On the levels view, in line with *Political Liberalism*, certain political principles may be supported by a variety of comprehensive moral doctrines. Think of how many different comprehensive moral doctrines may be able to agree that we ought to make collective decisions in a deliberative democratic manner, that we ought to respect a certain system of basic rights and liberties and avoid extreme socio-economic inequality, and that we ought to have a humane criminal justice system. In this way, utilitarians, Kantians, Aristotelians, and Scanlonian contractualists, among others, may agree on the same set of political principles for governing the basic structure of society, even if they offer competing comprehensive moral foundations for those principles. At the political level, there is a fact of the matter about which political principles are the correct ones—for instance, which liberties and entitlements citizens should have—but there is no fact of the matter about the correct comprehensive moral foundations for those principles, such as whether utilitarianism, Kantianism, or some other moral doctrine is true. This is analogous to our earlier point that, at the macro-physical level, there is a fact of the matter about whether water in a kettle is boiling, but no fact about the precise micro-states of all the underlying water molecules. Similarly, there is no political-level fact about whether human beings are created in the image of God, whether one ought to confess in order to go to Heaven, and whether one ought to adhere to the Categorical Imperative in one's personal life. Those questions are settled only at the comprehensive moral level.

This does not imply that all moral facts are absent from the political level. Rather, those moral facts on which all relevant competing comprehensive moral doctrines agree, such as the fact that—in standard situations—killing innocent people is wrong, still hold at the political level.

---

[3] "Realization", in our discussion of "multiple realizability", refers to the instantiation or grounding of some higher-level fact in some configuration of lower-level facts, not to the fulfilment of whatever it is that certain normative principles require of individuals and/or society. We thank David Estlund for prompting us to clarify this point.

So, the most non-controversial portion of morality is preserved at the political level. That is the portion of morality on which there is an overlapping consensus among all the relevant competing comprehensive moral doctrines. We can think of the normative facts that lie within this overlap as coarse-grained moral facts that are multiply realizable. Such facts are settled even at the political level, although their comprehensive normative foundations are left open.[4]

How to define the set of possible normative worlds at the political level and which such world is the "correct" one—in the sense of specifying the correct body of normative facts at the political level—are further questions, which must be discussed separately. Our focus up to this point has been on the *structure* of the levels view. We have explained how one can draw the distinction between moral facts and normative political facts in a levelled framework. That said, our interest is in specifying the two levels in a way that is consistent with a liberal outlook. So, what we are proposing is a liberal version of the levels view.

4. Inadmissible Facts versus Inadmissible Evidence

One might think that the idea of treating certain issues as indeterminate at the political level is similar to the familiar idea that certain evidence is not admitted in the courtroom, such as evidence that was acquired in a procedurally incorrect way. The legal rules of evidence may exclude such evidence from consideration even if, privately, a rational agent would consider it epistemically relevant; that is to say, the evidence could lead to an opinion change in a rational agent who had access to it. The problem with such evidence is not its epistemic irrelevance, but its legal inadmissibility.

Perhaps, then, what the levels view suggests is that political theorizing is analogous to the activity of legal reasoning in the courtroom, namely governed by certain rules of evidence, which specify which evidence is

---

[4] The fact that political-level discourse and moral-level discourse overlap in some of their terms (such as the use of notions like *permissibility, obligation, right, wrong,* etc.) does not undermine the claim that the totality of normative facts at the political level is thinner (more coarse-grained) than the totality of normative facts at the comprehensive moral level.

admissible and which is not. Though tempting, this is the wrong way to think about the levels view. We must distinguish between two theses:

- the thesis that certain kinds of evidence are inadmissible in certain contexts;
- the thesis that at a particular level of description we can only invoke facts at the relevant level and not facts at other levels, especially lower-level facts.

The first thesis characterizes legal reasoning in the courtroom (Rawls 1996, p. 221). But it is the second that characterizes political theorizing, according to the levels view. Note that the first thesis is epistemic: its sole concern is the question of which evidence we may use in certain contexts. The second thesis is ontic: it is concerned with the facts of the matter we may posit. (For discussion of a more epistemic view, see Estlund 2012, p. 271.)

Deeming some evidence inadmissible—for instance, evidence gained through a forced confession—is not the same as refraining from positing a relevant fact of the matter. In a criminal trial, we certainly assume that there are facts about who did it, how and when they did it, who may have helped them, what their motives were, and so on. For this reason, we seek to establish those facts on the basis of the best evidence we have. Sometimes we cannot reliably know all the facts, or there may be restrictions on the evidence we may use, such as when some evidence was gathered in an inadmissible way. But the existence of the facts themselves is not in question.

By contrast, at the political level, the reason why we should refrain from considering, for instance, religious testimony is not merely that such evidence is inadmissible, while we may still assume that there are religious facts, albeit ones we may not conclusively know. Rather, our reason for not considering religious testimony is that, at the political level, we cannot assume the existence of religious facts in the first place. Similarly, we should not assume the truth of atheism for political purposes. At the political level, we should not take a stand on this issue at all: we should treat the issue as indeterminate. At the comprehensive moral level, we *can* assume that there is a fact of the matter. Moral theories can in principle have religious or metaphysical commitments.

But the comprehensive moral level is not the one at which political theorizing should be conducted, according to the levels view.

By analogy, consider whether religious testimony should be considered in medicine. Imagine a patient asking a doctor whether to pray to attain spiritual salvation. Presumably, the doctor would say that this question is outside the domain of medicine: there is no medical fact on this matter. It is not that there is a medical fact, but the relevant evidence is inadmissible. If that were the case, the medical profession would have to approach the issue as an instance of decision-making under uncertainty. It might then be appropriate for doctors to try to give the best advice under the uncertainty, for instance by invoking Pascal's wager argument. If God exists, praying might lead to spiritual salvation, not praying to a worse outcome; and if God does not exist, praying would not be much of a sacrifice anyway; so perhaps praying is all-things-considered advisable. But doctors do not give this advice. In fact, we would be suspicious of any medical professional who engaged in such reasoning. What this suggests is this. On our established views about the proper domain of medicine, there is no medical fact about religious matters, simpliciter. That is why religious testimony is not relevant to medicine. By contrast, there are facts about religious matters in theology, and religious testimony is relevant to theological investigations. Analogously, the levels view asserts that, when we engage in normative argumentation at the political level, we must not presuppose that there is a fact of the matter about the existence of God, spiritual salvation, and other comprehensive moral questions. In sum, the distinction between admissible and inadmissible facts, as drawn by the levels view, is different from the distinction between admissible and inadmissible evidence, as familiar from the courtroom.

5. Why Should We Accept the Levels View?

So far, we have introduced the levels view and have used it to distinguish between the ontologies of moral and political theory, taking Rawls's *Political Liberalism* as inspiration. We now want to show that the levels view, in the Rawlsian liberal version we propose, has a number of attractive features. In particular, we suggest that it satisfies three key desiderata that— we think—any good account of normative political ontology should meet:

1. *Consistency with the aim of political theorizing*: Political theory should answer the question of how to live together under circumstances of pluralism.
2. *Consistency with the core liberal conviction that "you can't push people around in the name of what you think is right"* (Korsgaard 2008, p. 318): Public decisions, which may be informed by political theory, should not be based on reasonably contested moral or religious views, even if one believes them to be correct.
3. *Consistency with Occam's Razor principle*: In any domain of inquiry, one should not posit more, or fewer, facts than necessary to account for the relevant evidence.

Given space constraints, we are not able to show that the levels view is the only account of normative political ontology that satisfies those three desiderata, but our discussion should show, at least, that the levels view satisfies them in a clear and compelling way. Of course, the desiderata themselves are not uncontroversial. For instance, supporters of G.A.-Cohen-style, fact-free political theorizing are likely to reject Desideratum 1, which presupposes a more practical understanding of the aim of political theorizing (e.g., Cohen 2008). Desideratum 2 may be rejected by those who find liberal principles unconvincing and also by those who defend respect for persons' liberties on comprehensive—for example, autonomy-promoting—grounds (e.g., Raz 1986; for discussion, see Nussbaum 2011). Desideratum 3 should be fairly uncontroversial. The less readers are convinced by our desiderata, the less they will be convinced by our version of the levels view. Still, the desiderata are sufficiently widely accepted to make our exploration worthwhile. Moreover, even the acceptance of one or two of the desiderata would lend some support to the levels view.

5.1 Consistency with the Aim of Political Theory

As Rawls noted, in a pluralistic society, stable and peaceful cooperation is hardly possible if disagreeing parties insist on imposing their comprehensive views on one another (Rawls 1996, pp. 140–4). The levels view, by prescribing political agnosticism regarding comprehensive moral doctrines, rules out the legitimacy of such imposition from the start.

In response, one might suggest that peace and stability could be obtained through autocracy, thereby suppressing pluralism. However, this option is not only morally reprehensible—certainly from a liberal perspective—but also pragmatically dubious. The costs involved in suppressing pluralism would be extremely high, and it is not clear how successful or sustainable such suppression could be, even setting aside its immorality. To a lesser extent, the same could also be said about an approach that imposes a relatively benign but still comprehensive moral doctrine on society as a whole. The answers given to normative questions by such an approach would be unlikely to convince the proponents of other comprehensive moral doctrines. By contrast, the levels view is set up to accommodate the circumstances of pluralism, and it gives us a principled methodology for answering normative political questions under such circumstances. So, the levels view fits the aim of political theorizing in contemporary societies.

5.2 Consistency with Core Liberal Convictions

The levels view clearly accommodates the conviction that one ought not to impose one's reasonably contested views on others. To develop this point, we need to say more about the nature of moral disagreement. In moral discourse, we ask questions such as the following:

- How ought we to act, or not to act?
- Why ought we to act in that way?

Answers to the first question typically take the form of verdicts about permissibility and obligation. Answers to the second typically refer to the underlying values or reasons. Philosophers, and people in general, notoriously disagree on both questions. These disagreements are largely intractable: there is no publically accepted procedure for resolving them (Waldron 1998). For some people, the answer to moral questions lies in religion, for others it lies in intuition, for still others it lies in rational deliberation, and so on. None of the people in question are obviously mistaken or irrational. They are responsive to evidence on empirical matters, and their thinking is coherent. Furthermore, despite their moral disagreements, their views may all be compatible with basic liberal principles. As Rawls puts it, they may all qualify as "reasonable", in a moralized sense of the term (more on this in Section 6; on ambiguities in Rawls's notion of reasonableness, see Nussbaum 2011, sect. IV).

In the face of intractable moral disagreements, liberals typically acknowledge that they may not unilaterally impose their contested views on others, for instance through state coercion.[5] Such imposition would be contrary to the core liberal commitment to respect for persons as free and equal agents (on the "respect" principle, see Larmore 1999). In Martha Nussbaum's words, "it is especially violative of persons to impose a scheme of value upon them" (2011, p. 20). The levels view captures this tenet of liberalism. At the political level, we recognize only a thin domain of normative facts and corresponding truths: those that are acceptable from the perspective of all reasonable comprehensive views. By contrast, we do not assume the existence of facts about comprehensive moral matters, such as matters of interpersonal morality, religion, and metaphysical foundations. Furthermore, we use certain level-specific concepts and categories in political theorizing, such as concepts of political obligation and permission, reasonableness in a public sense, and so on. These are distinct from (and at most partly overlap with) the concepts and categories employed in moral theorizing, such as moral obligation and permission and an array of richer notions in terms of which we express moral reasons.

Faced with these claims, critics may raise an objection familiar from the literature on *Political Liberalism* (see, e.g., Callan 1997, chap. 2, Enoch 2017, and Arneson 2014; for discussion, see Daniels 1996). Is it not irrational or even schizophrenic

- to accept that in the political realm, due to intractable disagreement, one should not appeal to comprehensive doctrines, and use thinner, political concepts and categories,
- and yet to continue to hold on to those comprehensive doctrines privately?

---

[5] Exceptions may be those liberals who view liberalism as a comprehensive moral doctrine, for example, perfectionistic liberals.

Consider, for example, a liberal Catholic anti-abortionist. Would it not be absurd for him or her to believe that, at the moral level, there is a fact about whether abortion involves killing a moral person and also to believe that, at the political level, there is no such fact?

As Norman Daniels (1996, p. 152) puts the concern:

> Can people say to themselves, "Although I have fundamental values and beliefs that bear on this issue of behavior, I will refrain from raising them and consider only the reasons permitted by public reason?" Is this moral double bookkeeping a kind of multiple moral personality disorder?[6]

For those who share this worry, it might be tempting to offer one of the following suggestions, each of which is an alternative to the levels view.[7]

- *Moral uncertainty*: Given intractable disagreement, we should all be uncertain about our views (cf. Barry 1995).[8] The problems of political theory then require that we apply moral decision-making under uncertainty, instead of accepting the seemingly schizophrenic view that there are different normative facts at different levels.
- *Judgement suspension*: Given intractable disagreement, the rational thing to do is to suspend judgement (see the discussion in Leland and van Wietmarschen 2012, p. 745, and Enoch 2017). If we suspend judgement, we are no longer disagreeing. Hence the problem of disagreement disappears, and with it, the associated schizophrenia of assuming different sets of normative facts at different levels (for discussion of these sceptical objections, see Quong 2011, chap. 8).

In the following two subsections, we respond to each suggestion in turn.

5.2.1 Moral Uncertainty?

What about treating intractable disagreement as an indicator of moral uncertainty? It would then seem appropriate to answer all normative

---

[6] Note, however, that Daniels is unpersuaded by this critique.

[7] We thank Victor Tadros for discussion. For criticisms of the epistemic reading of *Political Liberalism*, see Enoch (2017).

[8] Barry (1995, p. 169) writes: "no conception of the good can justifiably be held with a degree of certainty that warrants its imposition on those who reject it".

questions about politics by applying our best theory of decision-making under uncertainty. On this picture, we may be uncertain about whether utilitarianism, prioritarianism, Kantianism, or some other moral theory is true, and so we may need to hedge our bets in deciding which political arrangements to recommend. Yet, it is assumed, there is a fact of the matter about the true moral theory. The limitations in political theory are then epistemic, not ontic, and we can uphold full-blown moral realism, even in politics.

We think this proposal is not viable. First, it is not clear that our established theories of decision-making under uncertainty can easily apply to moral matters, where the uncertainty is not about empirical facts, but about the requirements of morality. To apply those theories, we would have to accomplish at least three things:

- come up with an agreed specification of the set of possible normative worlds at the moral level; these would have to include one world in which utilitarianism is true, one in which Kantianism is true, one in which each religious view is true, and so on;
- assign subjective probabilities to these possible normative worlds, such as 0.25 to the utilitarian world, 0.25 to the Kantian world, and so on, while making sure these numbers are meaningful; and
- assign numerical utilities to the consequences of all possible choices (such as actions, policies, or institutional designs) in each possible normative world, where those utilities capture the moral value of each choice under the "true" moral theory in that world, while permitting comparability across different normative worlds; for instance, if lying is worse in a Kantian world than in a utilitarian one, then lying might correspond to a utility of −100 in the Kantian world and only to a utility −50 in the utilitarian one.

We suspect that, contrary to what some recent literature on moral uncertainty suggests, these three tasks pose insurmountable challenges (cf. Lockhart 2000). Of course, one could stipulatively postulate a utilitarian world, a Kantian world, a contractualist world, and so on, then assign some subjective probabilities to these worlds, and ask how good or bad, in numerical utility terms, various outcomes would be in each of them. This would seem to enable us to calculate the expected utility of various possible choices against the background of our moral uncertainty (for defences of such approaches, see Riedener 2015 and MacAskill 2016). However, whether this exercise is genuinely meaningful and whether it can be done in an agreeable way under conditions of pluralism are altogether different questions. The jury is still out on this.

Second, even if we set these difficulties aside, we are left with the problem that people intractably disagree about decision-making—moral or otherwise—under uncertainty. Should we be expected utility maximizers? Maxi-minimizers (who try to achieve the best possible worst-case consequences)? Risk-weighted expected utility maximizers (Buchak 2014)? And if so, what should our risk attitude be? Or should we adopt an altogether different decision procedure? In fact, people intractably disagree about the very question of whether the appropriate response to disagreement among competent thinkers is decreasing one's degree of belief in one's comprehensive moral view (see the literature on peer disagreement, as reviewed in Goldman and Blanchard 2015, sect. 3.4).

In sum, adopting a framework of decision-making under uncertainty and selecting a particular decision procedure within that framework will reproduce the same problems we identified in connection with identifying the correct substantive answers to normative questions. The moment we settle for a certain procedure for making decisions under moral uncertainty, we impose that procedure on others who reasonably disagree with it, contrary to what we called the "core liberal commitment".[9] The moral-uncertainty response to the problem of intractable disagreement is therefore theoretically dubious and morally unappealing, at least from the liberal perspective with which we have started.[10]

---

[9] Note that the levels view should not be interpreted as involving decision-making under moral uncertainty. According to the levels view, cases of intractable moral disagreement are not instances of uncertainty; rather, they are instances of indeterminacy. This is because, at the comprehensive moral level, the levels view does not instruct proponents of the competing moral doctrines to abandon their views. At the political level, by contrast, the levels view takes there to be no fact of the matter in such cases. So, we are not dealing with moral uncertainty at either of these levels. Furthermore, at the political level, the levels view does not impose any commitment to controversial moral facts on anyone.

[10] For comprehensive reservations about epistemic versions of political liberalism, see Enoch (2017).

5.2.2 Suspending Judgement?

Let us turn to the second response to the "schizophrenia" worry, namely that, in the face of intractable disagreement, the rational response is to suspend judgement altogether. The problem of disagreement would then disappear: we would hold no views on any contested issues.

This suggestion is at odds with our moral phenomenology. It would imply that virtually everyone is irrational in a pluralistic society. Given intractable disagreement about moral matters, we ought to suspend judgement, thereby abandoning most if not all of our moral commitments. But this is not what most people, including apparently very rational ones, do. A view that leads us to regard those we ordinarily consider rational as completely irrational is one of which we should be suspicious.

The levels view tells us that we should suspend judgement only at the political level, by assuming a thinner set of normative facts at that level and using only political-level concepts and categories. This is faithful to our moral experience. As liberal-democratic citizens we accept that we shouldn't impose our convictions on others in the face of intractable moral disagreement, but as private individuals we hold on to our contested convictions and shape our lives around them (Macedo 1995, p. 474).

Consider again the example of a liberal Catholic who holds the following beliefs: at the comprehensive moral level, there is a fact about whether abortion involves killing a moral person; and at the political level, there is no such fact. Are these beliefs really in tension? Recall our earlier observation that, in medicine, there is no fact of the matter about whether one should pray for spiritual salvation, while there may be such a fact in morality or religion. This claim is unlikely to elicit any charges of schizophrenia. Now imagine you went to a judge or a government official—that is, someone responsible for making public decisions—and asked them: "Does abortion involve killing a moral person?" Presumably, they would respond: "I am the wrong person to answer this question in my capacity as a public official. At most, I can say something about *legal* personhood. The law is silent about *moral* personhood; there is no *legal* fact of the matter about it."

This hypothetical dialogue puts pressure on the claim that there is something incoherent in holding that there are different facts at the moral and political levels. The burden of proof is on the objector to tell us why the official's response is incoherent, when it seems obviously correct. And if this response is not incoherent, then neither is the liberal Catholic's belief that while there is a fact about moral personhood at the comprehensive moral level, there is no such fact at the political one, which is similar to the level at which state officials and judges operate.

Reservations about our argument are likely to be motivated by the temptation to collapse moral and political levels, or to suggest that the latter should "mirror" the former. This, however, is a substantive view about the structure of normative ontology, and one that suggests that normative ontology is "flatter"—less "multi-levelled"—than we have argued. Appeal to this substantive view, which is distinct from the levels view, is no response to our claim that the levels view is free from incoherence or schizophrenia.

5.3 Ontological Parsimony and the Levels View

The picture of normative ontology suggested by the levels view is also more in line with Occam's Razor principle than its comprehensive rivals. Let us explain. Given the prominence of moral realism in philosophical debates, philosophers often assume that some comprehensive moral theory must be true. While it is widely accepted that we do not conclusively know which moral theory is true, the existence of a fact of the matter is seldom put into question by moral philosophers—at least outside anti-realist circles. However, the assumption that there is a fact of the matter, which we must "merely" discover, is a demanding one, and it is far from obvious that this assumption should be the default, especially when it comes to politics.

In science, but also in philosophical ontology in Occam's tradition, the leading methodological principle is that we should not posit more features of reality—that is, more facts, entities, or properties—than needed in order to account for the *relevant evidence* concerning the *matter of interest*. Suppose we are interested in the ontology of physics. Electromagnetic fields, for instance, were not part of the original Newtonian ontology of the world. Maxwell's electrodynamics, however, showed that we need to invoke them as new unobservable features of the world in order to make sense of certain observable phenomena.

For this reason, we now accept their reality. By contrast, the ether was an ingredient of reality postulated at some point, but it turned out to be explanatorily dispensable, and so we no longer believe that it exists.

What does Occam's Razor imply for the normative domain? Let us start with comprehensive moral questions. It may well be true that *if* we are interested in explaining what makes an action right or wrong (our matter of interest) *and* we take our personal comprehensive moral judgements as our "data points" (the relevant evidence), *then* an indispensability argument might be given for realism about certain normative facts. Specifically, it might be that, without positing a rich normative ontology, we would not be able to account for our normative "data" about comprehensive moral questions in an adequate manner. A rich ontology of moral facts might offer the best explanation of our personal moral landscape.

But even if this correctly characterizes the methodology of *moral* theorizing, the matters of interest and relevant evidence are different in *political* theory. First, the matter of interest will now be political morality and social organization, as opposed to the sorts of moral questions within comprehensive morality. Second, while treating one's personal judgements as relevant evidence may be defensible in matters of personal morality, it appears problematic once we turn to matters of public concern. Regarding public matters, "relevant evidence" should be publically ascertained. This implies that contested personal normative judgements won't count as relevant data points in political theorizing. And so, those judgements will also fail to constitute data points whose explanation makes a richer normative ontology indispensable.

These observations suggest that, at a political level, the kind of rich normative ontology that full-blown moral realists accept is hard to defend. At best, we might be able to defend a less demanding form of normative realism, restricted to a thinner ontology of normative facts: facts concerning matters of social organization on which the evidence is publically ascertained. These are precisely the facts on which we can establish an overlapping consensus in Rawls's sense.

So, the question to ask is not "why should we accept that our political ontology is thin", but "why not"? The burden of proof should fall on those who wish to posit more facts in order to address a given set of normative questions, not on those who wish to posit fewer facts, especially when the evidence for those facts is intractably contested.[11]

5.4 An Analogy

Suppose the politics department of a university is hiring a new assistant professor in political theory (for a similar example, see Quong 2016). The department is split between analytic theorists and postmodernists, who have competing comprehensive views about what counts as good scholarship. The decision about whom to hire is of great public significance in the department: everyone has to live with it. Consider the following, rather different, ways of conducting the hire.

Procedure 1: Colleagues deliberate about whom to hire, each appealing to his or her own comprehensive views about excellence in research. The discussion turns nasty. Through the arguments they offer for and against hiring various candidates, faculty members end up making accusations at each other. The analytic theorists accuse their colleagues of sloppiness, charlatanism, and ideological pontificating. The postmodernists lament their colleagues' parochialism, sophistry, and narrow-mindedness. No consensus is found. The top candidate for each side is deemed unappointable by the other. Resigned to the need to fill the position, the department votes. The analytic side narrowly wins. A new hire is imposed on the department for reasons many of its members find deeply objectionable.

Procedure 2: In deliberating about whom to hire, colleagues with different comprehensive views look for common ground. Aware of their differences, they proceed by arguing from shared premises, abstracting away from their partisan views: the analytic theorists set aside the criterion of formal analysis, the postmodernists set aside the importance of

---

[11] A referee has raised the following objection: "The opponent of levels is not positing more total facts—they are resisting the levels view and arguing that there's just one level of normative facts and thus arguably fewer total facts. The proponent of levels is positing more total facts since they introduce more levels." We disagree, insofar as we are here referring only to normative facts at the political level. At that level, the proponent of the levels view is undeniably positing fewer facts. From the perspective of the political level, matters of comprehensive morality are simply left indeterminate. At the political level, there are no facts about them.

deconstruction, and so on. They focus on what they have in common. For example, they all agree that publishing in some generally recognized journals is an achievement (though they disagree about more specialist venues). They all agree that positive student evaluations are *prima facie* evidence of good teaching. They all agree that it would be desirable to hire someone who can teach the history of political thought. The deliberation proceeds in a civil manner. Colleagues fail to reach consensus on how candidates should be ranked, but they agree about some of them being in principle appointable. The issue is put to a vote, and again—let's suppose—an analytically oriented candidate is chosen. To be sure, the postmodernist group is disappointed, but not completely alienated. They can see some public reasons in support of the decision and feel that they have been treated respectfully by their colleagues.

Intuitively, we hope readers will agree, Procedure 2 is superior to Procedure 1. We will comment on why that is in a moment. First, we would like to look at the ontological presuppositions of Procedure 2. Importantly, it is not the case that, *for the hiring process*, participants assume that there is a comprehensive truth about the right approach to political theory but are uncertain about what that truth is: is it in line with postmodernism or with analytic methodology? If that were the case, the department would follow some procedure for decision-making under uncertainty. For instance, colleagues would assign certain probabilities to the correctness of the different methodological approaches and decide on that basis. But this is not what they do under Procedure 2.

Instead, they refrain from assuming the existence of a fact of the matter about whether postmodernism or analytic theorizing is better. *At the level of the department*, they bracket off certain questions and assume a thinner class of facts about what constitutes good scholarship—facts that lie at the overlap between their different partisan views. Doing so does not prevent them from holding on to their comprehensive views in their own circles. At a deeper level, they each continue to believe that one way of doing research is superior to the other. But they acknowledge that comprehensive facts about research methodology cannot be assumed at the level of their pluralistic department. Procedure 2, then, presupposes an ontological structure akin to the levels view.

Now why does Procedure 2 seem superior to Procedure 1? Several answers come to mind, which are analogous to the ones we have offered in the political case. First, Procedure 2 is likely to be conducive to the good functioning of a department, by ensuring peace and stability. Procedure 1, by contrast, may lead to conflict and disaffection. Second, Procedure 2 shows respect towards both sides of the debate, who reasonably disagree with each other. Of course, what counts as "reasonable" is often far from clear-cut; more on this below. Still, each side can see that the other consists of rational individuals acting in good faith. And each side can see the wrong involved in imposing a view on others based on reasons that those others consider deeply disagreeable. Third, given that the question "Whom should we hire?" can be answered independently of "deep facts" about research methodology, and given how contested that methodology is, Occam's Razor principle suggests that we should not posit more facts about that matter than strictly necessary for departmental purposes. Procedure 2 does exactly that.

6. Some Implications

We have argued that political theorizing should operate at a more coarse-grained level than moral theorizing and should be associated with a thinner ontology of normative facts. We now discuss two questions on which we have been silent so far. First, how should we determine the "political truth", that is, which normative facts should we posit at the political level? And, second, what would the proposed approach imply for the role of the political theorist?

6.1 How to Determine the Political Truth

On the levels view, what counts as "the political truth" depends on the society in question and its degree of reasonable pluralism.[12] To develop this point, we must say more about the difficult notion of "reasonableness".

---

[12] As should be clear, on the levels view, political theory need not dispense with the notion of truth (something that sets it apart from Rawls's original version of political liberalism). Our perspective is therefore cognitivist. That said, the levels view remains agnostic about complex meta-ethical questions about the nature of the moral truth. Compare the discussions in Cohen (2009), Quong (2011, chap. 8), and Estlund (2012).

For present purposes, we adopt the following simple definition. A comprehensive moral view is "reasonable" if it is (i) so far unfalsified by incontestable evidence and (ii) compatible with basic liberal requirements, including the prohibition on coercing others in the name of contested comprehensive doctrines.[13] Reasonable pluralism, then, is the presence of different reasonable views in a given society. According to our definition, a variety of moral views can count as reasonable, including many familiar examples: utilitarianism, prioritarianism, various forms of egalitarianism, Kantianism, Aristotelian virtue ethics, and so on. Likewise, many (tolerant) religious views will qualify as reasonable.

What we have given is a definition scheme. For example, we may use stricter or weaker standards of (i) the absence of falsification by incontestable evidence and of (ii) compatibility with basic liberal requirements. Our aim here is not to argue for a particular specification of (i) and (ii), but to make a structural point: whatever the criterion of reasonableness is, different degrees of reasonable pluralism will give rise to different specifications of the normative facts at the political level.

Crucially, the political-level facts should be multiply realizable at the comprehensive moral level, that is, supportable from the perspective of different competing reasonable moral views. The more such views we wish to accommodate, the thinner the resulting political-level facts will be. Ideally, we will be looking for what Rawls calls an "overlapping consensus" on political matters (Rawls 1996, lecture IV). "Political truths" should lie in the intersection of the "moral truths" according to the different reasonable moral views present in the society in question.[14] Proponents of different such views should each be able to endorse the agreed political principles from their own perspective: they may ultimately have their own comprehensive reasons for endorsing them, but they will still converge on the principles themselves.

In line with these observations, there is not just one political level, but several, corresponding to different political domains. The political level associated with a nation state may admit a richer ("thicker") specification of the normative facts than the political level associated with the

---

[13] Our characterization thus contains both a "thin" epistemic element and a "thin" moral one.
[14] This structure is also reminiscent of "supervaluationist" semantics for predicates which have competing admissible precisifications.

international arena. Indeed, some settings, particularly the international one, may exhibit forms of pluralism that transcend the reasonable or that will qualify as "reasonable" only after significantly weakening the standards of reasonableness; such settings pose challenges for political liberalism (a point familiar from Rawls 1999). For example, the principles of justice that are likely to be supported by an overlapping consensus within the United Nations will be dramatically thinner than those that will be supported by an overlapping consensus within a nation state.[15]

Ideally, the political-level facts should include facts about which procedures should be used for making collective decisions in the relevant domain when some issues need to be resolved on which there is no overlapping consensus. For instance, there is unlikely to be an overlapping consensus on many policy issues such as the precise tax rate, and yet a binding decision may still be needed. In such a case, we would like to attain an overlapping consensus at least on the legitimacy of the decision procedure itself.

6.2 The Role of the Political Theorist

On the levels view, the political theorist should formulate his or her arguments for a particular audience, namely everyone in the political domain. Political theory should not rely on the truth of claims that are reasonably contested within the society in question. This suggestion is familiar from the literature on political liberalism. Jonathan Quong (2011, p. 242), for example, argues that "[w]hen we go beyond the limits of the political, and try to provide the deep metaethical or epistemic foundations for political values and their priority, we are no longer engaged in political philosophy suitable for a well-ordered liberal society". In our terms, when we appeal to facts at a lower, more fine-grained moral level, we are no longer doing political theory "proper", but moral theory applied to political questions.

[15] Even within a given setting, such as a nation state, we may specify the political-level facts in thicker or thinner ways, depending on whether we are discussing constitutional arrangements, which should remain stable in the long term, or whether we are dealing with ordinary politics, where political commitments may be richer than at the constitutional level but more variable.

But what exactly does normative *political* theorizing involve? It involves seeking the truth at the political level. The levels view thus presupposes a cognitivist political meta-ethics: it refers to normative *truths* at the political level. Yet those truths must be found in the overlap between different reasonable comprehensive doctrines and be expressible using political-level concepts and categories. This places constraints on the kinds of arguments political theorists may put forward. As Rawls already suggested in *Political Liberalism*, these constraints are akin to those faced by Supreme Court Justices, who must answer legal questions not by marshaling their deep moral convictions, but by appeal to a restricted set of public reasons, as given by the relevant body of law (see Rawls 1996, pp. 231 ff.; for discussion, see also Waldron 2007).

Political theorists are not legal experts or judges. For them, identifying truths at the political level cannot be a matter of interpreting legal statutes, but it must be a matter of interpreting the public culture of the relevant society—another idea familiar from Rawls. Political theory, on this picture, needs to rely more heavily on empirical or sociological analysis, with the aim of interpreting the political-moral facts in the given society. This renders political theorizing more similar to the kind of interpretive exercise proposed by thinkers such as Michael Walzer (1987).[16] Perhaps surprisingly, then, a truly liberal approach requires that we re-orient political theory towards the kind of interpretive, sociologically informed methodology associated with "communitarian" approaches.

Many political theorists will baulk at this suggestion. This reaction may be, in part, due to the prospect of no longer having unconstrained freedom to invoke the rich methodology of moral theory, ranging from appeals to contested philosophical premises, and following an argument "wherever it takes us" to the use of far-fetched, sometimes outlandish thought experiments and other intuition pumps. Political theory according to the levels view is a more soberly disciplined activity.

However, might one not insist, with Jeremy Waldron, that "it ought to be someone's job to figure out whether [for example] torture is

---

[16] See also the so-called "practice-dependent" approach, as discussed in Sangiovanni (2008). Note that this would not remove disagreement from political theorizing. Different theorists are likely to defend different interpretations of the relevant overlapping consensus, given that such consensus needs to be unearthed, and is far from transparent.

objectively wrong in all circumstances and why"? And might one not agree with Waldron (2015, p. 124) that "[i]t is hard to see that this is not a task for political philosophers"? "[I]f it is not their task, whose is it?" We agree that it should be someone's task to think about these issues, but if what ultimately explains the wrongness of torture is a comprehensive moral fact, then the levels view suggests that it is the task of the moral (not the political) theorist to investigate it. However, there may well be a political-level truth concerning the wrongness of torture, which can be underwritten by a variety of different comprehensive moral truths. The political theorist would have to investigate the (im)permissibility of torture from that political perspective, not the comprehensive moral one.

Two further concerns may be put forward. The first is that doing political theory in line with the levels view involves a status-quo bias. The second is that refusing to engage with deeply contested comprehensive doctrines is disrespectful towards politically engaged citizens who fight for justice in the name of those doctrines.

The first worry—that the levels view is status-quo biased—echoes a complaint that liberals often raised against communitarians in the 1980s and 1990s. To defend the levels view, we begin by noting that a bias towards the status quo need not be bad: it depends on what the status quo is. As we have argued, our version of the levels view is meant to apply—like the later Rawls's—to liberal-democratic societies. So, the relevant status quo should ideally be one that is acceptable by liberal standards. Of course, the objector will insist that if political theory can only appeal to what "is already there" in a liberal public culture, resources will be limited for advocating progressive reform—for making a liberal society morally better. We find this worry misplaced, at least if one subscribes to what we called the "core liberal conviction". The worry presupposes that invoking the truth of contested moral doctrines in political argument could lead to a better society. But justifying reforms by reference to contested views is tantamount to renouncing liberalism, at least on our understanding of it. A society that appeals to comprehensive moral doctrines in order to justify state coercion is one in which individuals are being pushed around in the name of partisan and contested views. This is not a truly liberal society, and thus hardly morally superior from a liberal perspective. That said, progressive reforms can be politically justified if the status quo exhibits inconsistencies or contains illiberal elements, for instance if some existing laws or policies tacitly presuppose contested moral doctrines. Moreover, progressive reforms can be justified if the overlapping consensus itself shifts.

The second objection, put forward by David Enoch, suggests that by refusing to engage with the substance of deep moral disagreements, the political theorist treats his or her fellow citizens in a disrespectful, patronizing manner. Focusing only on facts at the political level seems equivalent to treating "some of the most deeply held beliefs of those engaged in the relevant disagreement as if they were mere preferences: For with mere preferences, arguably going second-order and impartial is precisely the way to go, and certainly engaging them in argument doesn't make much sense" (Enoch 2015, p. 136). There is no fact of the matter about which preferences are right and which are wrong. Preferences are not cognitive attitudes; they are conative. Similarly, so the objection goes, assuming that there is no fact of the matter about which comprehensive moral view is right fails to take seriously the proponents of such views.

We think that the levels view can be defended against this critique. The view does not deny the existence of facts about deep moral questions altogether. It simply asserts that those facts do not belong to the political level; they belong to a more fine-grained moral level. The levels view can therefore not be accused of treating fundamental moral commitments as if they were mere preferences. It is precisely because fundamental moral commitments are very important that it would be disrespectful to impose them on others who reasonably disagree with them and to use them to justify public policy.

7. Conclusion

We have suggested a way of demarcating the normative ontologies of moral and political theory, based on a "levels view" inspired by the philosophy of science and *Political Liberalism*. We have argued that this view is consistent with the aims of political theorizing in pluralistic societies, that it honours liberal convictions, and that it respects methodological principles of parsimony.

We conclude with some comments on the point and limits of our analysis. First, although we have framed the discussion around the distinction between moral and political theory, labels are not so important. Our interest is not in the question of what should be called "moral" or "political theory", but in distinguishing between different levels of normative analysis. Which labels we attach to them is secondary. What matters is vindicating the claim that, when it comes to justifying coercive state policies and binding public decisions, we may appeal only to a restricted set of normative facts and use political-level concepts and categories rather than comprehensive moral ones. This is the form of normative political theorizing we recommend.

Second, our defence of the levels view in its politically liberal form may raise the question of how it relates to the "domain" and "core values" views, and whether it really competes with them. After all, the levels view also implies that political theories (i) are concerned with the domain of public decisions (in line with the domain view) and (ii) deal with a distinctive set of normative facts (in line with the core-values view). So, what is special about the levels view? The view is special insofar as it does not merely *stipulate* that features (i) or (ii) define the difference between political and moral theory, as in the case of the domain or core-values views, but instead combines the two features and relates them to a more systematic approach to normative ontology.

Third, even those who are sympathetic to our version of the levels view may be skeptical about its real-world applicability. In the real world—especially when the overlapping consensus is rather thin—we often run out of arguments if we do not appeal to comprehensive moral convictions (see, e.g., Reidy 2000). This concern is legitimate, yet it does not invalidate the levels view. We have offered an ideal account of the facts to which we may appeal in normative political arguments. In the real world, we can at best approximate this ideal. We should appeal to as few comprehensive moral considerations as possible when we offer public justifications. In short, we should try to justify normative political claims in the spirit of the ideal, and the more a society departs from that ideal, the less liberal it will be. Nothing as neat and clear-cut as the ideal itself is likely to be realized in practice. But this does not invalidate the levels view as a regulative ideal.[17]

References

Arneson, Richard (2014) "Rejecting the Order of Public Reason," *Philosophical Studies* 170: 537–44.

Barry, Brian (1995) *Justice as Impartiality*, New York: Oxford University Press.

Buchak, Lara (2014) *Risk and Rationality*, Oxford: Oxford University Press.

Callan, Eamonn (1997) *Creating Citizens*, New York: Oxford University Press.

Carter, Ian (2015) "Value-freeness and Value-neutrality in the Analysis of Political Concepts," pp. 278–306 in David Sobel, Peter Vallentyne, and Steven Wall (eds.), *Oxford Studies in Political Philosophy*, vol. 1, New York: Oxford University.

Cohen, G. A. (2008) *Rescuing Justice and Equality*, Cambridge, MA: Harvard University Press.

Cohen, Joshua (2009) "Truth and Public Reason," *Philosophy & Public Affairs* 37(1): 2–42.

Daniels, Norman (1996) "Reflective Equilibrium and Justice as Political," pp. 144–76 in *Justice and Justification*, Cambridge Studies in Philosophy and Public Policy, Cambridge: Cambridge University Press.

Dennett, Daniel (1991) "Real Patterns," *Journal of Philosophy* 88(1): 27–51.

Enoch, David (2015) "Against Public Reason," pp. 112–42 in David Sobel, Peter Vallentyne, and Steven Wall (eds.), *Oxford Studies in Political Philosophy*, vol. 1, New York: Oxford University Press.

Enoch, David (2017) "Political Philosophy and Epistemology: The Case of Public Reason," pp. 132–65 in David Sobel, Peter Vallentyne, and Steven

[17] We are grateful to the audiences at the Graduate Workshop in Political Philosophy (Hamburg, April 2016), the LSE-Princeton Workshop (Princeton, May 2016), the Fudan-Harvard-NYUAD conference on Justice (Shanghai, July 2016), the UCD Politics Seminar (Dublin, November 2016), the Political Philosophy Seminar (Berlin, January 2017), the Moral, Political and Philosophical Workshop at KCL (London, November 2017), and the 6th Annual Workshop for Oxford Studies in Political Philosophy (Pavia, June 2018) for questions and comments. Special thanks to Paul Billingham, Ian Carter, David Estlund, R.J. Leland, Thomas Parr, Kevin Vallier, David Zuluaga Martínez, the editors, and an anonymous reviewer, for extensive written comments.

Wall (eds.), *Oxford Studies in Political Philosophy*, vol. 3, New York: Oxford University Press.

Estlund, David (2012) "The Truth in Political Liberalism," pp. 251–71 in Jeremy Elkins and Andrew Norris (eds.), *Truth and Democracy*, Philadelphia: University of Pennsylvania Press.

Fodor, Jerry (1974) "Special Sciences (or: The Disunity of Science as a Working Hypothesis)," *Synthese* 28(2): 97–115.

Goldman, Alvin, and Thomas Blanchard (2015), "Social Epistemology," in Edward N. Zalta (ed.), *The Stanford Encyclopedia of Philosophy*, summer edition <http://plato.stanford.edu/archives/sum2015/entries/epistemology-social/>.

Jackson, Frank, and Philip Pettit (1990) "Program Explanation: A General Perspective," *Analysis* 50(2): 107–17.

Korsgaard, Christine (2008) "Realism and Constructivism in Twentieth-Century Moral Philosophy," pp. 302–26 in *The Constitution of Agency: Essays on Practical Reason and Moral Psychology*, New York: Oxford University Press.

Larmore, Charles (1999) "The Moral Basis of Political Liberalism," *Journal of Philosophy* 96(12): 599–625.

Larmore, Charles (2013) "What Is Political Philosophy?" *Journal of Moral Philosophy* 10(3): 276–306.

Leland, R. J., and Han van Wietmarschen (2012) "Reasonableness, Intellectual Modesty, and Reciprocity in Political Justification," *Ethics* 122(4): 721–47.

List, Christian (2018) "Levels: Descriptive, Explanatory, and Ontological," *Noûs*, published online (early view) <https://doi.org/10.1111/nous.12241>.

List, Christian, and Peter Menzies (2009) "Non-reductive Physicalism and the Limits of the Exclusion Principle," *Journal of Philosophy* 106(9): 475–502.

List, Christian, and Kai Spiekermann (2013) "Methodological Individualism and Holism in Political Science: A Reconciliation," *American Political Science Review* 107(4): 629–43.

Lockhart, Ted (2000) *Moral Uncertainty and Its Consequences*, New York: Oxford University Press.

MacAskill, William (2016) "Normative Uncertainty as a Voting Problem," *Mind* 125(500): 967–1004.

Macedo, Stephen (1995) "Liberal Civic Education and Religious Fundamentalism: The Case of God v. John Rawls?," *Ethics* 105(3): 468–96.

Nozick, Robert (1974) *Anarchy, State, and Utopia*, New York: Basic Books.

Nussbaum, Martha C. (2011) "Perfectionist Liberalism and Political Liberalism," *Philosophy & Public Affairs* 39(1): 3–45.

Owens, David (1989) "Levels of Explanation," *Mind* 98(389): 59–79.

Putnam, Hilary (1967) "Psychological predicates," pp. 37–48 in W. H. Capitan and D. D. Merrill (eds.), *Art, Mind, and Religion*, Pittsburgh: University of Pittsburgh Press.

Quong, Jonathan (2011) *Liberalism without Perfection*, New York: Oxford University Press.

Quong, Jonathan (2016) "Disagreement, Equality, and the Exclusion of Ideals: A Comment on *The Morality of Freedom*," *Jerusalem Review of Legal Studies* 14(1): 135–46.

Radford, R. A. (1945) "The Economic Organisation of a P.O.W. Camp," *Economica* (New Series) 12(48): 189–201.

Rawls, John (1996) *Political Liberalism*, New York: Columbia University Press.

Rawls, John (1999) *The Law of Peoples: With "The Idea of Public Reason Revisited"*, Cambridge, MA: Harvard University Press.

Raz, Joseph (1986) *The Morality of Freedom*, Oxford: Clarendon Press.

Reidy, David A. (2000) "Rawls's Wide View of Public Reason: Not Wide Enough," *Res Publica* 6(1): 49–72.

Riedener, Stefan (2015) "Maximising Expected Value under Axiological Uncertainty: An Axiomatic Approach," DPhil thesis, University of Oxford.

Rossi, Enzo, and Matt Sleat (2014) "Realism in Normative Political Theory," *Philosophy Compass* 9(10): 689–701.

Sangiovanni, Andrea (2008) "Justice and the Priority of Politics to Morality," *Journal of Political Philosophy* 16(2): 137–64.

Schaffer, Jonathan (2003) "Is There a Fundamental Level?," *Noûs* 37(3): 498–517.

Waldron, Jeremy (1998) "Moral Truth and Judicial Review," *American Journal of Jurisprudence* 43(1): 75–97.

Waldron, Jeremy (2007) "Public Reason and 'Justification' in the Courtroom," *Journal of Law, Philosophy and Culture* 1(1): 107–34.

Waldron, Jeremy (2015) "Isolating Public Reasons," pp. 113–38 in Thom Brooks and Martha C. Nussbaum (eds.), *Rawls's Political Liberalism*, New York: Columbia University Press, 2015.

Walzer, Michael (1987) *Interpretation and Social Criticism*, Cambridge, MA: Harvard University Press.

Williams, Bernard (2005) *In the Beginning Was the Deed: Realism and Moralism in Political Argument*, Princeton, NJ: Princeton University Press.

Wittgenstein, Ludwig (1922) *Tractatus Logico-Philosophicus*, London: Kegan Paul.

8

Relevance Rides Again?

Aggregation and Local Relevance

Aart van Gils and Patrick Tomlin

I Introduction

Often institutions or individuals are faced with decisions where not all claims can be satisfied. Sometimes, these claims will be of differing strength. In such cases, we must decide whether or not weaker claims can be aggregated in order to collectively defeat stronger claims. Some deny that such aggregation is ever permissible (Taurek, 1977; Munoz-Dardé, 2005; Thomas, 2012; Doggett, 2013). Call this *Anti-Aggregation*. However, this position seems unduly restrictive when claims are close in strength. For example, consider:

Case 1. You can save one person from death, or some larger number of people, N1, from paraplegia.

According to Anti-Aggregation, no matter how large N1 gets, we should save one person from death. But imagine N1 were one hundred, or one thousand, or one million people. It seems implausible that we should allow so many people to suffer paraplegia in order to save a single life. This may push us toward what we can call *Pure Aggregation*, a view under which there is no restriction on aggregating claims, no matter how weak they are. However, this kind of position is vulnerable to two famous kinds of examples, the most well-known and oft-discussed of which are T. M. Scanlon's 'World Cup Case' and F. M. Kamm's 'Sore Throat Case':

Aart van Gils and Patrick Tomlin, *Relevance Rides Again? Aggregation and Local Relevance* In: *Oxford Studies in Political Philosophy Volume 6*. Edited by: David Sobel, Peter Vallentyne, and Steven Wall, Oxford University Press (2020). © Aart van Gils and Patrick Tomlin.
DOI: 10.1093/oso/9780198852636.003.0008

Case 2. *Scanlon's World Cup Case*: Suppose that Jones has suffered an accident in the transmitter room of a television station. Electrical equipment has fallen on his arm, and we cannot rescue him without turning off the transmitter for fifteen minutes. A World Cup match is in progress, watched by many people, and it will not be over for an hour. Jones's injury will not get any worse if we wait, but his hand has been mashed and he is receiving extremely painful electrical shocks. Should we rescue him now or wait until the match is over? Does the right thing to do depend on how many people are watching—whether it is one million or five million or a hundred million? (Scanlon, 1998: 235.)

Case 3. *Kamm's Sore Throat Case*: Suppose…that we have a choice between saving A's life and saving B's, and alongside B is C who has a sore throat. Our drug that can save B's life can also in addition cure C's sore throat (Kamm, 1998: 101).

Here is what Pure Aggregation would say about these cases. In Scanlon's case, provided the number of viewers were large enough, it would have us allow Jones to suffer the agonizing shocks in order to allow the many viewers to enjoy the football. In Kamm's case it would have us save B and C over A, since C's claim against a sore throat added to B's claim against death would outweigh A's claim against death. Both of these are entailments that many find counter-intuitive.

These two cases offer two different challenges to Pure Aggregation. Scanlon's case is an example of what we can call a *one vs. many* case— one strong claim (Jones's) is pitted against many weak claims (those of the viewers). Kamm's case is an example of what we can call a *tie-break* case—a seemingly trivial claim is all that separates two otherwise equally matched groups of much stronger claims.

Many people are not attracted to either extreme view—Case 1 speaks against Anti-Aggregation, while Cases 2 and 3 speak against Pure Aggregation. Therefore, they seek a middle way, which we can call *Limited Aggregation*. The best-known version of Limited Aggregation, versions of which both Scanlon and Kamm endorse, is a view known as the *Relevance View*. The idea of the Relevance View is that weaker claims can be aggregated against stronger claims when they are sufficiently close in strength to be 'relevant' to the stronger claim, but not when they are 'irrelevant' to the stronger claim. So, for example, claims against paralysis can be aggregated against a claim against death, but claims to watch the World Cup, or to avoid a sore throat, are 'irrelevant' and thus should not be counted.

The clearest articulation of this Relevance View is Alex Voorhoeve's 'Aggregate Relevant Claims' (ARC), which states:

1. Each individual whose well-being is at stake has a claim on you to be helped. (An individual for whom nothing is at stake does not have a claim.)
2. Individuals' claims *compete* just in case they cannot be jointly satisfied.
3. An individual's claim is *stronger*:
   a. the more her well-being would be increased by being aided; and
   b. the lower the level of well-being from which this increase would take place.
4. A claim is *relevant* if and only if it is sufficiently strong relative to the strongest competing claim.
5. You should choose an alternative that satisfies the greatest sum of strength-weighted, relevant claims (Voorhoeve, 2014: 66–7).

The Relevance View provides judgments in line with common intuitions across Cases 1, 2, and 3: provided N1 were large enough, it would require saving the many against paraplegia in Case 1, but it would require saving Jones in Case 2, and would allow for either A or B and C to be saved in Case 3 (Kamm advocates tossing a coin).[1]

Although the Relevance View vindicates our intuitions in these three cases, the Relevance View has always attracted criticism, often for the way it handles more complex cases (see, e.g., Halstead, 2016). These complaints have been extensively discussed, and replied to (e.g., Voorhoeve, 2014: 75–86). However, the Relevance View has recently come under renewed attack. In 'On Limited Aggregation' (hereafter

---

[1] Although Voorhoeve's view has this attractive implication in Kamm's case, strictly speaking Voorhoeve (2014: 67) restricts his theory to cases in which each member of a group has the same strength of claim.

OLA[2]), one of us (Tomlin, 2017) shows that when we consider complex cases involving groups of claims of diverse strength, the Relevance View suffers from an important ambiguity and seemingly fatal counter-intuitive entailments (OLA: 232–60).

In response to these problems, Victor Tadros has articulated a new version of the Relevance View, which he calls *Local Relevance* (Tadros, 2019). We will explain this view in depth in the next section. The key idea is that 'relevance' is not all-or-nothing: a claim is not relevant or irrelevant to some decision simpliciter. Rather, a claim can be relevant to some competing claims but not others, and therefore even if it is irrelevant to the strongest claims within a situation, it can still affect the decision as to which group to save in a limited way. The view is promising, and, as we will show, seems to get around the cases that OLA presents as objections to the original Relevance View as articulated by ARC. However, the general idea of Local Relevance is vague—it isn't clear exactly how to apply it to decisions about whom to save.

In this chapter, we want to explore and examine this view more closely. We will, first, introduce a more tightly-specified version of the Local Relevance view, called *Sequential Claims-Matching*. We will then show how Sequential Claims-Matching is able to meet the challenges presented in OLA. However, Sequential Claims-Matching faces difficulties and ambiguities of its own. In particular, we show that whilst it can deliver intuitive results in the OLA cases and in one vs. many cases, such as Scanlon's World Cup Case, it struggles to capture the intuition that Kamm's Sore Throat Case is designed to elicit and cannot necessarily rule out allowing tie-breaks in such cases. We will also show how there are two important ambiguities within the view that any would-be advocates will need to address. Finally, we briefly present an alternative version of Local Relevance, *Strongest Decides*.

One vs. many cases and tie-break cases are important objections to Pure Aggregation, and the Relevance View allows us to vindicate both objections on the same grounds, giving a unified anti-aggregative rationale, whilst still allowing us to reject Anti-Aggregation. However, in our view, the most promising account of Limited Aggregation, namely Local

---

[2] We will refer to this paper as OLA throughout to save Tomlin from having to refer to himself in the third person. Or at least from having to do so again after this note.

Relevance, will only justify Scanlon's judgment in the World Cup Case, and *not* Kamm's judgment in the Sore Throat Case. Therefore, we seek to pull apart the two most famous objections to purely aggregative views. It may be that our intuitions about tie-break cases can be vindicated via some other route, but, we will argue, this cannot be based upon the best understanding of when claims are relevant.[3]

Before we begin our examination of Local Relevance and Sequential Claims-Matching, a word on method. In exploring Local Relevance, we will focus largely on whether it is able to vindicate core Limited Aggregation intuitions. Obviously, any full theory of Local Relevance will need to do more than this: for example, it will need an account of the deeper justification or rationale for the view, and to take a stand on how to distinguish which claims are relevant to which.[4] While these are important tasks, it is clear from the wider literature that the search for a plausible position on aggregation which treads the middle ground between Anti-Aggregation and Pure Aggregation is *driven by* our intuitive responses to cases. Therefore, any defensible Limited Aggregation theory must both match our intuitions *and* have a firm theoretical grounding.

In this chapter we seek to make progress on the first half of this coin—the search for an approach to aggregation that can make sense of common intuitions. This should help inform the search for a deeper justification: once we have a sense of which view looks intuitively plausible, we will have a better sense of what kind of deeper justification can be offered for it. Obviously, this must be an ongoing process of reflective equilibrium, but we cannot try to 'do it all' in this chapter.

As a result, this chapter deals with many hypothetical cases designed to show particular results, and they are quite complex. In order to be as clear as possible about what each case shows, we will both walk the reader through how a given view will handle the case and provide a brief summary of what we think the important upshot of the case is. For those

---

[3] Alternative ways might involve appealing to a general form of pluralism (Ross, 2002); (Lang and Lawlor, 2015), or specifically by balancing aggregate goodness of satisfied claims with the unfairness of unsatisfied claims Lawlor 2006; Peterson 2009; Peterson 2010; Hirose, 2015).

[4] Voorhoeve (2014: 79–82) proposes a test based on the personal prerogative. Kamm (2015) rejects this approach.

happy to trust us, they can read the brief summary and ignore the detailed description of how and why we end up there.

II Local Relevance

In this section, we will briefly outline the ambiguity which OLA identifies in the Relevance View, and the principles which OLA shows different versions of the Relevance View to violate. (We will use these principles to test Local Relevance and the particular version of it that we will focus on, Sequential Claims-Matching, throughout the chapter.) We will also introduce in greater detail Tadros's Local Relevance idea.

For the Relevance View to get off the ground, it needs to distinguish between those claims that are relevant within a choice situation and those that are not. For a claim to be relevant, it needs to be sufficiently strong in comparison with some other claim. Let us call this latter claim the 'anchoring claim'. In standard cases in the literature, it is always clear what the 'anchoring claim' is. For example, in Case 2, the 'anchoring claim' is clearly Jones's claim against suffering agonizing shocks, whilst in Cases 1 and 3 the 'anchoring claim' is the claim against death. OLA exposes an ambiguity in the Relevance View. There are two different anchoring rules we might endorse. In simple cases, like Cases 1, 2, and 3, these two anchoring rules identify the same anchoring claim. But when we consider more complex cases, these two rules suggest different answers to the question of which claim is the anchoring claim. These two anchoring rules are:

Anchor by Strength: in order to be relevant, a claim must be sufficiently strong relative to the *strongest overall* claim in the competition.

Anchor by Competition: in order to be relevant, a claim must be sufficiently strong relative to the strongest claim *with which it competes*.

OLA shows that these anchoring rules violate the following compelling principles. Anchor by Competition violates:

Equal Consideration for Equal Claims: all claims of equal strength ought to be given equal weight in determining which group to save.

Anchor by Strength violates:

The Principle of Addition: merely adding a claim to a group of claims cannot *lessen* that group's choice-worthiness, compared with a fixed alternative.

In addition, Anchor by Strength violates a similar though importantly different principle that OLA does not discuss:

The Principle of Strengthening: merely strengthening a claim within a group of claims cannot *lessen* that group's choice-worthiness, compared with a fixed alternative.

In his 'Localized Restricted Aggregation', Victor Tadros introduces an important distinction between 'Global Relevance' and 'Local Relevance' (Tadros, 2019). Under Global Relevance, claims that are judged to be irrelevant to an anchoring claim are irrelevant to the overall decision concerning which group to save. By contrast, under Local Relevance, if a weaker claim is judged irrelevant in comparison with an anchoring claim, while the weaker claim cannot counter-balance or outweigh the anchoring claim, it can counter-balance or outweigh other, weaker, claims with which it competes and thus remain part of the overall decision about which group to save. In sum, according to Global Relevance, claims are either relevant or irrelevant simpliciter to a decision. According to Local Relevance, claims can be relevant to some competing claims but not others. Both Anchor by Competition and Anchor by Strength are Global Relevance views.

The core idea of Local Relevance is interesting, but it admits of many potential interpretations.[5] We know that claims are not relevant or irrelevant simpliciter, but this does not tell us how to decide between two groups of claims in messy cases where the groups are made up of claims of diverse strength. It is clear from Tadros's paper that we must 'match up' claims, allowing them to counter-balance, or neutralize, claims to which they are relevant. However, there are many ways that we might go about doing this 'matching'. In the next section, we will

---

[5] In response to Horton (2018), Tadros (2019: Section IV) refined his own version somewhat.

introduce a more precise version of Local Relevance, which specifies
how to match claims, before testing it against the OLA principles.[6]

III   Sequential Claims-Matching

The central insight of Local Relevance is that claims are not to be judged
relevant or irrelevant simpliciter. This insight is captured by this more
precise view, Sequential Claims-Matching, suggested to us by Garrett
Cullity.[7] Sequential Claims-Matching provides a procedure through which
we can decide which of two competing groups to save. Furthermore,
this way of proceeding, in which we start with the strongest claim in the
competition, as if it has a *pro tanto* claim to be saved which must be
matched or defeated by claims relevant to it, seems like a natural extension
of the Limited Aggregation approach. Limited Aggregation seeks to walk
the middle ground between Anti-Aggregation and Pure Aggregation, and
to combine personal and impersonal perspectives.[8] According the strongest claim a *pro tanto* claim to be saved seems to do justice to the personal,
Anti-Aggregative, perspective.

Sequential Claims-Matching

I.   Identify the strongest claim-type T1. Does one group contain more
individuals with claims of type T1 than the other?

   If not, remove all T1-claims from consideration, and proceed to Step V.

   If so, match each T1-claim from the group with fewer T1-claims to a
T1-claim from the group with more T1-claims, and remove the matched
claims from consideration.

II.   Now consider the remaining T1-claims. Does the other group contain claims of types that are relevant (i.e., sufficiently strong relative to)
claim-type T1?

---

[6] For an alternative OLA-inspired response to Tadros, see Horton (2018).

[7] OLA (252–7) suggested a similar 'matching' procedure for 'quasi-competition' cases (cases
where some subset of one large group must be saved) but did not consider this kind of procedure for 'competition cases' (where we must save one group or the other). OLA argues that
quasi-competition cases are actually more analogous to many policy decisions.

[8] For similar approaches in the literature that look to combine and/or balance personal and
impersonal perspectives, see Kamm's (five different versions of) "Sobjectivity" (1998: chapters
8–10; 2007: 34–6, 39, 50) and Thomas Nagel's (1989, 1995) "View from Nowhere" vs. "View
from Somewhere."

If not, you should decide in favor of the group with the remaining T1-claims.

If so, proceed to Step III.

III.   Do the relevant competing claims outweigh the T1-claims?

If not, you should decide in favor of the group with the remaining T1-claims.

If so, proceed to Step IV.

IV.   Match the set of remaining T1-claims to a set of relevant competing claims with comparable weight, and remove the matched claims from consideration.

V.   Now consider the remaining unmatched claims. Of these, identify the strongest claim-type T2. Repeat the above procedure.

VI.   Continue until either:

>   a.   one group contains unmatched claims, in which case you should decide in favor of that group; or
>
>   b.   neither group contains unmatched claims. Then it is not the case that you should decide in favor of one group over the other (though you must save one).[9]

Sequential Claims-Matching is, as you can see, complicated.[10] Nevertheless, the key idea is fairly simple: can the anchoring claim be matched by claims relevant to it? If not, we should meet the anchoring claim. If so, the anchoring claim is 'matched' to claims relevant to it, and all those claims are then set aside, since they counter-balance one another.[11] We now identify the strongest remaining claim, that becomes the new anchoring claim, and the process begins again.

Before we proceed to testing Sequential Claims-Matching against the OLA principles identified above, it may be helpful to show how it works

---

[9] We leave it open here whether in such a situation an agent has a free choice, or whether she must choose via a fair procedure such as a coin toss.

[10] As formulated here, Sequential Claims-Matching only applies to two-group cases. It may become more complicated still for three-group cases. The following seems like the most plausible procedure for three- or more-group cases: first, eliminate all groups with *no* claims relevant to the strongest overall claim. Second, conduct a series of pairwise comparisons using Sequential Claims-Matching. If a single group emerges, save that group. If no single group emerges, then it isn't the case that you must save one group over the others. We are grateful to Garrett Cullity for comments here.

[11] 'Set aside' here does *not* mean 'cancelled'. If the claims were cancelled, then two equally strong claims would cancel each other and nobody would have a claim to be saved. We're grateful to Mike Otsuka for useful comments here.

in a simple case. This will also allow us to introduce our way of presenting cases. In the following table, on the left-hand side is the strength level of the claim, Level 1 being the strongest. Under headings Group A and Group B are the numbers of claims at each level within each group, each claim being held by a distinct individual. For shorthand, we will refer to claims at Level 3 in Group B as B3 claims.

Suppose that relevance extends two levels up. That is, Level 3 claims are relevant to Level 1 claims, but Level 4 or Level 5 claims are *not* relevant to Level 1 claims. Furthermore, imagine that two claims at Level x precisely match one claim at the level above. So, for example, one claim at Level 1 will be precisely matched by two claims at Level 2, and those will be precisely matched by four claims at Level 3. Unless we state otherwise, these stipulations also apply to all cases hereafter.

Here is our initial case:

Case 4

Level	Group A	Group B
1	1	
3		5
5	3	

Here is how Sequential Claims-Matching would handle this case.

First, it would identify A1 as the initial anchoring claim. There are no B1 claims to match A1 with, so we see whether there are weaker but relevant claims in Group B. There are—the five B3 claims. Four of these B3 claims will precisely match the A1 claims, so we take these four B3 claims and the A1 claim which are then set aside, as they counter-balance one another. The one remaining B3 claim then becomes the new anchoring claim. There are no A3 claims with which to match the remaining B3 claim, and so we look to see if there are weaker but relevant claims in Group A. There are—the three A5 claims. However, three A5 claims do not match one B3 claim (since four Level 5 claims precisely match one Level 3 claim), and so we would save Group B in this case.

Sequential Claims-Matching has attractive implications in key cases that OLA uses to undermine Anchor by Competition and Anchor by Strength. Against Anchor by Competition, OLA (240–1) shows that adding equal numbers of equally strong claims to two groups will force us to switch groups. Even stranger, when one additional claim is added to one group (Group A), and a billion equally strong claims are added to another (Group B), Anchor by Competition may require us to switch from saving Group B to saving Group A (OLA: 242). Both of these counter-intuitive entailments result because Anchor by Competition violates Equal Consideration for Equal Claims: it allows that claims in one group will be relevant, while claims of equal strength in another will not, as they compete with different 'anchoring claims.'

Sequential Claims-Matching does not have these odd implications in the cases that OLA considers. This is because it allows that as soon as claims of strength X in one group are relevant, all such claims are relevant.

OLA (244–7) shows that Anchor by Strength has even odder implications: adding a very strong claim (such a claim against death) to a group of weaker claims would force us to switch *away* from saving that group, even if the competing group is not altered at all. This violates the Principle of Addition. Again, Sequential Claims-Matching would avoid this implication. Since relevance is determined by whether or not a claim is relevant to claims it competes with, adding a single claim could not suddenly rule as irrelevant claims within its own group.

Thus far we see that Sequential Claims-Matching is a better-specified version of Tadros's Local Relevance view, and that it is preferable to both Anchor by Competition and Anchor by Strength in that it provides more intuitively attractive judgments in the key cases presented in OLA. In the rest of the chapter, however, we will show that Sequential Claims-Matching faces difficulties and ambiguities of its own.

IV Sequential Claims-Matching and Sore Throats

Recall that there are two famous objections to Pure Aggregation. The first, exemplified by Scanlon's World Cup Case, is the *one vs. many* case. As well as handling the more complex cases introduced in OLA and Section IV of the present chapter, Sequential Claims-Matching would have no problem with such cases. The strongest claim (the 'one') would be the initial anchoring claim, and it would not be matched by any relevant claims (the 'many' being irrelevant) and so we would meet the strongest claim (e.g., we would save Jones in Case 2).

The second objection, exemplified by Kamm's Sore Throat Case, is the *tie-break* case. Here, however, we will show that Sequential Claims-Matching as we have defined it thus far would not be able to vindicate Kamm's intuition and would allow the sore throat to break the tie. We will then consider four possible amendments to Sequential Claims-Matching which will allow us to vindicate the intuition, but which are found wanting in other, more serious, ways. Therefore, we recommend rejecting the Sore Throat intuition, as the lowest caliber bullet of those on offer.

Case 3 Upshot: Sequential Claims-Matching will recommend saving B and C (a life and a sore throat) over A (a life).

Consider how Sequential Claims-Matching would handle Case 3 (Kamm's Sore Throat Case). Step I of Sequential Claims-Matching requires that we identify the strongest claims, and that where there are equal numbers of such claims, they are matched to each other and set aside. So, we would put aside A's claim against death, and B's claim against death. Step V of Sequential Claims-Matching states that we should then identify the next strongest claim, and that becomes the new anchoring claim. In Case 3, this would be C's claim against a sore throat. That claim is unmatched and so we would save B and C over A according to Step VI.

Therefore, as it stands, Sequential Claims-Matching only meets one of the two prominent objections to Pure Aggregation that in turn motivate the desire to find a plausible version of Limited Aggregation. The original Relevance View, which relied on Global Relevance, ruled out considering small claims such as sore throats, when much more serious claims were on the table. However, as a Local Relevance view, Sequential Claims-Matching never takes claims *fully* off the table. It therefore allows C's sore throat to act as a tie-break in Case 3.[12]

Could Sequential Claims-Matching be altered so that it can vindicate common intuitions in the Sore Throat Case? We will now consider four ways to alter or supplement Sequential Claims-Matching so that it can avoid having this counter-intuitive implication in the Sore Throat Case.

---

[12] We are grateful to an anonymous referee for helping us to describe the structural differences between Kamm's Irrelevant Utilities view and Sequential Claims-Matching.

Response 1

The first, seemingly obvious, way that we could try to fix this problem would be to amend Step V. The problem arises because the two claims against death counter-balance each other out, leaving us with an unmatched claim against a sore throat, which becomes the new anchor. But sore throats are irrelevant to claims against death, and so it seems troubling, from a Limited Aggregation perspective, to allow a sore throat to determine who lives and who dies. Claims that have been 'set aside' should still be allowed to determine whether remaining claims are relevant. We could alter Sequential Claims-Matching so that when it comes to considering 'new anchoring claims', we only consider those claims which are relevant to the weakest of those claims that have been previously matched and set aside. For example, in Case 3, A and B's claims may have been set aside, but since C's claim is relevant to neither of these, it should not be allowed to become a 'new anchor'. Consider this replacement for Step V:

Step V*:   Now consider the remaining unmatched claims. Are any of them relevant to the weakest claim that has previously been matched?
   a.   If so, identify the strongest claim-type T2. Repeat the above procedure.
   b.   If not, then it is not the case that you should decide in favor of one group over the other (though you must save one).

In Case 3, Step V* would not allow C's sore throat to condemn A to death. However, while Step V* can save the Sore Throat Case intuition, it comes at a price too high to pay: Sequential Claims-Matching using Step V* would violate the Principle of Addition and the Principle of Strengthening.

To see this, consider Case 5, which is a two-stage case. Initially we have a comparison between two groups. Then some additional claims are added to one or both groups. (See OLA and Horton, 2018, for use of this method.) From here onward, numbers in brackets represent claims added at the second stage.

Case 5

Level	Group A	Group B
1	1	
2		2
3		(1)
5	5	

Case 5 Upshot: Sequential Claims-Matching (incorporating Step V*), would initially not require us to save one group over the other. By adding a claim to Group B, we would then be required to save Group A.

According to Sequential Claims-Matching using Step V*, we would handle this case in the following way. At Stage 1, A1 would be the initial anchoring claim. That claim would be precisely matched by the two B2 claims. So, the A1 claim and the B2 claims would be set aside. The remaining five A5 claims are not relevant to the B2 claims, and so we would end in a tie.

At Stage 2, we add in the single B3 claim. This would fundamentally alter the structure of the case. For now, after having matched A1 to the B2 claims, we *would* have a new anchoring claim, namely the B3 claim. This would qualify as a new anchoring claim as it is relevant to the previously matched B2 claims. This B3 claim, however, would 'activate' the previously irrelevant A5 claims, which would not only match but outweigh the B3 claim, so we would save Group A. Therefore, by adding a claim to Group B we would switch from a tie, and viewing both groups as equally choice-worthy, at Stage 1, to saving Group A at Stage 2. This would clearly violate the Principle of Addition, which, recall, states that:

The Principle of Addition: merely adding a claim to a group of claims cannot *lessen* that group's choice-worthiness, compared with a fixed alternative.

A similar case (call it Case 5*) shows that Sequential Claims-Matching would also violate the Principle of Strengthening. Imagine that instead of adding the B3 claim, it was initially a much weaker claim (e.g., a Level 15 claim) that became much more serious at Stage 2. If it becomes a B3 claim at Stage 2, the same process described above would go through, and so the claim moving from B15 to B3 would force us to switch from viewing both groups as equally choice-worthy to choosing Group A, in violation of the Principle of Strengthening.[13]

Given that this way of vindicating the Sore Throat intuition comes at such a high price, we are back to allowing sore throats to break ties between equally-matched claims against death.

Response 2

Here is a second way in which Sequential Claims-Matching might be amended to avoid it having to allow the sore throat to make the difference in Case 3, without violating the Principles of Addition and Strengthening.[14] This amendment retains and builds upon the amendment examined in Response 1 (i.e., Step V* is retained). Return to Case 5. What goes wrong there, for Sequential Claims-Matching (amended to incorporate Step V*), is that the addition of the B3 claim 'activates' the five A5 claims, which not only match the B3 claim, but *outweigh* it. This means that we go from a situation in which both groups were regarded as equally choice-worthy to a situation in which Group A is favored, even though a claim was added to Group B.

This could be avoided if we refuse to allow the A5 claims to *outweigh* the B3 claim, but rather only allow them to 'match' or 'disable' the B3 claim. If the role of the A5 claims is restricted in this way, then all they can do is counter-balance the B3 claim, preventing it from tipping things in Group B's favor, and so the addition of the B3 claim would leave us where we were after Stage 1, namely in a tie.

In his original formulation of the idea of Local Relevance Tadros states that while a claim may lack force against a stronger claim to which it is not relevant, it can still 'retain such force for other aspects of the overall decision [about which group to save]. For example, it may counter-balance other [claims]' (Tadros, 2019). Tadros leaves it open here what kind of roles weaker claims might play but gives the *example* of counter-balancing. The amendment to Sequential Claims-Matching we are

---

[13] We are grateful to Anna Mahtani and Alex Voorhoeve for useful discussion here.
[14] This has been proposed in discussed by both Victor Tadros and Alec Walen.

considering here would restrict weaker claims to *only* counter-balancing stronger claims, therefore not allowing them to outweigh them. So, in Case 5, at Stage 2 all the A5 claims can do is match the added B3 claim (even though there is enough of them to outweigh the B3 claim in a 'straight fight').

Note that the claim here cannot be that weaker claims are *always* restricted to counter-balancing rather than outweighing stronger claims to which they are relevant. If that were the case, Sequential Claims-Matching would deliver the implausible recommendation in Case 1 that no matter how large the number of people facing paralysis got, we would only ever consider them to have matched the claim against death. So, we need a more precise and complex articulation of this restricted role for weaker claims. We propose this:

Restricted Role: Claims can only counter-balance, but not outweigh, claims to which they are relevant if they are also competing with claims with which they are not relevant.

This may sound confusing, but again a simple example will illustrate the point of Restricted Role. Restricted Role would allow the claims against paralysis to outweigh the claim against death in Case 1, but would only allow the A5 claims to match, but not outweigh, the B3 claim in Case 5, because the A5 claims also are in competition with the B2 claims. This makes sense within the Local Relevance view, because while the A5 claims are relevant to the B3 claim, they are not relevant to the competition between the A1 claim and B2 claims, and so, we might think, should only be able to neutralize the B3 claim, without affecting the competition between the stronger claims.

However, we have concerns about this view. Consider, first, the following case:

Case 6

Level	Group A	Group B
1	1	
3		5
5	(10)	(10)

Case 6 Upshot: At Stage 1, Sequential Claims-Matching with Restricted Role would instruct us to Save Group B. We then add equal numbers of equally strong claims to both groups. This leads to a tie at Stage 2.

At Stage 1, the five B3 claims are relevant to, and outweigh, the single A1 claim. We then add, at Stage 2, ten Level 5 claims to each side. We would expect adding equal claims like this to leave everything else the same. Indeed, it is precisely this intuition on which Tadros relies in order to show how Local Relevance performs better than Global Relevance (in a case he calls 'Adding People' (Tadros, 2019: section III)). However, on the version of Sequential Claims-Matching we are considering here, adding these equal claims would result in a tie.

The A1 claim is the initial anchoring claim. This is matched by four B3 claims, leaving one B3 claim as the new anchoring claim. This is matched by four A5 claims, leaving six A5 claims as the new anchoring claims. These are matched by six of the ten B5 claims, leaving four B5 claims unmatched. Under Sequential Claims-Matching as we originally considered it, these four B5 claims would carry the day in favor of Group B.

However, under the current proposal, they are irrelevant, and will not be counted. Since B5 claims compete with an A1 claim to which they are irrelevant, they can only disable or match claims to which they are relevant, and so beyond the six B5 claims required to match the A5 claims, B5 claims can make no difference. Thus, we would have a tie, in violation of the key intuition that has been used to show why some version of Local Relevance is necessary, that adding equally strong claims of equal numbers to the groups should not alter which group is to be saved.[15]

In addition, this violates Equal Consideration for Equal Claims. *All* of the A5 claims matter—the more A5 claims we have, the more that speaks in favor of saving Group A. A5 claims can not only match but *outweigh* the B3 claims. B5 claims, however, matter only insofar as they match A5 claims, and so four of them are not counted.

Some have declared themselves happy to let go of Equal Consideration for Equal Claims. It is surely a far weaker bullet to bite than, say, the

---

[15] In response to Horton (2018), Tadros accepts that sometimes adding claims of unequal numbers but equal strength should cause us to switch to saving the group to which fewer claims have been added. However, as we have stressed here, he accepts the intuition that this is unacceptable in cases such as Case 6 and 6*. Tadros (2019, sections III–IV).

Principle of Addition. But it isn't just the principle that should cause us to reject Response 2. The counter-intuitive cases, independently, weigh heavily against it. As we have already noted, Case 6 is a variant of the kind of case that was used as a rationale for Local Relevance. Further, imagine, at Stage 2, that we added five A5 claims and one million B5 claims (call this Case 6*). The five B5 claims would be treated equally to the five A5 claims, since it would match it. But the 999,995 other B5 claims would be superfluous. We would go from saving Group B to a tie, even though we had added equally strong claims to both sides, but with numbers heavily in favor of Group B. This is counter-intuitive.

This view would also leave us with a lot of ties: in going down the chain of matching claims to claims, as soon as we got past the point at which the claims were relevant to the strongest claim, we would be in 'matching only' territory. Complex, real-world, cases, would therefore almost always end in a tie.

Response 3

A third way of amending Sequential Claims-Matching so as to capture the Sore Throat intuition, is suggested by the way that Tadros attempts to escape this conclusion. Tadros tries to use the fair procedure of tossing a coin between A and B to exclude or outweigh C's claim. It is plausible that the value of a fair procedure would explain our intuitions in the Sore Throat Case. After all, for many, the intuition is not merely that you are not required to save B and C over A, it is that you are required to toss a coin.[16]

Tadros tries to bring in this kind of consideration via two routes. The first is to claim that A has an interest in a chance of being saved, and C's claim is irrelevant to A's interest in having that chance. The second route is to claim that tossing a coin is a fair procedure that has independent value, and that C's claim is not sufficiently strong to outweigh that value.

These two routes look importantly different. The first incorporates interests in chances to be saved *within* the Sequential Claims-Matching framework: A's interest in having a chance at survival is strong enough

---

[16] We are grateful for comments from an anonymous referee here.

to deem C's claim *irrelevant*.[17] The second claims that fair procedure is an independent value, and the difference between the groups (i.e., C's claim) is not sufficient to warrant abandoning that value. This does not rely on C's claim being irrelevant.

Incorporating a concern for chances within the Sequential Claims-Matching procedure is undermotivated and leads to counter-intuitive results. Meanwhile, relying on fair procedure, or the distribution of chances, as an independent value is not so much an amendment of Sequential Claims-Matching as downgrading it to only *pro tanto* guidance, in competition with other considerations.

If this is right, then our intuitions in tie-break cases can only be explained by entirely different considerations from those that explain our intuitions in one vs. many cases. Scanlon's World Cup viewers have irrelevant claims; whilst Kamm's sore throat victims have relevant claims, but those claims (or the difference between the two groups) are outweighed by some alternative value. Recall that the original Relevance View appeared to explain both intuitions. Sequential Claims-Matching is only able to vindicate the one vs. many intuitions—something else, on this third response, must take care of the tie-break cases.

So, only Tadros's first route is an *amendment* to Sequential Claims-Matching that could see it vindicate the Sore Throat intuition from the inside, by ruling C's claim to be irrelevant. There seem to be two ways to understand A's claim to holding a lottery—via A's interest in the chance of being saved, or via A's moral claim to a fair procedure.

If A's claim to a chance to be saved is based on the cost of going from a 50% chance to be saved to a 0% chance of being saved, this would surely be counter-balanced by B's interest in going from a 50% chance to be saved to a 100% chance to be saved. B has an equally strong interest in *avoiding* the lottery as A has in holding the lottery. This would still leave C as a tie-breaker.

If A's claim to a 50% chance of being saved is based on that being *fair*, then it must be that fairness declares that a fair coin is the correct procedure *prior to C's claim being dismissed as irrelevant*. But this is far from

---

[17] Kamm sometimes appears to adopt this reasoning—that the sore throat is too weak a claim compared with the claim to a *chance of life*. At other times she appears to claim that the sore throat is too weak compared to the claim against death. See Kamm (2005: 13), where both types of reasoning are on show.

uncontroversial. In addition, once we *moralize* claims, allowing them to depend on fairness, for example, we have moved a long way from the Relevance View and the account of claims with which we began.

Even if A's interest in a 50% chance can be explained, however, this amendment has counter-intuitive implications:

Case 7

Level	Group A	Group B
1	1	1
2		
3		(1)
4	3	

Case 7 Upshot: At Stage 1, the groups are equally choice-worthy. We then add a claim to Group B, and this addition requires us to save Group A.

At Stage 1, A1 and B1 have equal claims. According to Tadros, the A4 claims are irrelevant to B1's claim *and* (let us stipulate) B1's claim to a fair procedure. So, we would view both groups as equally choice-worthy and hold a lottery. However, at Stage 2, within the Sequential Claims-Matching framework, the addition of the B3 claim changes things. It is relevant to A1's claim, and so, absent other considerations, would act as a tie-breaker. However, it would also 'activate' the A4 claims, as they are relevant to it, and we would then move to the usual 'back and forth' of Sequential Claims-Matching. The A4 claims would not only be relevant but would outweigh the B3 claim, and so we would save Group A. So, adding a claim to Group B at Stage 2 would move us from a lottery to saving Group A. This violates the Principle of Addition.

Response 4

An alternative way to save Kamm's Sore Throat intuition within Sequential Claims-Matching would be to endorse the idea of 'rough equality' (see Hirose, 2015: 35). That is the idea that the scales of justice should not be finely tuned. As we go down the Sequential Claims-Matching process, so long as the groups are held to be 'roughly equal', then it is not the case that we must save one group over the other. If we consider Case 3, we can see that the claims of A and B are precisely matched, and so the addition of C's sore throat doesn't take us out of the zone of 'rough equality', and so it is not true that we must save B and C over A.

We have several concerns about this line of thinking. One problem that advocates of 'rough equality' will surely come up against is that in specifying this view they will need to decide whether what counts as 'rough equality' is a constant or contextual matter. To explain: in Case 3, if the 'rough equality' view is to save the Sore Throat intuition, one sore throat cannot tip the scales. But is this because of the broader context (where two lives are also at stake) or because sore throats never tip scales? On the latter view, under which sore throats cannot be difference-makers, we would end up viewing two sore throats as 'roughly equal' to one. This seems implausible. But on the other view, under which what counts as 'rough equality' is contextual, or proportional, to what is at stake, then we will end up viewing 1,001 lives as 'roughly equal' 1,000. We find this counter-intuitive, though some have endorsed this claim (Kamm, 1998: 103; though see 2007: 33).

Our second response to 'rough equality' is to wonder *why* (other than it vindicating the tie-break intuition) we should prefer 'scales of justice' that ignore seemingly morally-relevant information. When pressed on this, advocates of the view seem to rely on the following kind of case. Imagine you could save the life of a 20-year-old or a 21-year-old. Both have the same life expectancy. Therefore, one is deprived of one more year of life than the other.[18] If this translates into a stronger claim for the 20-year-old, then, without rough equality, we should save the 20-year-old over the 21-year-old. Many find this counter-intuitive.

While we agree with the intuition that we are not required to save the 20-year-old in this case, we do not think this case provides much backing for the idea of 'rough equality' in cases of multiple claims. In essence, the issue is that the two cases raise two importantly different questions. Case 3 raises the question of how we should balance different people's claims of different strengths against one another. The question raised

---

[18] [18]For competing accounts of the moral relevance of this, see McMahan (2003: 165–74); Broome (2004: 241–53).

when choosing between two people of roughly similar ages, however, raises the question of how to establish the strength of a claim. All those who reject Pure Aggregation will endorse the idea that the 'separateness of persons' matters in some way, and so we should be careful in reading straight across from a case in which what is at stake is *how strong* a claim is to a case in which what is at stake is whether, or to what extent, a claim *counts*. For example, we don't think the choice between saving a 20-year-old or a 21-year-old is the *same* as the choice between saving a 20-year-old or a 20-year-old *and* a person with one year of quality of life left (if they are saved).

However, even if we accept 'rough equality', problems remain. One, which we will describe in detail below as 'A Further Problem', is that 'rough equality' will still sometimes allow one headache to determine who lives and who dies. Another is that even if 'rough equality' explains why we shouldn't let the headache break the tie in Case 3, then the *rationale* for tossing a coin in Case 3 is *entirely distinct* from the rationale for saving Jones in Case 2. In other words, even if Sequential Claims-Matching combined with a commitment to 'rough equality' saves the anti-aggregative intuitions in Cases 2 and 3, there is no single underlying rationale that explains both.

The original Relevance View, if accepted, would explain both intuitions. But 'rough equality' and Sequential Claims-Matching are wholly distinct. One can accept Sequential Claims-Matching without accepting 'rough equality', and one can accept 'rough equality' without accepting Sequential Claims-Matching, or indeed any Limited Aggregation view—'rough equality' could be attached to Pure Aggregation, for example. Indeed, not only are Sequential Claims-Matching and 'rough equality' distinct positions, one might even say that they are somewhat in tension with one another. Sequential Claims-Matching seems to offer us a precise method for determining which group to save. To throw the vague idea of 'rough equality' over the top of that procedure may undermine its merits.

A Further Problem

Thus far in this section we have been considering whether Sequential Claims-Matching can accommodate the intuition that a sore throat cannot decide who lives and who dies in a tie-break case. We have considered four ways of doing so, and there are, at the least, concerns with each. However, even if Sequential Claims-Matching can be modified or supplemented such that we can avoid this entailment in tie-break cases, no version of Sequential Claims-Matching can escape the entailment that a single sore throat will sometimes decide who lives and who dies. Consider, for example, Case 8.

Case 8

Level	Group A	Group B
1	1	
2		3
3	3	
4		3
5	3	
...	...	...
99	3	
100		2 (+1)

Case 8 Upshot: At Stage 1, we have a tie. At Stage 2, through the addition of another B100 claim (a very weak claim), the tie is broken and we save Group B. As such one very weak claim determines whether the strongest claim in the competition, A1, is met.

Imagine in between Level 5 and Level 100, the pattern of three claims in Group A at each odd-numbered level, and three claims in Group B at each even-numbered level continues. Sequential Claims-Matching (as originally conceived) would then handle this case as follows. The A1 claim would be the initial anchoring claim. Two B2 claims would match it, leaving one B2 claim as the new anchoring claim. That would be matched by two A3 claims, leaving one A3 claim as the new anchoring claim. This process would continue all the way down, until one A99 claim was left as the anchoring claim. This would be matched by the two B100 claims, leaving us with a tie. However, at Stage 2, if we add another B100 claim—an extremely weak claim—this would tip things in favor of Group B, meaning that that extremely weak claim is decisive. Therefore, whether or not that additional B100 claim is present could decide whether A1 lives or dies.

This entailment could be avoided if we endorse the Restricted Role for weaker claims, considered in Response 2, since then the additional B100 claim added at Stage 2 could only counter-balance the A99 claims, which were already counter-balanced. However, consider a modified version of the case (Case 8*), in which we start with only one B100 claim. This single B100 claim would fail to counter-balance the A99 anchoring claim, and so we would save Group A at Stage 1. Adding in a second B100 claim at Stage 2 would counter-balance the A99 claim, and so take us to a tie. So, even if we accept Restricted Role, the single B100 claim would again be decisive, even though it is extremely weak in comparison with the strongest claims in play.

Of course, 'rough equality' would still rule out a single headache making the difference in Case 8, but all 'rough equality' can do is to kick this can further down the road. If we keep adding headaches to Group B, at *some point* we will emerge out of the zone of 'rough equality' and find ourselves in the zone of inequality. Therefore, while it may be difficult to find the exact place where it occurs, a single headache will still take us from a tie to saving Group B.

Summary of Section IV

In this section we have shown how Sequential Claims-Matching as we originally formulated it cannot capture Limited Aggregation intuitions in tie-break cases. We then considered four ways in which Sequential Claims-Matching could be amended in order to get around this problem, but each seemed to generate further difficulties for the view, causing us to violate the very principles which OLA had shown the Relevance View to violate. In addition, in non-tie-break cases such as Case 8, we still wouldn't be able to avoid a single very small claim making all the difference. Our sense here, is that the advocate of Limited Aggregation should reject the tie-break intuition, though we accept that not all advocates of Limited Aggregation will feel able to do so.

Even if Sequential Claims-Matching is accepted as we originally formulated it, or some alternative version is put forward, however, two key ambiguities about the view remain, which we will now describe.

V Ambiguity 1: How Should We Match Claims in Sequential Claims-Matching?

We have noted how Tadros's explanation of Local Relevance view seems to require us to 'match up' claims with one another, so that they can counter-balance other claims to which they are relevant. Sequential Claims-Matching is a clear advance on the loosely-specified Local Relevance view because it clearly outlines a process by which we should match up claims. Nevertheless, it still contains an ambiguity concerning how to 'match up' claims. The relevant step within the Sequential Claims-Matching view is as follows:

IV.   Match the set of remaining T1-claims to a set of relevant competing claims with comparable weight, and remove the matched claims from consideration.

This step shows how anchoring claims must be matched with claims that are relevant to them. However, more than one kind of claim can be relevant to a single anchor, and in such a case we need a procedure to decide which of the weaker claims to match with the anchor. Consider this case:

Case 9

Level	Group A	Group B
1	1	
2		3
3	2	
4	4	
5		
6		20

Case 9 Upshot: A B2 claim can be matched with *either* A3 or A4 claims. Whether the B2 claim is matched with A3 or A4 claims determines which group is saved. Sequential Claims-Matching provides no guidance as to which is preferable.

The A1 claim would be the initial anchoring claim. This claim is matched by two B2 claims, leaving the remaining B2 claim as the new anchoring claim. Here is where the ambiguity concerning how to match up claims comes in. Both the A3 and A4 claims are relevant to the B2 claim. Either the two A3 claims or the four A4 claims would exactly counter-balance the one remaining B2 claim. However, whether we match the B2 claim either with the two A2 claims or the four A4 claims will decide which group we will save.

Suppose, first, that we match the B2 claim with the two A3 claims. These are all the A3 claims there are, and so we move one level down in order to identify the next anchoring claim. The A4 claims become the new anchoring claims. What is crucial here is that the twenty B6 claims are relevant to the A4 claims and outweigh them. So, matching in this way means that we would save Group B.

But now let's suppose that when we have the remaining B2 claim as the anchoring claim that we match it with the four A4 claims. That would mean that the only claims that are left in the competition are two A3 claims and twenty B6 claims. But B6 claims are not relevant to A3 claims. There could be any number of B6 claims but they could never outweigh a single A3 claim. So, the two A3 claims are unmatched. Therefore, were we to match claims in this way, we would save Group A.

This case shows that there is an ambiguity in how we match claims on Sequential Claims-Matching that could be decisive in deciding which group to save. What Sequential Claims-Matching requires, therefore, is a principled way in which to determine how we match claims in this kind of case. We have been able to conceive of three rival possibilities, all of which have some plausibility, but which would give conflicting advice in Case 9.

The first possibility is the following:

Match to the Strongest Competing Claim: Anchoring claims should be matched with the strongest unmatched claims with which they compete.

This rule has some plausibility. Sequential Claims-Matching in general has a structure which encourages us to look at the 'next level down'—that is, after all, the next claim in the sequence. It also seems a non-arbitrary and clear way to decide how to match up the claims. In Case 9, Match to the Strongest Competing Claim would have us match the B2 claim to the A3 claims, leaving the A4 claims to be outweighed by the B6 claims. Therefore, we would save Group B.

The second possibility is the following:

Match in the Interest of the Overall Strongest Claimant: Anchoring Claims should be matched in whatever way is in the interest of strongest overall claimant.

Limited Aggregation generally has, of course, much in common with Anti-Aggregation. Anti-Aggregation is concerned, above all else, with the person who possesses the strongest claim. Limited Aggregation doesn't hold this concern above all else—it would allow the weaker claims to outweigh the strongest claim in Case 1—but it is plausible to think that it would inherit this general priority to the worst off. Match in the Interest of the Overall Strongest Claimant says that when there is a plurality of ways of matching up claims within the confines of Sequential Claims-Matching, and where different ways of matching would produce different outcomes (as in Case 9) we should, in essence, allow the person possessing the overall strongest claim in the competition to choose how we should match up the claims. In Case 9, A1 is the strongest claim. If we match the B2 claim with the A4 claims, this leaves the A3 claims unmatched, since they are 'out of reach' of the B6 claims. And so, Group A would win, which is, of course, what A1 would want.

The third possibility is as follows:

One or the Other: when there is an ambiguity over how to match up claims, and different ways of doing so would require saving different groups, then it is not the case that you should decide in favor of one group over the other (though you must save one).

This view takes the ambiguity we have noted in this section not as something to be rectified, but rather as to reveal that we are not required to save one group over the other. Since the Sequential Claims-Matching process can be used to justify saving either group, we cannot say that we are required to save one group over the other. In such circumstances, it may be that we are permitted to choose, or are required to toss a coin.

Advocates of Local Relevance owe us an account of how to match up claims with one another. Sequential Claims-Matching provides such an account. However, there remains an ambiguity in that even within the strictures of that more precise theory, there can be more than one way to match up claims. So, advocates of Sequential Claims-Matching will need to further specify the view.

VI   Ambiguity 2: Partial Leftovers

Thus far we have been considering cases in which two claims at one level *precisely* match one claim at the level above. However, it is unlikely that things will always be quite so neat, especially given how small the differences between claims can be. For example, even if one accepts that two claims at Level 2 will precisely match one claim at Level 1, imagine if one of the Level 2 claims becomes ever so slightly stronger (e.g., if it is a claim against partial paralysis, the loss of use of one more finger). Does this remain a Level 2 claim with no additional weight? Surely not. But equally implausible is that it would become a Level 1 claim, and double in weight.

To put things more concretely, many health systems use Quality Adjusted Life Years (QALYs) or Disability Adjusted Life Years (DALYs) to measure the strength of claims. Imagine a case in which a single person facing the loss of 50 QALYs faces three people facing the loss of 20 QALYs each. The single strongest claim outweighs two of the weaker claims and is defeated by three of the weaker claims; 2.5 of the weaker claims precisely match the stronger claim.[19]

If whole numbers of weaker claims do not precisely match stronger claims, we need to decide how to handle the 'partial claims' that are left over once the matching has taken place. To make things clearer, consider this case. In this case, 2.5 claims at Level x precisely match one claim at the level above.

---

[19] For related discussion, see Kamm (2005: Section VII, 15–18). Kamm's discussion clearly indicates that lesser claims must compete with leftovers but is ambiguous between our Full Claim Relevance and Partial Relevance.

Case 10

Level	Group A	Group B
1	1	
2		3
3		
4		
5	20	

Case 10 Upshot: Following Sequential Claims-Matching, 0.5 of a B2 claim is left over from the first round of 'matching' and becomes the new anchor. But it is ambiguous in Sequential Claims-Matching whether the twenty A5 claims need to be relevant to that 0.5 of a B2 claim or to a full B2 claim. Which route we take, determines whether the twenty A5 claims are relevant and so which group we save.

A1 is the initial anchoring claim. It is matched by 2.5 B2 claims, seemingly leaving half a B2 claim as the new anchoring claim. There is an ambiguity about what kinds of claims should be considered relevant to this partial B2 claim. The key question is whether the twenty A5 claims are relevant to the half B2 claim. If it were a full B2 claim, then there would be no ambiguity, since Level 5 claims are not relevant to Level 2 claims. However, in this case, there is half a Level 2 claim remaining. In order to be relevant, should we demand that the A5 claims are relevant to a full B2 claim or a half B2 claim? This suggests two possible principles.

Full Claim Relevance: To be relevant, a claim must be relevant to the claim with which it competes (e.g., the full B2 claim).

Partial Claim Relevance: To be relevant, a claim must be relevant to the proportion of the claim with which it is in competition (e.g., the half B2 claim).

On the one hand, we could imagine one of the B2 claimants objecting to small A5 claims being considered relevant to her far weightier claim. On the other hand, it seems unfair to expect A5 claims to have to be relevant to a full B2 claim when they are only in competition with half a B2 claim.

In our view, Partial Claim Relevance seems the right view. However, this again raises the issue of sore throats. Imagine a case in which there is a partial leftover of 1/1,000 of a very serious claim. Very weak claims, which would only need to be relevant to (and not necessarily equal to) the leftover, could then tip the balance. This adds to the case for advocates of Limited Aggregation letting go of the tie-break intuition.

VII   An Alternative Version of Local Relevance

We began by highlighting how Tadros's Local Relevance was promising. We sought to provide a more concrete version through Sequential Claims-Matching and have discussed at length the merits and problems of this view. One ambiguity we highlighted (in Section V) concerns how to match up claims with one another. One suggestion we offered was to Match in the Interest of the Overall Strongest Claimant. However, we have only considered this within the confines of Sequential Claims-Matching. But why not match in the interest of the overall strongest claimant more generally? So, whenever we face cases with groups of claims of diverse strength, if there is any way to match the claims such that the strongest claimant would have her claim met, then we should allow this. The basic idea here is that we take from Anti-Aggregation the priority for the worst off and we allow that to dictate the way in which claims are matched. Call this view *Strongest Decides*. Here is an example where this view would deliver a different verdict from Sequential Claims-Matching:[20]

Case 11

Level	Group A	Group B
1	1	
3	3	3
5		10

---

[20] We draw here on cases presented in Horton (2018), though we put them to different ends here.

Case 11 Upshot: Sequential Claims-Matching would tell us to save Group B. Strongest Decides, by contrast, would tell us to save Group A.

Sequential Claims-Matching would first match two B3 claims with the A1 claim, leaving one B3 claim as the new anchoring claim. That would be matched by one A3 claim, leaving two A3 claims. Finally, these two A3 claims would be outweighed by the ten B5 claims. So, we would save Group B.

Strongest Decides, by contrast, would have the A1 claimant decide how we match claims in this case. It is in A1's interest to have the three A3 claims be matched with the three B3 claims, as such taking all these claims out of consideration. This would leave A1's own claim and ten B5 claims. Level 5 claims are not relevant to a Level 1 claim, and so we would save Group A.

Here is a potential problem with Strongest Decides: it may violate Equal Consideration for Equal Claims.[21] It is clear that, in some cases, there will be more than one way of 'matching up' claims, and the way that would be favored by the person with the strongest claim may be one in which some, say, Level 5 claims are matched with claims to which they are relevant, while other Level 5 claims are matched with claims to which they are not relevant. Therefore, in the 'matching scheme' the strongest claim would select, some Level 5 claims will be counted (as they're relevant to the claims they're matched with) and others will not (as they're not relevant to the claims they're matched with).

While that much is clear, it is not clear whether this in fact violates Equal Consideration for Equal Claims. OLA (241) makes it clear that *any* plausible view will not advocate Equal *Treatment* for Equal Claims, for when we have two groups with equal claims on both sides, we will end up saving one group and not the other. What OLA objected to, and Equal Consideration for Equal Claims attempted to articulate, was that *at the outset* some views ruled that some claims of a certain strength mattered, and other claims, of the same strength, did not. Strongest Decides does not do this.

Strongest Decides only really comes into play when there is a plurality of ways in which to 'match up' claims with one another. Since equal

---

[21] We are grateful to Bastian Steuwer for pressing this worry.

claims can always be matched to each other, claims of equal strength will never be ruled as irrelevant *at the outset*: there is always a potential 'match up' in claims in which all claims of the same strength are relevant. The strongest claim is able to dictate which 'match up' is chosen *as a tie-breaker*. This may involve choosing a 'match up' in which some Level 5 claims are relevant and others are not. Is this like accepting that we will save some Level 5 claims and not others, which is surely acceptable? Or is it like ruling out some Level 5 claims but not others at the outset? Or, is it like neither? Equal Consideration for Equal Claims may need to be further refined. Or perhaps it must be abandoned. Perhaps it didn't properly articulate what Anchor by Competition was getting wrong. At any rate, this is an issue that advocates of Strongest Decides must confront.

VIII Concluding Remarks

This chapter is an exploration. Many of us would like to avoid biting the bullets of the extreme Anti-Aggregation and Pure Aggregation positions. Limited Aggregation therefore seems our best hope. But as OLA shows, the Relevance View (or what Tadros calls 'Global Relevance') is open to potentially devastating objections. Tadros's version of Limited Aggregation, 'Local Relevance', is attractive, but can be fleshed out in a variety of ways. It is this idea that we have sought to precisify and explore. We have done this by, first, providing a clearer and more tightly-specified version of the idea, Sequential Claims-Matching; and, second, by subjecting that view to scrutiny. We have found that Sequential Claims-Matching stands up well against alternative versions of Limited Aggregation in terms of the OLA cases. But it suffers from problems and ambiguities of its own.

First, it does not seem able to vindicate some of the key intuitions that have motivated the search for Limited Aggregation cases (those elicited from 'tie-break' cases). We considered several possible refinements to Sequential Claims-Matching which might allow it to account for these intuitions, but each was found either to be wanting or to rest the vindication of those intuitions on alternative values from outside the Sequential Claims-Matching procedure. This seems like a considerable cost when compared with Global Relevance Views, like ARC, which were able to explain our judgments about tie-break and one vs. many cases in the same way. One option is for the advocate of Local Relevance to let go of the tie-break intuitions, and, on reflection, this is the route that we ourselves would recommend. What is distinctive about Local Relevance is that no claim is ever 'ruled out' altogether. This means that one tiny claim can always make the difference between who lives and who dies. This seems counter to some of the intuitions and commitments that drive the Relevance View but is, in our view, the smallest caliber bullet to bite having precisified the view.

Second, while it is clearer than Tadros's view on how to match claims, there are two important ambiguities within Sequential Claims-Matching: an ambiguity about how to match up claims, and a further ambiguity about how to handle what we have called partial leftovers. Thus, we have shown that Sequential Claims-Matching, at best, needs to be further specified. In addition, we have articulated an alternative version of Local Relevance: Strongest Decides. This view tracks more closely to the Anti-Aggregation view, giving the strongest claim under consideration a defeasible right to be saved. However, this view potentially conflicts with the Equal Consideration for Equal Claims principle. We recommend further scrutiny of this view, and the principle it seems to violate.

In conclusion, we offer an interim report on Local Relevance. The general idea admits of several possible interpretations. We need a clear sense of which versions appear to be the most plausible, both in terms of how they handle key cases, and the sort of deeper justifications which can be offered on their behalf. Even within these versions, there are ambiguities, for example, on how to handle partial leftovers. Second, while Local Relevance offers intuitively plausible responses to some cases, since it does not fully rule out any claims, no matter how weak, as completely irrelevant, it will struggle to handle cases, like tie-break cases, in which one small claim 'tips the balance'.[22] Our recommendation is to

---

[22] There are further potential problems with Local Relevance. In particular Joe Horton (2018) has shown cases in which it appears to violate this principle:

> *The Principle of Net Addition*: Adding claims of equal strength but differential numbers cannot make the group to which more claims are added less choice-worthy compared with the group to which fewer claims are added.

To be clear: this is our attempt (with help from Mike Otsuka) to articulate a principle which Horton's cases show Local Relevance to violate. Horton doesn't try to articulate such a principle.

bite this bullet. The alternative seems to be to downgrade Local Revelance to only being a *part* of the aggregative story. Further work is needed to see whether these challenges can be met, or whether some alternative version of Limited Aggregation, abandoning altogether the focus on 'relevance' is the best hope for those who wish to tread the tightrope between the extremes of Anti-Aggregation and Pure Aggregation[23].

References

Broome, J. (2004). *Weighing Lives.* Oxford: Oxford University Press.

Doggett, T. (2013). Saving the Few. *Noûs, 47*(2), 302–15.

Halstead, J. (2016). The Numbers Always Count. *Ethics, 126*(3), 789–802. https://doi.org/10.1086/684707

Hirose, I. (2015). *Moral Aggregation.* Oxford: Oxford University Press.

Horton, J. (2018). Always Aggregate. *Philosophy & Public Affairs, 46*(2), 160–74. https://doi.org/10.1111/papa.12116

Kamm, F. M. (1998). *Morality, Mortality Volume I: Death and Whom to Save From It.* Oxford University Press. https://doi.org/10.1093/0195119118.001.0001

Kamm, F. M. (2005). Aggregation and Two Moral Methods. *Utilitas, 17*(01), 1–23. https://doi.org/10.1017/S0953820804001372

Kamm, F. M. (2007). *Intricate Ethics: Rights, Responsibilities, and Permissible Harm.* Oxford: Oxford University Press. http://public.eblib.com/choice/publicfullrecord.aspx?p=415447

Kamm, Frances M. (2015). Bioethical Prescriptions. *Journal of Medical Ethics, 41*(6), 493–95. https://doi.org/10.1136/medethics-2014-102543

Lang, G., and Lawlor, R. (2015). Numbers Scepticism, Equal Chances and Pluralism: Taurek Revisited. *Politics, Philosophy & Economics, 15*(3), 298–315. https://doi.org/10.1177/1470594X15618967

Lawlor, R. (2006). Taurek, Numbers and Probabilities. *Ethical Theory and Moral Practice, 9*(2), 149–66. https://doi.org/10.1007/s10677-005-9004-4

---

[23] We are grateful to Mike Otsuka, audiences at LSE and Pavia, two anonymous referees, and Peter Vallentyne for useful feedback. We are especially grateful to Garrett Cullity for the suggestion of Sequential Claims-Matching, and subsequent comments.

McMahan, J. (2003). *The Ethics of Killing: Problems at the Margins of Life*. New York: Oxford University Press.

Munoz-Dardé, V. (2005). The Distribution of Numbers and the Comprehensiveness of Reasons. *Proceedings of the Aristotelian Society*, *105*, 191–217.

Nagel, T. (1989). *The View from Nowhere* (first issued as an Oxford University Press paperback). New York: Oxford University Press.

Nagel, T. (1995). *Equality and Partiality*. New York: Oxford University Press. https://doi.org/10.1093/0195098390.001.0001

Peterson, M. (2009). The Mixed Solution to the Number Problem. *Journal of Moral Philosophy*, *6*(2), 166–77. https://doi.org/10.1163/174552409X402331

Peterson, M. (2010). Some Versions of the Number Problem Have No Solution. *Ethical Theory and Moral Practice*, *13*(4), 439–51.

Ross, D. (2002). *The Right and the Good*. (P. Stratton-Lake, ed.). Oxford University Press. https://doi.org/10.1093/0199252653.001.0001

Scanlon, T. M. (1998). *What We Owe to Each Other*. Belknap Press of Harvard University Press.

Tadros, V. (2019). Localized Restricted Aggregation. *Oxford Studies in Political Philosophy*, *5*.

Taurek, J. M. (1977). Should the Numbers Count? *Philosophy & Public Affairs*, *6*(4), 293–16.

Thomas, A. (2012). Giving Each Person Her Due: Taurek Cases and Non-Comparative Justice. *Ethical Theory and Moral Practice*, *15*(5), 661–76. https://doi.org/10.1007/s10677-012-9358-3

Tomlin, P. (2017). On Limited Aggregation. *Philosophy & Public Affairs*, *45*(3), 232–60. https://doi.org/10.1111/papa.12097

Voorhoeve, A. (2014). How Should We Aggregate Competing Claims? *Ethics*, *125*(1), 64–87. https://doi.org/10.1086/677022

Index